The Prophetic Milton

The Prophetic Milton

WILLIAM KERRIGAN
University of Virginia

UNIVERSITY PRESS OF VIRGINIA
Charlottesville

The University Press of Virginia

First published 1974

Library of Congress Cataloging in Publication Data

Kerrigan, William, 1943–
The prophetic Milton.

1. Milton, John, 1608–1674—Criticism and interpretation. I. Title. PR3588.K47 821′.4
74–6118 ISBN 0–8139–0512–5

Printed in the United States of America

To

Edward Tayler

Acknowledgments

INSEPARABLE for the last five years, the author and his book have been associated with several institutions. At Middlebury College, where the book was a project, I benefited from the subdued but passionate conversation of Professor Madelon Gohlke and from the sweet cantankerous wisdom of Professor William Sharp. At Columbia University, where the book was a dissertation, my manuscript was read with extraordinary perception by Professors James Mirollo and Jeffrey Ford. At the University of Virginia, where the book was a book at last, I have profited from the intellectual companionship of a number of my colleagues, particularly from the uncanny lucidity of L. A. Beaurline, the rhetorical acumen of Richard Waswo, the unaffected good sense of Leopold Damrosch, and the feisty scholarship of James Earl. I am also grateful for the encouragement of Hoyt and Gail Duggan, John and Jane Casey, Kurt Olsson, Robert Kellogg, Arthur Kirsch, Alan Howard, Arnold Rampersad, Edward Berry, Anthony Winner, and David Levin. Final revisions were financed by the generosity of the Research Committee of the University of Virginia. I was assisted in preparing the manuscript by the meticulous, inerrant Patricia Ruth. Barbara Damrosch sacrificed much for this book.

I have been notably fortunate in my teachers. Ronald Rebholz and H. Bruce Franklin of Stanford University offered their time and intelligence with a ready tolerance more impressive to me each year that I myself deal with undergraduates. Joseph Mazzeo and Jacques Barzun of Columbia University provided models of urbane accomplishment so spacious that I am still, years later, assimilating their example. Especially I wish Yvor Winters were alive to read this book. Often out of sympathy with Milton and always the opponent of inspired creation, he would probably have considered my argument either outrageous or, if true, an unanswerable brief for the literary damnation of John Milton. But surely no few sentences of this book were written to be understood, ideally, by that crusty old dogmatist with whom I have been speaking in the privacy of my being for well over a decade.

To the man to whom this book is dedicated, Edward Tayler of Columbia, my debt is largest and (as the convention goes) least expressible within the convention of scholarly acknowledgment. His guidance, literary and more than literary, constitutes one reason why the author and his book have indeed been inseparable. He remains the best of my teachers.

To thank Amelia Burnham Kerrigan, flesh of my flesh, the articulate silence between her eyes and mine must, and will, suffice.

Charlottesville, Virginia
January 1974

Contents

The Prophetic Milton

Introduction

SEVERAL generations of Miltonists have fought the good fight against enemies such as Middleton Murry, Ezra Pound, T. S. Eliot, Robert Graves, F. R. Leavis, and William Empson. No doubt these battles on the printed page formalized innumerable less articulate skirmishes, now happily forgotten, in the classrooms of English and American universities. Today, however, all this warfaring passion seems to have subsided. Miltonists must surely have won a respectable portion of those lesser encounters, for each year more committed scholars emerge from the graduate schools. Critical work either implicitly or explicitly favorable to John Milton is now proliferating at a delirious pace, making him as much a specialty item as Shakespeare. The last major statement of the adversary position was William Empson's *Milton's God* (1961), more an attack on Christianity that on Milton. James Holly Hanford, E. M. W. Tillyard, C. S. Lewis, Rosemond Tuve, A. S. P. Woodhouse, Merritt Hughes, and William Riley Parker are dead. A book has been written on the "Milton controversy" of this century.[1] As the holy war and its honorable warriors recede into the past, it may be time to assess the achievements of our side and begin, with a caution born of utmost respect, to defend Milton against his friends.

The recent appearance of Parker's *Milton: A Biography* supplies convenient ground for this assessment.[2] These two volumes supercede the six volumes of David Masson, and not only because of their convenient format. An imaginative and

[1] Patrick Murray, *Milton: The Modern Phase, a Study of Twentieth-Century Criticism* (London: Longmans, 1967).

[2] Clarendon Press: Oxford, 1968. Hanford also wrote a biography, *John Milton, Englishman* (New York: Crown Publishers, 1949). Tillyard's *Milton* (Chatto & Windus: London, 1930) is organized according to the chronology of the works and contains much biographical information. The same is true of Marjorie Nicolson's *John Milton, a Reader's Guide to His Poetry* (New York: Farrar, Straus, 1963). But Parker is the first scholar to attempt a replacement for David Masson's *The Life of Milton* (London, 1859–94).

resourceful scholar himself, Parker incorporates the fine work of Hanford, Tillyard, J. Milton French, Harris Fletcher, and many others. His first sentence establishes a tone of dignified intimacy welcome in an undertaking of such ambition: "Let me say at once that I like Milton as a person." Despite moments in which disarming honesty becomes frantic wit, the prose sustains this tone remarkably well. The biography, no monument to impersonal scholarship, is the lifework of a good man who admires a greater man. Parker does not betray the life to documents about the life; the first volume presents a coherent, readable narrative, and the weighty footnotes of the second volume defend this narrative as fully as one could wish. Inviting his readers to enjoy a greater man, the biographer refuses to license their participation without also requiring the exercise of judgment. Parker confronts almost every conceivable objection to Milton as both a man and a literary artist. Without undue affectation, he imagines the anti-Miltonist over his shoulder and speaks to him as one rational judge to another. They discuss the lordly attitude toward women, the mocking hatred for opponents, the wrenching of biblical texts to erect premises for a sect of one. Readers of all persuasions should be grateful for this integrity, since the Parker biography will occupy the imaginative center of Milton studies for years to come.

But the successes of *Milton: A Biography* force us to take special notice of its defects. Parker all but ignores one traditional objection to his subject. There is little mention of the special communion between Milton and God. The most revealing paragraph occurs in the preface:

> When the boy grew to manhood and saw his destiny more clearly, he eventually came to think of himself as a Spokesman, as a Chosen One, not by whom, but through whom, Truth was to be made known. This was not mysticism, but rather an impersonal faith in human Reason, together with a half-classical, half-Calvinistic belief in 'election'. Although there was great pride there was also genuine modesty in the conviction. . . . He, the Spokesman, was comparatively unimportant; his words, God-directed, were imperative. If the distinction between the man and the voice became at times hazy in the man's thinking, it is understandable. The distinction was nevertheless real—real to him, that is. [I, vii]

This brief passage illustrates the tendency throughout. The biographer presides over a linguistic metamorphosis. The pejorative "mysticism" fades into the admirable "human Reason." The "genuine modesty" of John Milton neatly balances his "great pride." Instead of risking the word "prophet," Parker chooses to capitalize the word "Spokesman"—a device which gives birth to a new concept, the "Spokesman" of God, left undefined and therefore entirely private. Though he spoke for God, the faith of Milton was "impersonal." He was no more assured of his God than any of the "half-classical, half-Calvinistic" elect. The final distinction between "the man" and "his voice" seems hazy in Parker's thinking. Why should this poet have considered "his words, God-directed" more important than himself, the speaker of those words? Why is it "understandable" that Milton became "hazy" about the relationship between himself and God? With respect to divine inspiration, at least, whatever was "real" to John Milton is clearly not "real" to his incredulous biographer. Comfortable words canceling disturbing words, Parker exercises the power of verbal transformation to create a safe Milton out of a dangerous Milton. Completing this transformation, the biographer can presumably "like Milton as a person."

The linguistic metamorphosis of mysticism into reason, pride into humility, and prophecy into election is a tactic common to the tradition that Parker summarizes. Most commentators, assuming some kind of special intimacy between Milton and his God, have avoided a detailed examination of the subject. This restraint has extended beyond the province of the biographer to the proper concerns of the literary critic. It is rare indeed to find a critic interested in discovering with any precision the connection between Milton's art and his aesthetic of literary creation, for in the work of Milton this aesthetic is inseparable from his psychological effort to attain and retain a sense of divine purpose. To mention one extreme, there has been no responsible attempt to psychoanalyze Milton in this century of lay analysts.[3] There are, perhaps, good reasons not to encourage such an attempt, however responsible; a mediocre piece of historical scholarship is nowhere near so disastrous in its effects as an equally mediocre piece of psychoanalysis. But the guardians of Milton's reputation seem

[3] Maud Bodkin based her famous *Archetypal Patterns in Poetry: Psychological Studies of Imagination* (New York: Oxford University Press, 1934) on a reading of *Paradise Lost.* I find this work, like most of the literary progeny of Jung, ponderously irresponsible. For a more cautious use of Jungian archetypes, see Wayne Shumaker, *Unpremeditated Verse* (Princeton: Princeton University Press, 1967). Freudian vocabulary appears here and there in the impressionistic Milton criticism of J. B. Broadbent and William Empson.

unusually hesitant about psychological speculation. Though Tillyard distinguished between the "conscious" and "unconscious" significance of *Paradise Lost,* this daring vocabulary announced rather timid perceptions.[4] What he considered unconscious meanings were, as unconscious meanings go, circumspect and genteel: the author of the great Christian epic inadvertently displayed his admiration for Satan and his boredom with Christ, his hidden skepticism about prelapsarian joy and his secret pessimism about human history. Certainly an embarrassment, this argument has not attracted many defenders. The terms "conscious" and "unconscious" impose an alien psychology on the creation of *Paradise Lost,* obscuring the older psychology that produced this great epic. Milton worked with the vocabulary and assumptions of prophetic inspiration. His "unpremeditated verse" has nothing to do with "unconscious verse" or "autotelic art." Yet the influential Miltonists have been reticent about psychological speculation itself, whether the vocabulary be modern or historical. Consequently, they have invested the whole issue of inspired creation with an aura of forbidden knowledge. Like Parker, they have tended to translate his apparent "mysticism" with respect to divine authority into more familiar, more comfortable notions. The inspired poet has suffered from a conspiracy of tactful disinterest.

Of the major scholars, Hanford alone treated divine inspiration in any detail, with any sense of its importance. He wrote in 1939: "following the movement of Milton's ideas on inspiration we have touched on what seems to me the centre of his spiritual biography."[5] These ideas are surely not at the center of the Parker biography. Perhaps the embattled Miltonists feared that an extended discussion of prophecy and inspiration might deliver Milton into the hands of the anti-Miltonists, for most of that reactionary group admitted to a genuine antipathy toward the historical Milton, the damnably proud revolutionary who signed the death warrant of Charles I.[6] Miltonists answered objections to the art but tended to ignore objections to the man as irrelevant, unfair, or unnegotiable. In *Paradise Lost in Our Time* (1945),

[4] Pp. 218–44. A. J. A. Waldock chastized Tillyard for this lapse in Paradise Lost *and Its Critics* (Cambridge: Cambridge University Press, 1964), pp. 119–38.

[5] "That Shepherd Who First Taught the Chosen Seed: A Note on Milton's Mosaic Inspiration," *UTQ,* 8 (1939), 417.

[6] See Murray, pp. 66–86.

Douglas Bush offered an enormously energetic defense of Milton's humility.[7] The sober Milton of this distinguished scholar was sage in his Christianity, serious in his humanism—obedient to a rational God in all his endeavors. He had a mind too fine to be violated by an irrational or inhumane idea. If Bush is a fair indication, it must have seemed necessary for the defensive Miltonist to dwell on right reason and Christian humanism, discounting in one way or another those places where the narrator of *Paradise Lost* claims to write unpremeditated verse, see mystical visions, and nightly to experience prophetic dreams. Reading Milton was the pleasure of a rational man, the greater pleasure of a rational Christian. He understood the place of humanity in a universal hierarchy of authority. More a Renaissance artist than a Puritan enthusist, this great poet was, despite the irregularities of his theology, a largely orthodox defender of reason, liberty, and social tolerance. To an extent, Milton the Christian humanist had no psychological disposition, no peculiarity of spirit whatsoever. He inherited and, when writing at his best, transmitted the finest thought of the finest men who preceded him. His genius was simply the Christian culture of the renaissance. His uniqueness resided in artistic power, not in prophetic authority. The Milton who inspired the prophetic voices of Blake, Wordsworth, and Shelley was as much a myth as heroic Satan.

Interpreters of the major poems have tended to approach them as imaginative and scholarly expressions of Christian humanism—which indeed they are. What has emerged is an impressive synthesis of traditional scholarship and the techniques of the New Criticism, a synthesis nowhere so prevalent and successful as in Milton criticism. Glancing through the work on Shakespeare over the last ten years, one notices a tremendous variety of critical technique and vocabulary; every sort of literary sensibility can find a home in the varied continent of Shakespeare studies. But Milton criticism is more disciplined, more unanimous. His interpreters generally begin with a pattern of allusion or metaphor in one of his works. Traced to its origins in intellectual history, this pattern can be seen to represent one or more abstract propositions. For example, when the serpent appears before Eve and arranges his subtle folds to achieve maximum height, Milton compares

[7] University of Toronto Press: Toronto, 1945, pp. 29–57.

him to an orator. To elucidate this passage, the common expositor would discuss the history of attitudes toward classical oratory and its methods of persuasion. Relating Milton to this history, he would discover that the attitudes of the Puritan preachers, with their emphasis on plain speech, inform the Miltonic simile. At this point in the poem, Milton wished to contrast the oratorical manner of Satan with the clear, unadorned, pointedly chaste speech of God in Book III and the servants of God throughout the poem. The interpreter can now proceed to discuss Milton's conception of persuasion with reference to the history of that conception, discovering which traditional attitudes toward public speech are associated with Satan, which with God. Having made these connections, the interpreter may conclude with a brief reconstruction of Milton's beliefs about the public use of language as evidenced by his dramatization of Heaven, Hell, and Eden. Milton criticism thus practiced tends to reverse the actual process of literary creation: as the author began with intellectual allegiances and then created his poem, the critic begins with the poem and recreates the intellectual allegiances. Such criticism demonstrates the relationship between art and intellectual tradition, poetic and philosophical language, without violating the historicity of the text. But the critic labors under an illusion if he believes that he has, through the application of his methods, escaped from the artless material of the biographer. Ending in the reconstruction of the choices of an intellect, most contemporary studies of Milton represent a specialized form of biography; to say that Milton held certain attitudes about oratory and expressed them in certain passages of his epic is to write one minute portion of his biography. It is, indeed, the most cautious sort of biographical statement imaginable. The Miltonic intellect, recreated piece by piece in article after article, merges into the copious background of culture and tradition. Fixed in our literary quarterlies is a Milton almost anonymous, almost a culture unto himself. He is the careful creation of exceedingly meticulous biographers who have, consciously or unconsciously, eclipsed the prideful Milton of Pound, Eliot, Murry, and Leavis.

The approach from intellectual tradition, moving backwards through the creative process, has been applied to the invocations of *Paradise Lost.* Here, in its response to some of the finest verse in our language, the group biography of an anonymous Milton reveals its most serious limitations. For the language of the invocations is not essentially a propositional language, offering rational statements to be considered as logical or illogical, true or false. Milton alludes to various metaphysical conceptions of light at the opening of Book III, and several critics, noting these allusions, have attempted to reconstruct a Miltonic "metaphysic of light." [8] But these reconstructions ignore the overt intent of the invocation. This passage does not communicate abstract theological propositions to the reader of the poem. It does not communicate with the reader of the poem at all; addressed to God, the language performs a gesture of prayer toward God. Insofar as the invocations do speak to the reader, they seem more in the nature of imaginative autobiography than abstract theology. They tell who is writing the poem, how he is writing, when and under what conditions he is writing. Above all, they present the requests of the poet and introduce the answers of God. Those answers comprise the epic we read: *Paradise Lost* is framed by the gestures of human prayer and divine response. The invocations dramatize the composition of the poem and "pretend" that the poem is being composed as the reader proceeds. In Book VII, "Half yet remains unsung"—the truth, of course, is that half yet remains unread, for the remaining books have been already "sung" in the pages still unturned. The epic insists on the drama of its creation, preserving in a finished work of art the full process of the finishing. As we read the invocations, then, we confront a series of statements that take the form of "I am writing this poem now." Through which intellectual and cultural traditions can this kind of poetic statement best be apprehended? One might construct a history of self-reference in epic poetry, a history of invocations.[9] But this technique, if used exclusively, would transform imaginative autobiography into the impersonal conventions of a lost genre. A history of invokers and of the divine favor granted them seems more to the point. However, the pretense of "I am writing this poem now" suggests that our primary emphasis should concern this "now" in relation to the past of this poet. In a sense there is no need to reverse the creative process from

[8] See, for example, Don Cameron Allen, "Milton and the Descent to Light," *JEGP*, 60 (1961), 614–30 and A. B. Chambers, "Wisdom at One Entrance Quite Shut Out," *PQ*, 42 (1963), 114–19.

[9] Robert M. Durling defends this procedure in the introduction to *The Figure of the Poet in Renaissance Epic* (Cambridge: Harvard University Press, 1965).

expressions of art to historical choices of belief, for the invocations represent the creative process itself. Moreover, the aesthetics of inspired creation direct attention, not to the nature of the artifact, but to the act of making, which is in turn an event in the life of the artist. Critics must become, more overtly than usual, biographers, recreating the history of the Miltonic "I" and his relationship to the Miltonic "God." It is this intellectual tradition, this historical context, that *Paradise Lost* invokes.

Pressing a fine distinction, sophisticated readers may wish to divide the fictional autobiography of the invocations from the life written by William Riley Parker. But this separation would violate one of the nearly unanimous and most admirable tenets of Milton criticism. As practiced in Milton studies, historical scholarship assumes the refutation of any crude version of the intentional fallacy. Critics recover lost traditions and search for possible sources because they hope to learn what Milton, in all probability, intended to mean. Of course from a certain perspective the "I" of the invocations is not at all "John Milton." But John Milton clearly intended the fit readers of *Paradise Lost* to connect the epic poet with the zealous Puritan: both blind men were fallen on evil days, surrounded by evil tongues. Literary critics often assume this autobiographical dimension without examining the critical implications of their assumption. Learned in the arts of narrative, they use the term "narrator" for the speaker of *Paradise Lost* precisely as they would use this term to designate the speaker of a novel by James or Conrad. That is sophisticated delusion, betraying both Milton the artist and Milton the man.

Like all intellectual disorders, this one manifests itself in an imprecise vocabulary. What are the appropriate names for the creator of *Paradise Lost*? Often critics vary the tedious repetition of "Milton," "poet," "narrator," and "author" with the designation "poet-prophet." The term is an English amalgam uniting two of the three meanings of the Latin *vates* —"priest," "poet," and "prophet." Writing "poet-prophet" for "Milton," the critic assumes that he and his audience hold a communal definition to which he can appeal without explanation. But this definition does not exist, and "poet-prophet" is critical jargon. In Milton studies, as in most literary criticism, the bastard word blurs all the prerequisite distinctions. Is the poet a prophet like Isaiah, a prophet like Tiresias, or a prophet like Nostradamus? Furthermore, the term derives from a classical language. Is Moses as much a "poet-prophet" as Virgil? Exactly how can this word apply to a Christian poet in the late renaissance? Any reader of Milton understands that, time and again, he attempted to define the proper relationship between classical and Christian art. "Poet-prophet" fails to account for this obsessive concern. Milton wrote in *The Reason of Church Government* that the ability to create poetry is "the inspired guift of God." The editor of this pamphlet in the Yale *Complete Prose Works* annotates the sentence with references to Plato, Sidney, and Spenser: "Milton's doctrine of inspiration is partly Platonic (*e.g.,* Phaedrus, 265), the belief that God gives directly the ability to make poetry to a few specially chosen persons. They must, however, be persons of learning and ability. Two of his great predecessors believed the same. Sidney highly approved what he thought Plato said, 'a verie inspiring of a divine force, farre above man's wit.' . . . To Spenser poetry was 'a divine gift and heavenly instinct not to be gotten by laboure and learning, but adorned by both.' Argument, October Eclogue." [10] But Sidney did not "highly" approve of divine inspiration. If anything, he highly disapproved. "E. K." wrote the Argument to the October Eclogue, not Spenser; and for several reasons this "great predecessor" could not have much influenced the author of *Paradise Lost.* Both supposed sources deal primarily with the classical *vates.* The Christian *vates* of *Paradise Lost,* praying for divine illumination, catalogues the classical prophets in a willful act of memory:

> nor sometimes forget
> Those other two equall'd with me in Fate,
> So were I equall'd with them in renown,
> Blind *Thamyris* and blind *Maeonides,*
> And *Tiresias* and *Phineus* Prophets old.
> [III.32–36]

He cannot "forget" those prophets he hopes to equal "in renown." Milton associates mere "renown," fame under the sun, with the pagan seers. Here he performs the necessary ritual of remembering them, protecting the future of their renown. But the immortal longings of the Christian poet are surely to achieve what Moses achieved, soaring far above the

[10] *The Reason of Church Government,* ed. Ralph A. Haug, in *The Complete Prose Works of John Milton,* ed. Don M. Wolfe *et al.* (New Haven: Yale University Press, 1953–66), I, 816.

classical *vates*. Milton did not learn about this bolder flight from Sidney and "E. K." Offering a vague theory about "partly Platonic" inspiration and "great predecessors," the Yale editor places an essential statement about prophetic inspiration in a wholly classical, secular, and literary context. He performs in his footnote a scholarly version of the linguistic metamorphosis in *Milton: A Biography,* creating a safe tradition for a potentially dangerous sentence. Milton, the annotator assumes, harbored no unexpected or untraditional ambitions, but wished to be a "poet-prophet" on the familiar model of Sidney and Spenser. Miltonists—defensive about his ambition, appreciative of his humanism—find many ways to neutralize his constant identification with the prophets of God.

I have attempted to study that identification, trying to recover what Hanford believed "the center of his spiritual biography." My researches indicate that Milton was profoundly indebted to a long theological tradition of defining and categorizing the kinds of prophetic inspiration in the Bible. The two opening chapters set forth a brief history of this tradition in theological, literary, and political thought. Though recognizable as the history of an idea, these chapters examine at various points the psychological effects of this idea on particular men. For a history of prophecy is, above all, a history of psychological events—a history of righteous postures. Divine afflatus has always authorized special men to undertake special labors. Prophecy appears throughout history as a protection against wrongdoing and falsehood, a kind of invulnerable authority. It is most noticeable as a tone of voice, an attitude toward men derived from a necessarily hidden attitude toward God; no one experiences prophecy except the prophet. I have therefore tried to write a history of prophets rather than a history of prophecy. In this way I hope to avoid some measure of the historical determinism inherent in similar studies. Although my prose may inevitably suggest as much, an abstract conception of "prophecy" does not move intact from mind to mind; throughout Christian history the Spirit has graciously accommodated itself to the eccentricities of the individual spirit. Also, I am convinced that Milton developed his prophetic stance as a private response to an unusually various tradition. He never examined his belief in prophecy as he examined his belief in mortalism or divorce. Mortalism was a rational argument, but prophecy was a mode of intimate action. Quintessentially a Protestant, Milton experienced his God in the heart. And if this unique experience took the form of traditional conceptions, one need not conclude that the experience was any the less unique. Linguistic philosophers show that certain ideas are not expressible in a given language. Intellectual historians show that certain ideas are not probable in the expressions of a given language at a given time. Accepting both principles, I assume that the connection between intellectual tradition and unique belief is less direct the more intense and psychologically necessary the belief. Though the man who believes be shaped by what he believes, he will also tend to reshape his belief in a form peculiar to his disposition. The unexamined surfaces of our minds are the most perfectly traditional because they are the most fully public. I hold conventional ideas about "fatherhood." But my sense of myself as a father, though doubtless shaped by the history of fatherhood, cannot easily be translated into public and traditional discourse—the more engaged I am, the more unique I am. Milton believed himself a prophet. The traditional idea became inseparable from the self who had received that tradition. He spoke as a prophet, rarely of the prophet, and this belief in intimate impulse and divine favor sustained him through most of his life. When he spoke in public of his inner accord with God, his language was proud and passionate—but guarded, poised, and often impenetrable. Master of the conventions of public discourse, this man excelled in the rare art of speaking intimately before an audience. So I try to strike a balance between available tradition and the unique experience of John Milton.

The final chapters deal with *Samson Agonistes.* I choose this work, less understood than *Paradise Lost,* in part because the drama seems to represent the negative case. No prophet introduces *Samson Agonistes,* no prophet dramatizes the course of his inspiring. I am interested, then, in the implications of this apparent absence. With no prophetic narrator, the language establishes a kind of prophetic authority between itself and the reader. I examine the activity of this language with respect to tragic catharsis, typological history, and theological metaphor. Milton's Samson has often been understood as a characterization proceeding from traditional notions about the biblical Samson. Critics have suggested the relevance of Samson the saint, Samson the martyr, Samson the type of

Christ, and Samson the figure in Western literature.[11] But the biblical Samson was also a conventional example of a certain kind of prophet. The drama portrays a zealous warrior charged by God with the liberation of his nation, exactly the prompting experienced by Milton himself at the beginning of the Puritan Revolution. So, for an investigation of the prophetic Milton, both visionary poet and zealous pamphleteer, *Samson Agonistes* is not at all the negative case: it is a prophetic poem about another sort of prophetic burden. This perspective, I think, clarifies the relationship between *Samson Agonistes* and the other major poems, between Samson and the missing inspired narrator.

I have offered several reasons for the neglect of prophetic inspiration in Milton criticism. There are other reasons more difficult to discuss, more problematic to dismiss. Perhaps divine guidance is better left unexamined in so great an artist. To expose his sense of prophetic impulse is, unquestionably, to worry the tact of the scholar and, arguably, to tax the good will of the poet's audience. For many of us cannot "believe" in this phenomenon. Of course many of us cannot believe in God and Christ, an inability which results in serious problems for the modern reader of *Paradise Lost.* But this inhibition differs significantly from the first. Admirable men believed in Christianity and continue to believe in it; the religion is respectable and more, because so much splendid thought and fine feeling would be inconceivable without the faith. The history of Christian prophecy, however, turns upon a violent discontinuity. Until recent centuries, prophecy at times gave authority to the voices of powerful men with impressive purposes. A brief survey of the word "prophecy" and its derivatives in the seventeenth century suggests the honor attributed to this relationship with God. A "prophet" could be either a teacher, preacher, poet, or inspired interpreter of the Bible. The name could apply to someone within or without the church, to someone with an extraordinary or institutional min-

[11] For Samson as saint and martyr, see Michael Krouse, *Milton's Samson and the Christian Tradition* (Princeton: Princeton University Press, 1949); Kenneth Fell, "From Myth to Martyrdom: Toward a View of Milton's *Samson Agonistes,*" *ES,* 34 (1953), 145–55; Ann Gossman, "Milton's Samson as the Tragic Hero Purified by Trial," *JEGP,* 61 (1962), 528–41, and "Samson, Job, and 'the Exercise of Saints,'" *ES,* 45 (1964), 212–24. For Samson as a character modeled on previous characters, see Watson Kirkconnell, *That Invincible Samson: The Theme of* Samson Agonistes *in World Literature* (Toronto: University of Toronto Press, 1964).

istry. If applied to someone with an extraordinary, temporary, and biblical mission, the word "prophet" comprehended the variously important degrees of inspiration from Samson to Moses. In biblical exegesis, the words "prophet" and "prophecy" were sometimes virtually indistinguishable from the word "type": expositors made no clear division between foreshadowing and foretelling.[12] The noun "prophesying" often referred to the Zwinglian Bible readings, or "prophesyings," prosecuted by Elizabeth and her bishops.[13] As a verb the word denoted everything from Delphic writhings to something so broad as "to have an opinion" or "to know," as in Jeremy Taylor's *The Liberty of Prophesying* (1647). This wide usage indicates that fundamental emotions attached to the idea of prophecy in the seventeenth century—emotions which the users of language appropriated for various "improper" contexts. The proper emotional center of the word "prophet" was in the context of the Bible, particularly the Old Testament. Moving the word from this context, from the source of its impact, the users of language gave biblical dignity to teachers, preachers, and poets. The word "prophet" called forth an easy, immediate emotion; writers and speakers drew on this emotion for rhetorical purposes. When enough of them drew on it for the same purpose, the improper context became an acceptable and commonly understood residence. Judging from its many homes, "prophecy" evoked desirable associations.

The word commanded such power of response because renaissance Christians viewed history in terms of the Bible.

[12] George Wither, in *A Preparation for the Psalter,* Spenser Text Society (London, 1884), defined the unity of the Testaments as follows: "All that was either sayd or done in the one, were but types or Prophecies of such as were to be performed in the other" (p. 97). In the Richard More translation of Joseph Mede's *Clavis Apocalyptica,* there is no clear distinction between "prophecy," "type," and "allegory" (*The Key of Revelation* [London, 1643], pt. I, pp. 101–4).

[13] Daniel Neal, *The History of the Puritans* (New York, 1843–44), I, 242–44, 286–88, 310–14, 404; *Harrison's Description of England in Shakespeare's Youth,* ed. F. J. Furnival (London, 1877), I, 17ff.

Bishop Grindal was dismissed because he favored these prophesyings which tended to minimize the difference between the minister and the congregation. In *Of Reformation* Milton referred to Grindal as the "best of Elizabeth's divines." See *The Works of John Milton,* ed. Frank Patterson *et al.* (New York: Columbia University Press, 1931–38), III, 13. Unless otherwise noted, future references to Milton's prose use this edition, cited in my text as CE (Columbia Edition). I use this edition because it is complete; whenever appropriate I have checked quotations against those works included in the edition of Wolfe *et al.*

Through those clear spectacles they saw and understood the formal patterns of all chronicles, past and present and future. Having inspired prophets in ancient Israel, God would continue to provide some form of prophecy to guide His people and manifest His Word. Since the death of Milton, we have found other books and other vocabularies through which we know the world. Though the Bible has almost survived, the decline of prophecy, weakened at its emotional center, has been absolute. In poetry the dissolution was gradual. The "prophets" who followed Milton, like Blake and Yeats, created their own homespun religions, discarding the traditional presuppositions of Christian culture. The new "poet-prophet," defining his prophetic tradition with increasing eccentricity, spoke his fiery words from the margins of culture. The prophetic stance of renaissance poets assumed the expectations of an audience, a public willing to attend and likely to be moved. There was, by the time of Yeats, no cultural response to prophecy against which a poet could assume his dignity, call forth his power. In the work of Yeats, the prophetic voice touched its old biblical center only through the harebrained inclusiveness of Madame Blavatsky. The one contemporary "poet-prophet" seems to be Allen Ginsberg, that saintly apotheosis of Walt Whitman, Timothy Leary, and Alan Watts.

The decline in other contexts was even more complete. Throughout history prophecy sometimes attracted the crackpot and the charlatan, appealed to the most vicious kind of religious sensibility; now only such men are willing to accept the word "prophet" as their due title. Teachers who wish to dignify their office call themselves "revolutionaries" or "cultural guardians." Unlike Oliver Cromwell, no modern politician delights in being called a "prophet," for this term is associated with pejorative phrases such as "prophet of doom." In our day the word "prophet" reeks of occult mediums, radio preachers, California madness, the Bible Belt, fakery, and fanaticism. History has betrayed the inspired poet. Though he worked within the framework of traditional theology, Milton chose to organize his psychic life about a posture destined to become, in a future he himself might be said to have predicted, thoroughly discredited. *Paradise Lost* is not a monument to dead ideas—for Christian art continues to flourish and men continue to fall—but it is indeed a monument to a dead psychology. Milton seems intensely vulnerable in this regard. Of all the assumptions central to his art, none is likely to be more unpalatable to his modern audience than prophetic inspiration. Yet Milton, even at his most immodest, excites with the grandeur of his accomplishment. Again and again he embodied the relationship between liberty and constraint of which he wrote. Beginning from the narrowest of theological premises —that all truth is contained in the Bible—he developed a complex and unorthodox theology. Holding the most uncompromising sense of purpose—that he was a prophet inspired by God—he allowed himself unusual flexibility in the range of his pursuits, acting as teacher, pamphleteer, politician, historian, theologian, translator, editor, and poet. Accepting the most radical of aesthetics, one which others before and after him have used as an apology for artlessness, he acquired the skills of a consummate craftsman and ended the greatest master of rhythm and syntax in the history of English iambic verse. In the rigidity of his obedience lay the expansiveness of his freedom. While lowered eyes may comfort the modest reader, they inevitably lessen the stature of his poet. How, then, are we best to see? I assume throughout this study that I do in fact believe in prophetic inspiration. No doubt I have kept tradition, since there must be many an atheist critic who has written about *Paradise Lost* with all kinds of pious locutions. When reading Milton, it is fruitful to let his universe be the universe. But the spiritual biographer, reconstructing a lost psychology, often strains against the confinements of this decision. In those few places where I have permitted myself the insights of modern psychology, I have done so with some knowledge of what might be gained and what lost yet once more.

One of my best teachers used to argue that scholars who collect and publish the private letters of authors brutalize the rights of the dead. He believed in the rights of the dead. An artist offers the world what he wishes the world to have, and everything else belongs to oblivion. More is known of Milton than of any English writer who preceded him. We owe this knowledge to curious scholars and to our complicity in their gentle outrage. Biographers, spiritual or otherwise, assume that the rights of the dead pass with unquestioned justice to the living. Dead poets are dispossessed that learning may be advanced. Milton labors at the millstone, feeding our quarterly appetite for intellectual progress. We make him play before our gods. But even in his public works Milton sometimes expresses attitudes so private, so absolute and so necessary, as to confound the spirit of dispassionate inquiry. Before such intimacy one necessarily hesitates. For what is the difference between curiosity and *curiositas*? There have been moments during this endeavor when, the calm darkening among water-lights, I have felt a deep indefinable sense of trespass. I hope to have honored that vestige of conscience, that inward watch by which critics of literature may measure their privileges and their sins.

CHAPTER I

Prophets and Poets

The historian is a prophet looking backwards.
Schlegel, *Athenaeum*

RENAISSANCE apologists for the art of poetry never tired of reminding the unconverted that in ancient times the poet was honored with the name *vates*. In his *De Divinatione* Cicero gave this name to the kind of prophet inspired by divine frenzy. The dialogue records a sibling debate between Quintus Cicero, who argues that divination not only exists but reveals the speculative truths of theology, and Marcus Cicero, who ridicules such inflated propositions. Concluding his presentation with an appeal to proverbial wisdom, Quintus repeats a saying of Democritus for the benefit of his skeptical brother: *sine furore* it is impossible to be a poet, and since there are poets there must of course be prophets.[1] A history of responses to this wise old maxim forms a repetitive circle and not a straight progression toward novelty. Both Roman and renaissance commentators assumed, as a matter of ancient authority, the close connection between poetry and prophecy. In late classical and early patristic philosophy, prophecy became a subject of intellectual inquiry more or less isolated from poetry. When the two activities were united once more in renaissance literary criticism, the conclusions of the early churchmen regarding prophecy reappeared as new conceptions of poetic creation. In the unfolding of this circular history lies the proper intellectual context for the poetic and prophetic inspiration of John Milton.

Socrates outlines a theory of inspirational madness in the *Phaedrus*. "Mantic," he says, derives from "manic": insanity is a blessing from the gods, a mark of spiritual power.[2] The madness of the prophetess at Delphi—the madness of the Sibyl herself—suggests that young Phaedrus might reconsider his naive response to the irrational. Indeed, the young man might

[1] *De Divinatione* I.xxvii, in *De Senectute . . .* , trans. William A. Falconer, Loeb Classical Library (London, 1938), p. 226. The Loeb Classical Library is hereafter cited as LCL.

[2] *Phaedrus,* trans. H. N. Fowler in *Plato,* LCL (10 vols.; London, 1914–27), I, 467.

also contemplate the fine madness that comes from the Muses: "But he who without the divine madness comes to the doors of the Muses, confident that he will be a good poet by art, meets with no success, and the poetry of the sane man vanishes into nothingness before that of the inspired madmen" (p. 469). The whole notion is deeply ironic, part of the homosexual banter that pervades this dialogue at every point. Parodying the frivolous paradoxes of an Athenian orator admired by Phaedrus, Socrates interrupts himself to claim divine furor, since he is speaking in dithyrambics, and later interrupts again, claiming still greater inspiration for having slipped into heroic hexameters; if the new generation requires inspiration of its lovers, the ironic ardor of an aging Socrates will somehow acquire that fashionable virtue. Nevertheless this equation between the furious inspiration of poet and prophet, bolstered by a similar argument in the *Ion,* passed through the centuries without the qualifications of irony; one of the wonders of Christian classicism was an astonishing capacity for ignoring the complex tone of Platonic discourse. In the renaissance, followers of Aristotle emphasized the cool labor of poetic making and attempted to modify or discredit the artless vessel defined in Plato. Yet in places Aristotle himself seems to have sanctioned the theory of divine inspiration; and however ironically, the same idea was repeated by Cicero, Ovid, Horace, and the younger Seneca.[3] Perhaps it is not surprising that the renaissance critic often presented a Platonic conception of *furor poeticus,* then proceeded to define the techniques of imitation and to endorse the labors of revision. On the matter of inspiration, at least, these men received from classical culture a more or less unequivocal tradition. For in Greek mythology, the imaginative source of classical literature, both poetry and prophecy occurred under the auspices of Apollo; and in classical literature, the imaginative source of renaissance literature, Virgil invoked the same god who spurred the helpless Sibyl at the cave near Cumae.[4] The theory of Socrates found elegant support in the example of the poets.

Possibly the most interesting of the Greek texts concerned with the nature of prophecy are the *Moralia* of Plutarch, him-

[3] See *Ion* 533ff. Aristotle alluded to poetry as an "inspired thing" in the *Rhetoric* III.7. Cf. *Poetics* XVII. Other classical sources are Cicero, *Tusculan Disputations* III.iii–vi; Ovid, *Metamorphoses* I.1–5; Horace, *Epistulae Morales* CVIII.8ff.

[4] *Aeneid* VI.77–80, 98–103.

self a priest at Delphi, who considered many of the issues that later occupied Christian writers. He argued that one may account for the differences in the oracles from prophetess to prophetess by realizing that they were moved "each in accordance with her natural faculties." [5] Most of the early Fathers adopted the same explanation when discussing the variations of style and matter in the prophetic books of the Bible; like the Fathers, Plutarch thought it "foolish and childish in the extreme to imagine that the god himself after the manner of ventriloquists . . . enters into the bodies of his prophets and prompts their mouths and voices as instruments." [6] To solve the problem of how divinity communicates with men, Plutarch suggested that daimones or demigods, part human and part divine, act as mediators between the prophet and the deity (V, 377–79). Though rejecting this theory passionately, the Fathers assigned a similar function to the angels. Whatever their disagreements, Christians applauded the dignity with which this Delphic priest approached his subject. They shared his contempt for a fragment from Euripides: "The best prophet is always the best guesser" (V, 285). The quotation echoed from writer to writer, always with the same disapproval shown by Plutarch, until at last it appeared as a fine piece of sensible wit in Hobbes's *Leviathan*.[7]

Most importantly, Plutarch discussed the philosophical and psychological implications of foreknowing apart from literary creation. He understood that the Muses were originally "associates and guardians of the prophetic art." In the early days of Delphi responses were given in heroic verse, but history decayed, and the god of the oracle adapted himself to a more prosaic age. Even so, all men are potentially prophets. The prophetic power, however feeble, resides in human nature: "Just as the sun does not become bright when it bursts through the clouds, but is bright always, and yet in a fog appears to us indistinct and dim, even so the soul does not acquire the prophetic power when it goes forth from the body

[5] "The Oracles at Delphi No Longer Given in Verse," in *Moralia,* trans. Frank Cole Babbitt *et al.,* LCL (15 vols.; London, 1927–69), V, 275.

[6] "The Obsolescence of Oracles," *ibid.,* V, 377.

[7] Cf. *De Divinatione* II.v and *Leviathan,* ed. C. B. Macpherson (Aylesbury: Penguin, 1968), p. 97: "For the foresight of things to come, which is Providence, belongs only to him by whose will they are to come. For him only, and supernaturally, proceeds Prophecy. The best Prophet naturally is the best guesser, he that is most versed and studied in the matters he guesses at: for he hath most Signes to guess by." Here, but not elsewhere, Hobbes reduced prophecy to the cause-and-effect reasoning of science.

as from a cloud; it possesses that power even now, but is blinded by being combined and commingled with the mortal nature." [8] More than any other classical author, Plutarch developed the metaphorical equation of vision and prophecy, sight and foresight. "But I incline most to the opinion that the soul acquires towards the prophetic sight a close and intimate connection of the sort that vision has towards light" (V, 475). As this analogy suggests, human nature inclines toward foreknowing. The fact that few men receive oracles does not threaten the postulate—vision exists even when there is nothing to be seen.

Plutarch's dialogue on the letter *EI* at Delphi offers three possible meanings for this inscription. If Eustrophus is correct and the letter signifies the number five, then the god of the oracle can only be known through Pythagorean mysticism; the number five can be shown to be a structural principle in the creation of the universe, of music, of the human senses. Second, the letter may represent the conditional word "if," in which case the seeming discrepancy between logical demonstration and oracular prophesying disappears. "That the god is a most logical reasoner the great majority of his oracles show clearly; for surely it is the function of the same person both to solve and to invent ambiguities" (V, 211). This statement is remarkably deft and witty. In one brilliant stroke Plutarch toppled the dualistic division between madness and reason so evident in the *Phaedrus*. For centuries to come, Christians defended the obscure oracles of their God with a similar dualism, contrasting them to the logical discourse of philosophers. But ultimately this separation collapsed. With the clear presence of Christ the difficult ambiguities of the Old Testament disappeared: Christ answered the riddles and exposed the obscurities. The God of Moses spoke in dark oracles because at that time He wished to hide His truth from the unbelieving, the impure. Similarly the god of Delphi, though he spoke ambiguously, nonetheless promoted "logical reasoning as indispensable for those who are to apprehend his meaning aright" (V, 211). The conditional "if," then, implies the art of hypothesis, and the way to apprehend divine truth is not through number mysticism but through the syllogism. With its special relationship to conditional logic, the oracle

[8] V, 465–67. It is possible that the Christians who read this passage connected Plutarch's metaphor with the God of the Old Testament, who appeared to Moses in a cloud. See my discussion of "cloudless thunder" in chapter V.

implies something important about the nature of time. Prophecy concerns the future which results from the present which results from the past. All logical reasoning, all syllogisms depend on the same temporal divisions. Each logical hypothesis creates a present tense which in turn generates the past and future tenses: if *X* is, then *Y* has preceded; if *X* is, then *Z* will follow. Thus man, who always acts in the present tense, can receive prophetic knowledge only by discarding his awareness of the future and positing a hypothetical present tense. When we imagine the future, we imagine it as the present. Properly understood, foreknowing assumes a hypothetical present, not an imagined future. To study oracles is to confront the relationship between time and cognition. Oracles teach us, not simply about the future, but about the nature of time itself.

Ammonius presents the final solution. The letter signifies "Thou art" and must be compared to another inscription at Delphi, "Know thyself." God commands "Know thyself" and man replies "Thou art." Only the god properly "is," for in human time the present tense cannot really exist. Men assert what they may never possess. Like Socrates in the *Cratylus,* Ammonius argues that time is really indivisible because time is really motion: " 'It is impossible to step twice in the same river' are the words of Heraclitus, nor is it possible to lay hold twice of any mortal substance in a permanent state; by the suddenness and swiftness of the change in it there 'comes dispersion and, at another time, a gathering together'; or, rather, not at another time nor later, but at the same instant it both settles into its place and forsakes its place; 'it is coming and going' " (V, 241). How then can a man obey the command of the god? How can he know himself? "Dead is the man of yesterday, for he is passed into the man of today; and the man of today is dying as he passes into the man of tomorrow. Nobody remains one person, nor is one person; but we may become many persons, even as matter is drawn about some one semblance and common mould with imperceptible movement" (V, 243). Our very language, replete with verb tenses and temporal connectives, testifies to our "Not Being": "For time is something that is in motion, appearing in connexion with moving matter, ever flowing, retaining nothing, a receptacle, as it were, of birth and decay, whose familiar 'afterwards' and 'before,' 'shall be' and 'has been,' when they are uttered, are of themselves a confession of Not Being" (V, 243). Given our human language, one cannot speak of Apollo without a solecism. Often the god is identified with the sun, but that is metaphor and not identity. The sun moves in time and can be only an imperfect image of the eternal god. All things in time move naturally toward dissolution and decay. But Apollo interpenetrates the world of flux. Unable or unwilling to arrest this flowing, the god provides stability and, within the limits of recurring motion, a kind of permanence. Apollo is not responsible for natural disasters in human time, "else will the god be more futile than the poet's fancied child playing a game amid the sand that is heaped together and then scattered again by him, . . . fashioning the world that does not exist, and destroying it again when it has been created" (V, 249). On the contrary, "so far as he is in some way present in the world, by this his presence does he bind together its substance and prevail over its corporeal weakness, which tends toward dissolution" (V, 249).

If I interpret the dialogue correctly, the gift of prophetic speech is one of the ways in which Apollo binds together the ceaseless comings and goings of this world. Within time itself there is no possibility for knowledge, and insofar as man exists in time, man cannot be a proper object of his own inquiry. But human time is shaped and maintained by the eternal being of Apollo. At the mouth of the oracle time recedes into the timeless. The oracular responses, though ambiguous and prosaic, release us from the sequential motions of time. We participate, if imperfectly, in the motionless present tense of eternal being; reshaped by the oracle, human action becomes a proper object of human knowledge. Our participation in eternity is imperfect because we can stop time only by fiction, by language, by hypothesis. No human prophetess could receive the divine perspective intact, for the god himself cannot be known at all. When numbers, hypothesis, and metaphor collapse, we can only honor his presence: "But this much may be said: it appears that as a sort of antithesis to 'Thou art' stands the admonition 'Know thyself,' and then again it seems, in a manner, to be in accord therewith, for the one is an utterance addressed in awe and reverence to the god as existent through all eternity, the other is a reminder to mortal man of his own nature and the weaknesses that beset him" (V, 253). In both the original and the translation, this language is marvellously delicate. "May," "appears," "seems," and "in a manner" precede the two assertions of "is." The language both states and embodies the weakness of mortal speculation. A tentative philosopher honors his god with epistemological humility.

For Plutarch the mysteries of the oracle suggested, inevitably, the mysteries of time. A similar conception appears in Cicero's *De Divinatione:* "Therefore it is not strange that diviners have a presentiment of things that exist nowhere in the material world: for all things 'are' though, from the standpoint of 'time,' they are not present. As in seeds there inheres the germ, so in causes are stored the future events whose coming is foreseen by reason or conjecture, or is discerned by the soul when inspired by frenzy, or when it is set free by sleep" (I.lvi). The prophet, though he cannot step twice in the same river, may perhaps behold the same river more than one time. The world that will be sleeps in the bosom of the world that is. "Set free by sleep," the prophet awakens to the future. If a man can learn the future in the present, then there must be some sense in which the future already exists. Prophecy threatens our normal conceptions of "before" and "after" because it assumes a state of being where those notions have no meaning. The Christians who followed Plato, Plutarch, and Cicero also discovered that their prophetic religion assumed an antithesis between time and eternity: the letter *EI* means "Thou who art," and "Jehovah" means, in the Vulgate, "He who is." Yet the prophets of Jehovah were not frenzied women given to the arts of libation. They were not deceived in ecstatic trances; they understood their inspired words. Recognizing the differences between pagan and Christian oracles, the early Fathers attempted in varying degrees to assimilate the pagan philosophy that defined a *vates* so different from their own. Although the voice from the Delphic Oracle was branded as the Devil's very own, prophecy emerged as one of the many ways in which Athens might have something to do with Jerusalem. This brotherly rivalry became the rather confusing heritage of any man of the Renaissance hoping to write poetry both Christian and prophetic.

The early Fathers believed—and in the seventeenth century Milton still believed—that the supposed similarities between Greek and Hebrew philosophy were comprehensible in the light of history. Their argument was based on John 10.8, "All that came before me were thieves and robbers": for Moses was more ancient than Plato and, while in Egypt, had communicated the truth to Occidental cultures.[9] At best the Greeks only reiterated the insights of the Old Testament. At worst they profaned these sacred truths with blasphemous parody. Origen held fast to the notion that Plato read Moses even when his heathen opponent, Celsus, turned history around to suggest that Jesus read Plato.[10] However questionable his chronology may seem, the Christian was defeating the pagan without denying him all recourse to the truth.

But as he built the bridge he widened the gorge. The pagan oracles were, for Origen, the mouthpieces of Satan:

> Just as holy and stainless souls, when they have devoted themselves to God with entire affection and entire purity and have kept themselves apart from all contact with daemons and purified themselves by much abstinence and have been steeped in pious and religious exercises, acquire thereby a communion with the divine nature and win the grace of prophecy and of the other divine gifts, so, too, must we think that those who show themselves fit subjects for the opposing powers, that is, those who adopt a work and manner of life and purpose agreeable to them, receive their inspiration and become participators in their vision and doctrine.[11]

St. Paul accepted ecstatic prophecy as a gift of the Spirit but reminded the Corinthians that without the calmer gift of charity their prophecies would fail. In Eph. 4.11 he defined prophecy as an *ad extra* grace proceeding from the Spirit but unnecessary for salvation. It is a temporary gift and not a permanent office.[12] By the time of Philo, Clement, and Origen, the whole notion of ecstatic prophecy, whether Christian or pagan, had been identified with godless incontinence. A major cause of this revaluation was undoubtedly the presence of Montanus. Accompanied by two women, Prisca and Maxi-

[9] See Harry Wolfson, *The Philosophy of the Church Fathers* (Cambridge: Harvard University Press, 1956), pp. 21–23; Henry Chadwick, *Early Christian Thought and the Classical Tradition* (Oxford: Oxford University Press, 1966), pp. 13–15; R. P. C. Hanson, *Origen's Doctrine of Tradition* (London: S.P.C.K., 1954), pp. 157–74; Barbara K. Lewalski, *Milton's Brief Epic* (Providence: Brown University Press, 1966), pp. 10–11. Some version of this false history can be found in Josephus, Philo, Origen, Clement, Eusebius, Justin Martyr, and the early Augustine.

[10] Origen, *Contra Celsum* VII.58–61, trans. Henry Chadwick (Cambridge: Cambridge University Press, 1965), pp. 443–46. See also Augustine, *City of God* XXI.viii.

[11] Origen, *On First Principles,* trans. G. W. Butterworth (New York: Harper and Row, 1966), p. 226.

[12] See the commentary on Eph. 4:11 in B. F. Westcott, *Introduction to the Study of the Gospels* (Boston, 1863), pp. 399–444.

milla, this Phrygian seer claimed the direct revelation of the Holy Spirit. Much of what the Spirit revealed contradicted the established church. From all reports the performance of Montanus and his women must have resembled the savage writhings of Delphi. And if all Christians claimed, like Montanus, direct revelation, only anarchy could follow. Hippolytus wrote against the Montanist sect, maintaining that the institutional labor of conversion required the Spirit as surely as miraculous prophecy. The pagan oracles with their Apollonian ecstacies became models of pride, arrogance, and licentiousness. They were contrasted unfavorably to the *Sibylline Oracles*—a bogus compilation of Christian prophecies—and theologians quoted Plutarch and Cicero to prove that the pagan oracles had ceased forever at the birth of Christ, *summa propheta.*[13]

The true oracle resided between the cherubim. His prophets experienced no madness and no frenzy. As early as Irenaeus, Christians began to distinguish their own prophets from the mantic pagan *vates*. Plutarch had said that "the god of this place employs the prophetic priestess for men's ears just as the sun employs the moon for men's eyes. For he makes known and reveals his own thoughts, but he makes them known through the associated medium of a mortal body and

[13] On the influence of Montanus, see Henry Chadwick, *The Early Church* (Penguin: London, 1967), pp. 52–53; G. Salmon, "Montanus," in *A Dictionary of Church Biography,* ed. William Smith and Henry Wace (London, 1877–87), III, 935–45. The career of this shadowy heretic and the two women who attended him is recounted by Hippolytus, *The Refutation of All Heresies* VIII.xii, in *The Ante-Nicene Fathers,* ed. Alexander Roberts and James Donaldson, rev. A. Cleveland Cox (New York: Scribner's, 1907–13; rpt. of *The Ante-Nicene Christian Library* [Edinburgh, 1867–97]), V, 123–24 (hereafter cited as *ANF*). A surviving fragment of Asterius Urbanus (*ANF,* VII, 337) compares the serenity of the Hebrew prophet to the heated thrashings of the Montanist prophet. The most famous convert to this heretical sect was Tertullian, who fought against the Montanists as a young lawyer but eventually was converted to their beliefs and died outside his church.

The Sibylline Oracles, though Jewish in origin, were later added to by Christians. For a typical example of how the Fathers contrasted this collection with the pagan oracles, see Clement, *Exhortation to the Greeks,* in *Clement of Alexandria,* trans. G. W. Butterworth, LCL (London, 1919), pp. 57, 161. Norman Cohn discusses the relationship of these prophecies to medieval apocalyptism in *The Pursuit of the Millenium* (London: Secker and Warburg, 1957), pp. 15–21.

Plutarch, in "The Obsolescence of Oracles" (*Moralia,* V, 351–503), provided the primary source for the Christian belief that pagan oracles ceased at the Incarnation. Cicero also attested to the waning of Delphi in *De Divinatione* I.xix. For one example of how a Christian with literary ambitions made use of this notion, see the *Apotheosis* of Prudentius, ll. 434–48.

a soul that is unable to keep quiet, or, as it yields itself to the One that moves it, to remain of itself unmoved and tranquil, but, as though tossed amid billows and enmeshed in the stirrings and emotions within himself, it makes itself more and more restless" (V, 315). But Irenaeus believed that the Hebrew prophets, though justly indignant, found tranquillity in their labors of the Spirit. This passage from *Against Heresies* represents one of the earliest attempts to classify the kinds of prophecy in the Old Testament:

> For the prophets used not to prophesy in word alone, but in visions also, and in their mode of life, and in the actions which they performed, according to the suggestions of the Spirit. After this invisible manner, therefore, did they see God. . . . Moreover some of the arrangements concerning His summing up they beheld through visions, others they proclaimed by word, while others they indicated typically by means of outward action: seeing visibly those things which were to be seen; heralding by word of mouth those which should be heard; and performing by actual operation what should take place by action; but announcing all prophetically. . . . For by such means was the prophet—very indignant, because of the transgression of the people and the slaughter of the prophets—taught to act in a more gentle manner. . . . The mild and peaceful repose of His kingdom was indicated likewise. [IV.xx.8, in *ANF,* I,490]

The pagan oracle thrashed and moaned, "more and more restless," but the prophet of God is "taught to act in a more gentle manner." Justin Martyr, shifting the emphasis from gentle patience to sexual purity, also defined the true *vates* as a man of serene aspect. The Word of God could not have inspired classical culture: "The Word exercises an influence which does not make poets: it does not equip philosophers nor skilled orators, but by its instruction it makes mortals immortal, mortals gods, and from the earth transports them to the realms above Olympus. . . . the Word drives the fearful passions of our sensual nature from the very recesses of the soul; first driving forth lust, through which every ill is begotten—hatred, strife, envy, emulations, anger, and such like. Lust being once banished, the soul becomes calm and serene."[14] The true prophet is transported into serenity. Though such a statement may appear to represent a rather

[14] *ANF,* I, 272. Though accepted until the nineteenth century, this passage may be inauthentic. See also *ANF,* I, 276, for a passage about "the divine plectrum itself, descending from Heaven, and using the righteous man as an instrument like a harp or lyre."

inattentive reading of the biblical prophets, this formulation must be understood in a context of polemic. Irenaeus and Justin strained to defend prophecy as a religious phenomenon while at the same time discrediting a religion based to a large extent on prophecy and divination. The only possible solution was to create a distinction: the conception of prophecy split in two under the simultaneous pressures of exhortation and apology. Given a firm distinction between classical and biblical prophecy, the Christian could discredit his competitor without subverting the entire market. In the work of Origen, who described the entrance of God into His prophets as the descent of absolute tranquillity, one confronts the full consequences of this endeavor: "we learn to discern clearly when the soul is moved by the presence of a spirit of the better kind, namely, when it suffers no mental disturbance or aberration whatsoever as a result of the immediate inspiration and does not lose the free judgment of the will. Such for example were the prophets and apostles, who attended upon the divine oracles without any mental disturbance." [15] The mind of the Christian prophet is moved "without any mental disturbance." In his memoir of Plotinus, Porphyry told of the day when Origen walked into the hall just as Plotinus was finishing his lecture. The speaker blushed and could not continue. When Origen begged him to go on, Plotinus remarked, "The zest dies down when the speaker feels that his hearers have nothing to learn from him." [16] The psychological paradox of the moved and unmoved prophet derives from Greek philosophy.

In the Platonic dialogues motion itself has moral implications—there is no clear line between ethics and physics. The whirling universe of Heraclitus and Democritus lacks virtue because the conditions of motion and change frustrate knowledge: "How, then, can that which is never in the same state be anything? For if it is ever in the same state, then obviously at that time it is not changing; and if it is always in the same state and is always the same, how can it ever change or move without relinquishing its own form?" [17] In the *Cratylus,* Socrates speculates about the nature of language and posits an original name-giver who concealed a philosophy in mimetic words. Since most words reduce, etymologically, to motion,

[15] *On First Principles,* p. 227.

[16] Porphyry, "On the Life of Plotinus," in *Plotinus: The Ethical Treatises,* trans. Stephen MacKenna (Boston: The Medici Society, 1917–30), I, 14.

[17] *Cratylus,* trans. H. N. Fowler, in *Plato,* LCL, V, 189.

flow, and restraint, the primal name-giver must have been a Heraclitian philosopher who believed, with comic solipsism, that the whirligig of nature imitated the giddy motions of his own mind. Socrates often imagines that the name-giver was correct. If so, there are no absolutes to be known. "But we cannot even say that there is any knowledge, if all things are changing" (p. 189). A partial solution to this difficulty appears in the cosmology of *Timaeus* 35–38. The Creator, the All, moves in a circle. Such motion is perpetual and exempt from decay. Knowing this Creator, a man participates in his Being. The soul of the good and healthy man will imitate this divine example, unifying motion and rest like a hummingbird which beats his wings but does not move. Following his master, Plotinus also characterized the virtuous life as an escape from physical and psychic unrest. Though fastened to a turning world, the soul naturally moves toward the tranquil motions of eternity.[18]

The Fathers appropriated this Greek conception in order to separate the moved and unmoved prophet from the frenzied pagan diviner. In touch with God, the prophets were in touch with being. All kinds of extraordinary calm were attributed to the genuinely prophetic mind. Philo Judaeus, commenting on why Moses alone was allowed to approach God, defined inspiration with reference to the perfect stability of the Pythagorean monad: "But that 'Moses alone shall go up' is said most naturally. For when the prophetic mind becomes divinely inspired and filled with God, it becomes like the monad, not being at all mixed with any of those things associated with duality. But he who is resolved into the nature of unity, is said to come near God in a kind of family relation, for having given up and left behind all mortal kinds, he is changed into the divine, so that such men become kin to God and truly divine." [19] Pagan ecstasy, on the other hand, amounted to a shameless celebration of our first disobedience. Clement of Alexandria wrote that "Evoe," the cry of the prophetic Bacchantes, is really "Eva," which he in turn derived from the Hebrew "hevia" or female snake.[20] The pagan oracles writhed in intoxication, their serpentine motions

[18] *Enneads* I.4.5. in *Plotinus,* I, 61. Cf. *Enneads* IV.7.12.

[19] *Quaestiones et Solutiones in Exodum,* trans. Ralph Marcus, LCL (Cambridge, 1953), pp. 69–70. Clement made a similar remark about the monad in his *Exhortation* (*Clement,* p. 195).

[20] *Clement,* p. 31. In *Stromata* III.lxxx.2 Clement offered the traditional etymology: "Eve" derives from the word meaning "life."

manifesting the forbidden knowledge within. But divine fore-knowing was, like virtue itself, associated with the absence of violent psychological motion. In the *De Trinitate* Augustine divided prophecy into three kinds. The pagan *vates* was inspired by "spirits of the air," by devils; the Hebrew prophets were inspired either by angels "to whom God shows those things by His Word and His Wisdom, wherein both things future and things past consist" or else "so far borne upwards by the Holy Spirit, as to behold, not through the angels, but of themselves, the immovable causes of things future in that very highest pinnacle of the universe itself." [21] Transported to the heaven of "immovable causes," the greatest prophets were abstracted from corporeal and temporal experience—and hence removed from physical and mental restlessness. They stood serene on the pinnacle of the universe.

The Fathers insisted on the exemplary character of the prophets. Yahweh was mysterious, not random, and there was nothing arbitrary about His selection of mortal vessels. For this reason, Origen surmised in *Contra Celsum,* the prophetic Word included the biographies of its speakers:

> They were chosen by providence to be entrusted with the divine Spirit and with the utterances that He inspired on account of the quality of their lives, which was of unexampled courage and freedom; for in the face of death they were entirely without terror. And reason demands that the prophets of the supreme God should be such people. They make the courage of Antisthenes, Crates, and Diogenes appear as child's play. Indeed, because they spoke the Truth and freely rebuked sinners, they were stoned, sawn asunder, tempted, were killed by the sword; they went about in sheepskins, in goatskins, being destitute, evil entreated, wandering in deserts and mountains and caves and the holes of the earth; of whom earthly honour was not worthy. . . . The life of each prophet is to be found in the Bible. [VII.7]

Though inspiration stilled internal disquiet, the Hebrew prophets were chosen "on account of the quality of their lives"; God inspired tranquillity in men already "without terror." It was no calling for the faint at heart. Not all prophets were protected like Elijah—the body of Isaiah, it was believed, suffered mutilation. The courage of the prophets surpassed the heroism of Antisthenes, Crates, and Diogenes

[21] *De Trinitate* IV.xvii, trans. A. W. Haddan, rev. W. G. T. Shedd, in *Basic Writings of Saint Augustine,* ed. Whitney Oates (New York: Random House, 1948), I, 747. Augustine compared the prophet who understands the "immovable causes" to the prophet who speaks in ignorance of his own meaning.

as a man surpasses a child. In recognition of their achievement the religion attributed them great honors. Chosen to foresee the advent of Christ, they spoke of Him without fear of persecution and their prophetic words became a major proof of His divinity. For Origen the "strongest argument confirming Jesus' authority" was that "he was prophesied by the prophets of the Jews, Moses and those after him and even before him" (I.45). Patristic literature is filled with endless recitations of the prophetic Word. In text after text the Greeks and Jews were shown that the Old Testament prophets foretold the arrival of Christ. The demonstration of prophetic truth became the central strategy in the labors of conversion. Prophecy dominated Christian apologetics and continued to do so for well over a thousand years. In the seventeenth century Bishop Burnet was able to convert that dying reprobate, the Earl of Rochester, by showing him how Christ was foreseen by the prophets.[22] Quintus Cicero, quoting the Stoics, had reminded his brother that if there were gods, then there was divination, and if there was divination, then there were gods. Marcus fared unhappily among the Christians: his skeptical arguments were used to ridicule pagan oracles, while the arguments of Quintus were adapted to authorize both Christ and his prophets.[23]

By contrasting pagan ecstasy with Hebraic tranquillity, the early Fathers created what was, in effect, a new psychology for the man who would receive and pronounce the words of God. Blessed with unity and calm, courage and moral strength, the new *vates* is the possessor as well as the possessed. The inspiration of God does not violate essential humanity; according to Origen, the prophet retains "the free judgment of the will." But how can free will and divine inspiration exist at once? Philo Judaeus reversed the emphasis of Origen. The classical oracles exercised free will and attributed their own ambiguities to Apollo; the Hebrew prophets differed from these pagan diviners in adding nothing of their own to what they spoke: "For no pronouncement of a prophet is ever his own; he is an interpreter prompted by Another in all his utterances, when knowing not what he does he is filled with inspiration, as the reason withdraws and surrenders the citadel of the soul to a new visitor and tenant, the Divine

[22] See *Some Passages in the Life and Death of John Earl of Rochester, etc.* (London, 1677), pp. 56–57.

[23] Augustine enacted this historical irony in *City of God* V.ix.

Spirit which plays upon the vocal organism and dictates words which clearly express its prophetic message." [24] Philo obviously adapted the Platonic view of the artless prophet "knowing not what he does"—a mere puppet, deprived of reason and even awareness. Though Christian commentators like St. Jerome later tempered this position, Philo indicates an enduring problem in the history of prophetic literature and its interpretation. In a pure form, the Platonic theory of inspiration seems to reduce the prophet to a mechanical secretary whose greatest achievement is never to copy a mistake. If so, why insist on the exemplary character of prophets or the admirable calm of prophetic minds? Do prophets enjoy the mindless tranquillity of men with no decisions to make?

In places the Fathers did indeed suggest that the biblical prophets took dictation. Justin Martyr said that the divine Spirit used "righteous men as an instrument like a harp or lyre." [25] Athenagoras was even more direct: "While deprived of their natural powers of reason by the influence of the divine Spirit they uttered that which was wrought in them, the Spirit using them as His instruments, as a flute player might blow a flute." [26] Such metaphors, however, may not mean what they seem to mean. Both men also spoke of the "foreknowledge" of these unknowing instruments. In the nineteenth century, when the pressure of scientific discoveries made the problem of biblical inspiration and authority especially acute, Christian scholars turned to the patristic literature and discovered a fairly consistent theory of "plenary" inspiration.[27] Since the Fathers often wrote "the Spirit says" instead of "David says" or "Isaiah says," since they argued that the same Spirit spoke through the prophets as later spoke through the Apostles, they must have believed that the inspiration of Scripture was inerrant but not mechanical. Unlike Montanus, the biblical prophets spoke in the human third person and not the divine first person. Scripture was written by rational men endowed with divine illumination; every word in

[24] *De Specialibus Legibus* IV.49, trans. F. H. Colson, in *Philo,* LCL (London, 1935–39), VIII, 37–39.

[25] *ANF,* I, 276.

[26] *Leg. pro. Christ.* IX, quoted in *Inspiration and Interpretation* (Grand Rapids: Erdmans, 1957), p. 14.

[27] See Westcott, *Introduction to the Study of the Gospels;* William Sanday, *Inspiration: Eight Lectures on the Early History and Origin of the Doctrine of Biblical Inspiration* (Cambridge, 1893). The most impressive scholar of this school was Benjamin Warfield.

the Bible, therefore, can be read as if it had been spoken by God. By the time of St. Augustine this view was certainly the orthodox one. But a more recent historian, sympathetic to plenary inspiration, has admitted in an unguarded moment that the early patristic writing may contain "really no theory at all."[28] The fact is that prophetic inspiration was always assumed and its nature rarely discussed with any precision. Depending on which passages he chooses to emphasize, a commentator may have most of the Fathers contradicting themselves on this matter. The prevalent metaphors of the lute and the harp need not indicate the mechanical theory we definitely find in Philo and probably find in Athenagoras. The problem of free will and divine inspiration resides as much in the text as in the interpreters.

A paradoxical sense of the simultaneously active and passive prophet emerges clearly enough from the Scriptures themselves. "I John," says the author of Revelation, speaking the Word of God. The prophets refer to themselves in both the first and third person, as if owning and disowning their prophetic message: "I saw visions of God," Ezekiel writes, "The word of the Lord came expressly unto Ezekiel the priest." If Scripture is fully inspired by the Spirit, then Jeremiah speaks the Word of God while telling of his reluctance to speak the Word of God. When Origen considered Jer. 20.7, "O Lord, thou hast deceived me and I was deceived," he allowed for no mistake in the text: "none of the evangelists make mistakes or tell untruths" and "it is not right to say this about a holy prophet."[29] Even the most terrible words are therefore divine. Origen probably understood no unfamiliar contradiction in the idea of the prophet both free to speak and bound to speak the Word of God, for when taken together, the polar views of mechanical dictation and rational speech suggest the great achievement of the biblical prophets. Christianity tends to equate freedom with obedience: to become truly free, a man chooses to obey his God and assumes the yoke of the Gospels. Christian liberty is serving the Lord. Thus Origen wrote that the prophets "voluntarily and consciously . . . collaborated with the Word that came to

[28] J. Barton Payne, "The Biblical Interpretation of Irenaeus," in Walvoord, p. 15.

[29] Quoted in R. P. C. Hanson, *Allegory and Event* (Richmond: John Knox Press, 1959), p. 192.

them."[30] This prophetic collaboration between the free speaker and the divine Word enacts the paradox of Christian liberty. The Bible contains the lives of the prophets because the men who chose to speak were inseparable from the Word they obediently and inerrantly delivered. Though chosen, the free man chose to be so. Prophecy was at once the record of the Spirit and the autobiography of His free instrument.

If the example of Montanus worked toward the deemphasis of prophetic revelation in the immediate present, the threat of the Gnostics in general and Marcion in particular ensured the continued importance of Old Testament prophecy. Dividing the two Scriptures absolutely, Marcion argued that the true God was revealed for the first time at the birth of Christ, replacing entirely and forever the jealous, vain, incompetent, and brutal Yahweh. He found support in his understanding of the Pauline contrast between law and gospel, letter and spirit. The argument could be countered only by reinterpreting this contrast to harmonize the Old Testament with the New. The theory of inspiration provided one source of this harmony, but behind the theory of inspiration was the truth of prophecy itself. Although God sang one song to Israel and another song to Jerusalem, the old song mysteriously contained the new.[31]

The major instrument for harmonizing Hebraic with Christian was a technique of exegesis or, more precisely, a way of describing the relationship between history and eternity. From its inception in the Pauline epistles to its orthodox formulation in Augustine, typological exegesis served to redefine the "antithesis" that Plutarch discovered in the meanings of the Delphic inscriptions.[32] Augustine could still speak of time as the Heraclitian river into which no man steps twice. Glossing

[30] *Ibid.*, p. 195.

[31] Clement of Alexandria developed the metaphor of Christ as the Word of a New Song in the opening sections of his *Exhortation* (*Clement*, pp. 3–25). He referred to the classical precedents of Amphion, Arion, and Orpheus. See n. 53 below.

[32] The significance of typology for literary critics was demonstrated most tellingly by Erich Auerbach in his essay "Figura," reprinted in *Six Scenes from the Drama of European Literature*, trans. Ralph Manheim (New York: Meridian, 1959), pp. 11–76. In recent years this unique conception of allegory has been invoked regularly in the scholarly journals. For its origin in patristic theology, see Jean Danielou, *Origen*, trans. Walter Mitchell (New York: Sheed and Ward, 1955); G. W. H. Lampe and K. J. Woollcombe, eds., *Essays on Typology* (Naperville, Ill.: Allenson, 1957); Hanson, *Allegory and Event.*

Psalm 110, "He shall drink of the brook in the way, therefore shall he lift up his head," Augustine found himself in the shifting world of Plato, Plutarch, and Plotinus:

Let us consider Him drinking of the brook in the way: first of all, what is the brook? the outward flow of human mortality: for as a brook is gathered together by the rain, overflows, roars, runs, and by running runs down, that is, finishes its course; so is all this course of mortality. Men are born, they live, they die, and when some die others are born, and when they die others are born, they succeed, they flock together, they depart and will not remain. What is held fast here? what doth not run? what is not on its way to the abyss as if it was gathered together from rain? [33]

Following the Platonic tradition, Augustine reserved the assertion of being for God alone:

Should I say that these days of mine "are," and shall I rashly apply this word so full of meaning to this course of things passing away? To such a degree have I my own self ceased to "be," failing as I am in my weakness, that He escaped from my memory who said, "I AM HE THAT IS." Hath then any number of days any existence? . . . Everything is swept on by a series of moments, fleeting by, one after the other; there is a torrent of existences ever flowing on and on, a torrent of which He "drank in the way," who hath now "lift up His Head." These days then have no true being; they are almost gone before they arrive; and when they are come, they cannot continue; they press upon one another, they follow one after another, and cannot check themselves in their course. Of the past nothing is called back again; what is yet to be, is expected as something to pass away again: it is not as yet possessed, whilst as yet it is not arrived. [P. 114]

But the man who drank from this brook was also God. He made the waters run backward and the sun stand still in the sky. Before Abraham was, He is:

"The Lord hath said unto me, Thou art My Son, today have I begotten thee" (Psalm 2.7). Although that day may also seem to be prophetically spoken of, on which Jesus Christ was born according to the flesh; and in eternity there is nothing past as if it had ceased to be, nor future as if it were not yet, but present only, since whatever is eternal, always is: yet as "today" intimates "presentness," a divine interpretation is given to that expression, "Today have I begotten thee," whereby the uncorrupt and catholic faith proclaims the eternal generation of the Power and Wisdom of God, who is the only-begotten Son. [P. 3]

[33] Augustine, *Expositions on the Psalms,* in *A Select Library of the Nicene and Post-Nicene Fathers,* 1st ser., ed. Philip Schaff (Buffalo, 1886–88), VIII, 544 (hereafter abbreviated as *NPNF*).

In history the present has no being, while in eternity all things are present. Eternity is an endless instant in an endless day. Our sun revolves in the shadow of this eternal daylight. But the foretold advent of Christ complicates the antithesis between time and eternity suggested at Delphi. In Plutarch the relationship between our temporal sun and the eternal god Apollo remains essentially unchanged from human day to human day. When Apollo commands "Know thyself" and man answers "Thou art," the god reminds his followers of the absolute difference between his knowledge and their knowledge, his being and their lack of being. The Bible, however, is dynamic. The words and deeds of the Old Testament point forward in time to Christ and His church. They point forward to the interpenetration of time by eternity. Under the full will of God, the gospel light absorbs the Hebraic shadows. The veil fallen from the face of Moses, the kernel free from the husk, type runs into antitype. God is the architect of history, said Augustine, and "doth everything according to defined seasons"; in the Bible we find "the Old Testament revealed in the New, the New veiled in the Old" (p. 531). Knowing Apollo, Plutarch recognized the static, absolute difference between time and eternity. Knowing God, Augustine understood history, an unfolding record of the connection between time and eternity.

The practice of typological exegesis broadened the meanings of "prophet" and "prophetic." The method was applied to classical poetry, classical mythology, and all the books of the Old Testament. St. Jerome called Adam "the first man and first prophet." [34] Anyone who might be considered a "type" might also be considered a "prophet" in that he foreshadowed a future event. Augustine gave the name *propheta* to Noah and remarked, "I might not undeservedly call him a prophet, foreasmuch as the ark he made, in which he escaped with his family, was itself a prophecy of our times." [35] The poems of Virgil, the speculations of Plato, the myths of Orpheus and Hercules, the book of Genesis—all were in this sense "prophetic." The word "prophecy" broadened far beyond its ancient reference to the special language of a man in special communication with his god. The Bible abounded with prophets and oracles. The word "allegory" described not

[34] *In Epistolam ad Ephesios* III.v.32, in *Patrologia Latina,* XXVI, 535c.

[35] *City of God* XVIII.xxxviii, trans. Marcus Dods (New York: Random House, 1950), p. 646.

simply the visions of Isaiah and Ezekiel, but all holy Scripture. The narrative and historical sections of the Bible contained prophecies just as surely as Jeremiah and Daniel. Even the distinction between words and deeds tended to collapse: "the Prophets not only spoke, but also wrote what they spoke; nor did they write only, but also shadowed them forth by actions, as Abraham when he led up Isaac, and Moses when he lifted up the Serpent, and when he spread out his hands against Amalek, and when he offered the Paschal Lamb." [36] The Hebrew word *dābār* means both "speech" and "action." The deeds of the prophets were no less prophetic than their accounts of visions. Whenever the future was mysteriously foreshadowed in the Bible, that moment was prophetic and those involved in that moment were prophets; prophecy no longer required speech, no longer required a speaker. God created prophecy in temporal phenomena without the aid of a human instrument. The Fathers would have agreed that, strictly defined, prophecy is to speech what typological action is to time. But in practice the distinction between prophecy and typology was discarded along with the distinction between word and deed. Prophecy, once a foretelling of the future, became the character of time itself.

Delighting in prophecy, the Fathers found it everywhere. Nevertheless they recognized that the prophetic books, properly speaking, foretold the advent of Christ in a way clearly different from the rest of Scripture. The threefold division of the Bible into the Pentateuch, the Prophets, and the Hagiographa reflects this recognition. Moreover, the Fathers realized that the prophets wrote in a special style. They often contrasted this style to the logical discourse of philosophers. Justin Martyr attempted to convert Trypho the Jew with the already traditional argument that Christ was foretold in the Old Testament. He prefaced this argument with a statement about prophetic discourse: "For they did not use demonstration in their treatises, seeing that they were witnesses to the truth above all demonstration, and worthy of belief." [37] The prophets eschewed logical proofs; their language of belief was hyperbolic, parabolic, metaphorical. Clement of Alexandria compared the metaphors of classical and biblical authors. In pagan literature, figurative language "is effected through the voluntary departure from direct speech . . . for the sake of literary composition and on account of a diction useful in

[36] John Chrysostom, "Homily on Romans 1.2," in *NPNF*, 1st ser., XI, 339.
[37] *Dialogue with Trypho* VII, in *ANF*, I, 198.

speech." Prophecy, however, does not employ figurative language for the sake of beauty or persuasion: "But from the fact that truth appertains not to all, it is veiled in manifold ways, causing the light to rise only on those who are initiated into knowledge, who seek the truth through love." [38] Avoiding formal logic, the prophets avoided the intellectual fragmentation of schools and sects. All prophets foretold the same Christ, spoke the same Logos. The techniques of rational demonstration led the pagan philosophers to oppose each other. Illuminated by a light beyond nature, the prophets all agreed.[39] But the light of the prophets rose only on those already "initiated into knowledge." They agreed in such a way that only those who already agreed with them might agree with them; only the chosen could understand the chosen. The prophets spoke more directly to Christians of the new dispensation than to their Hebrew contemporaries. Clement argued that the prophets were parabolic in order that the heathens who read Moses might, as they did, misunderstand him and reveal their ignorance for all ages to see.[40]

Still and all, typological exegesis tended to blur the integrity of the prophetic books. The descriptions of prophetic discourse did not really arrest this tendency, for the same descriptions—absence of demonstration, parabolic metaphor to conceal the truth from evil men—were commonly applied to the Bible in general. All of Scripture spoke with one voice.[41] If all the sacred text is an oracle and all time a prophecy, then the prophet as a religious phenomenon ceases to require particular attention. The dreams and visions of the prophets had, in a sense, passed into history. After Christ and the Apostles, prophecy considered as a new revelation from God to His people through the medium of a single man was as dry as the Delphic Oracle. Christ summarized and concluded the era of prophetic vision. The prophets were the foundation, He the cornerstone of a church. "A mirror hath an image: all prophecy is an image of things future." [42] Christ would come again and the next coming might cast another image in the

[38] Clement, *Stromata* VI.xv, in *ANF,* II, 510. Clement said that the style of the Bible is "parabolic" in order that truth may stay hidden from the unregenerate—only a good man, apparently, can understand a good parable. But he made no clear distinction between the style of prophetic vision and the style of gospel narrative. See n. 45 below.

[39] Wolfson, pp. 17–20; Augustine, *City of God* XVIII.xl.

[40] *Stromata* VI.xv, in *ANF,* II, 510–11.

[41] Augustine, *Expositions on the Psalms,* in *NPNF,* 1st ser., VIII, 176.

[42] *Ibid.,* VIII, 617.

mirror of time. The Bible ends with Revelation. But Augustine provided an official formulation of human history, past and present and future, in his *De Civitate Dei.* Spreading the life of this world before him, Augustine translated all time between Creation and Apocalypse into the seven historical periods. The future was already in the present. The parabolic visions of the Bible became expository prose and official dogma. There was no longer any need for a new prophet bearing a new promise.

Many early theologians suggested that the parabolic gifts of Israel had passed to the Christian church. As the mystical body of Christ, the church mediated between time and eternity, interpreting the providential scheme. Sion, a type of the church, meant *speculata.* The church was a watchtower in history: "For she is Sion: not that one spot, at first proud, afterwards taken captive; but the Sion whose shadow was that Sion which signified a watchtower; because when placed in the flesh, we see into things before us, extending ourselves not to the present which is now, but to the future. Thus it is a watchtower: for every watcher gazes far. . . . Sion therefore is a watchtower, the Church is a watchtower."[43] The Lord had said to Isaiah, "Go, set a watchman, let him declare what he seeth" (Isa. 21.6). As the prophets had been to Israel, so the churchmen were to Christendom. The Fathers believed themselves to have inherited both the social function and the visionary powers of the biblical prophets. To define the nature and extent of their prophetic inheritance, they invoked an ancient principle of epistemology.

Plato's Ion claimed to experience poetic frenzy when interpreting Homer.[44] An inspired text needed an inspired reader, *furor poeticus* requiring *furor lectoris.* In the *De Divinatione* of Cicero, Quintus compares the interpreter and his oracle to the grammarian and his poet: "Men capable of correctly interpreting all these signs of the future seem to approach very near to the divine spirit of the gods whose will they interpret, just as scholars do when they interpret the poets" (I.xviii.34). For both Ion and Quintus, there must be a correspondence between the perceiver and the thing perceived whenever perception takes place. The man who knows something inspired becomes inspired himself—the subject takes on the same nature as the object known. The arguments of

[43] *Ibid.,* VIII, 500. [44] *Ion* 533ff.

Quintus and Ion, both dignifying the reader as a creator, represent a crude application of the correspondence theory of knowledge. This epistemological principle was developed in the mode of rational demonstration by Aristotle and, through the Philosopher, eventually appeared in Thomas Aquinas.[45] For my purposes here, I locate this epistemology in Plotinus, the friend of Origen whom Augustine said was Plato reborn.[46]

The theory begins with the problem of sensory perception. We know that the images we see are not objects—they are, obviously enough, images. Perception, then, always requires some concession to the human nature of the perceiver. Every object in the universe must partake of immateriality in order to be known by the immaterial soul. As received objects must be accommodated to the nature of receiving subjects, so subjects, in the act of receiving, take on the nature of objects. As the known becomes like the knower, the knower becomes like the known. In classical physics, vision is conceived of as an interaction between the "power" of seeing and the light of the object seen. One theory holds that the object seen joins with the power of sight and "propagates" or "multiplies" in the spatial continuum between itself and the eye. Thus the object is actually in the mind of the viewer—but only in a form acceptable to the nature of the viewer. These propagated forms are called "species" or "similitudes." Though he rejected the notion of propagation, Plotinus accepted the necessity of similitude between viewer and viewed: "The knowledge, then, is realized by means of bodily organs: through these, which (in the unbodied soul) are almost of one growth with it, being at least its continuations, the soul comes into something like unity with the alien, since this mutual approach brings about a certain degree of identity (which is the basis of knowledge)." [47] The mind takes on the form of what it knows. Hence, whatever we know must be conformable to the mind.

[45] John Herman Randall discusses the correspondence theory of truth in *Aristotle* (New York: Columbia University Press, 1960), pp. 81–107, 272–94. Ernst Cassirer locates this concept in the early renaissance in *The Individual and the Cosmos in Renaissance Philosophy,* trans. Mario Domandi (New York: Barnes and Noble, 1963), pp. 123–78. Etienne Gilson explains the scholastic use of the Aristotelian version of correspondence in *The Christian Philosophy of St. Thomas Aquinas,* trans. L. K. Shook (New York: Random House, 1956), pp. 214–35.

[46] This remark may be found in *Contra Academicos* iii.18.

[47] *Enneads* IV.5.1, in *Plotinus,* III, 103. Cleanth Brooks and William Wimsatt consider the influence of this idea on medieval aesthetics in *Literary Criticism, a Short History* (New York: Knopf, 1957), pp. 112–36.

Knowledge is correspondence. When Plotinus moved from vision to cognition, he simply transposed his terms. His epistemology is based on an analogy with sensory perception —on the metaphorical significance of "light," "vision," and "illumination." To know the good is to see the good. In this lovely passage from the *Enneads* the crucial transposition may be readily discerned:

> Withdraw into yourself and look. And if you do not find yourself beautiful yet, act as does the creator of a statue that is to be made beautiful: he cuts away here, he smoothes there, he makes this line lighter, this other purer, until a lovely face has grown upon his work. So do you also: cut away all that is overcast, labour to make all one glow of beauty and never cease chiselling your statue, until there shall shine out on your form the godlike splendour of virtue, until you shall see the perfect goodness surely established in the stainless shrine.
>
> When you know that you have become this perfect work, when you are self-gathered in the purity of your being, . . . when you perceive that you have grown to this, you are now become very vision: now call up all your confidence, strike forward yet a step—you need a guide no longer—strain, and see.
>
> This is the only eye that sees the mighty Beauty. If the eye that adventures the vision be dimmed by vice, impure, or weak, and unable in its cowardly blenching to see the uttermost brightness, then it sees nothing even though another point to what lies plain to sight before it. To any vision must be brought an eye adapted to what is to be seen, and having some likeness to it. Never did eye see the sun unless it had first become sunlike, and never can the soul have vision of the First Beauty unless itself be beautiful. [I.7.1, in *Plotinus,* I, 88–89]

The epistemology of metaphor led Plotinus around in splendid circles. To become beautiful, a man must already understand beauty—how else could he know what form to chisel within? To understand beauty, a man must already be beautiful—how else could he strain and see the uttermost brightness? Through Augustine, who also based his epistemology on the metaphor of divine "illumination," the correspondence theory of knowledge took root in the orthodox Christian tradition.[48] God is light, His Son is the light of the world. But this epistemology need not proceed by visual analogy. A man can learn nothing but what he is capable of learning. The definition of human

[48] Etienne Gilson traces the Neoplatonic version of correspondence in *The Christian Philosophy of St. Augustine,* trans. L. E. M. Lynch (New York: Random House, 1961), pp. 56–86, 105–11, 187–224, and *The Philosophy of St. Bonaventure,* trans. Illtyd Trethowan and F. J. Sheed (New York: Sheed and Ward, 1940), pp. 122–23, 129–30, 271–93, 404–30.

nature includes human potential. Therefore, whatever we learn was in our nature to learn. Everything known must conform to the nature of the knower and every knower must conform to the nature of the known: the Platonic theory of learning provided another channel by which this epistemological assumption reached the mainstream of Christian theology.

The correspondence theory of knowledge allowed the Fathers to replace prophecy with exegesis without a change in name. As Ion absorbed the inspiration of Homer by understanding Homer, so the reader of inspired Scripture might become himself inspired. Origen argued in *On First Principles* that the Bible was inspired because it did inspire: "if any one ponders over the prophetic sayings with all the attention and reverence they deserve, it is certain that in the very act of reading and diligently studying them his mind and feelings will be touched by a divine breath and he will recognize that the words he is reading are not the utterances of man but the language of God; and so he will perceive from his own experience that these books have been composed not by human art or mortal eloquence, but, if I may so speak, in a style that is divine" (p. 265). Origen's pupil, St. Gregory Thaumaturgus, thought his master inspired when interpreting the prophets by the same Spirit that inspired the prophets themselves. Anselm said the same of Laon, and John of Salisbury the same of St. Gregory the Great. In medieval iconography, a dove representing the Holy Spirit dictated biblical commentary to St. Gregory the Great.[49] Augustine, who wrote "with the help of God," used the correspondence theory of knowledge to argue that the Septuagint translators were as inspired as the original authors.[50] Glossing the prophetic visions, exegetes wrote with an authority similar to the prophets themselves. As the Word spread, so did the Spirit. The religion made its slow transition from an age of prophecy to an age of scholarship, and the Word delivered to the Hebrew prophets became the object of Christian contemplation.

"Behold," the Lord said to Jeremiah, "I am making my words in your mouth a fire and this people wood, and the fire shall devour them." In the cooler flames of exegesis, this

[49] Beryl Smalley, *The Study of the Bible in the Middle Ages* (New York: Philosophical Library, 1952), p. 12.

[50] *City of God* XVII.xliii, XX.xxix.

fire continued to devour. Text and interpreter burned alike. The Fathers had managed to seal up history against Montanist prophets while retaining the prophetic gift within the walls of the earthly Jerusalem. The medieval theologian, like the classical *vates,* unfolded the mysteries of time and eternity. And though the Spirit moved him away from parabolic visions and into discursive prose, still he authorized to some degree the ancient connection between poetry and prophecy. Classical metaphors acquired Christian tenors. God harmonized the spheres, Christ was a New Song or an instrument tuned on the cross. In this passage from his *Exhortation to the Greeks,* Clement of Alexandria first rejects the classical emblems of achievement and then, through metaphor, reappropriates them with a new meaning: "But as for you, if you long to see God truly, take part in purifications meet for Him, not of laurel leaves and fillets embellished with wool and purple, but crown yourself with righteousness, let your wreath be woven from the leaves of self-control, and seek diligently after Christ" (p. 27). Though Clement destroys the kernel, he preserves the husk. A Christian may still speak of laurels and fillets. Pagan learning, wrote St. Jerome, should become the captive bride of Christian hearts.[51] Classical literature and philosophy survived their own rejection.

The ancient *vates* remained most powerfully in the figure of David, who achieved the triple office of priest, king, and prophet: "In the progress of the city of God through the ages, therefore, David first reigned in the earthly Jerusalem as a shadow of that which was to come. Now David was a man skilled in songs, who dearly loved musical harmony, nor with a vulgar delight, but with a believing disposition, and by it served his God, who is the true God, by the mystical representations of a great thing. For the rational and well-ordered concord of diverse sounds in harmonious variety suggests the compact unity of the well-ordered city. Then almost all his prophecy is in Psalms." [52] The connection between musical harmony and the "well-ordered city" recalls the classical myths of Orpheus and Amphion, who sang civilization into being. The Christian God was also a lover of harmony. Singing in "well-ordered concord of diverse sounds," He created

[51] For the influence of Jerome on the Christian attitude toward pagan learning, see D. W. Robertson, *A Preface to Chaucer* (Princeton: Princeton University Press, 1962), pp. 337–65.

[52] *City of God* XVII.xiv, trans. Dods, p. 595.

the world in the Old Testament and, singing a New Song, recreated the world for New Testament Christians. God expressed Himself with imaginative truth in the harmonies of the Psalmist.[53] To sing of the harmonious revelations of God an earthly poet would, like David, imitate the divine music—both the harmonious movement of history and the harmonious voice of inspired Scripture. Knowing these harmonies, he might become harmonious. Understanding inspired language, he might become inspired.

But the fires of poetry are not the cool flames of exegesis. This hypothetical poet might find himself entangled in theological difficulties. Unless his inspiration were comparable to that of the original authors, why should he bother to retell the biblical stories? Why should an uninspired man presume to rewrite the words of God? If he chose to do so, must he slavishly repeat the sacred text? Would invention be blasphemous? If he were to claim inspiration, invent and elaborate, would he thereby assume the direct revelation of a Montanist? Moreover, any attempt to repeat the classical conventions of vatic inspiration might involve a conflict between religious and literary tradition. Apollo inspired his unconscious intruments with poetic frenzy. The Lord inspired his rational prophets with knowledge and tranquillity.

Isidore of Seville summarized and extended the early patristic teaching in his encyclopaedic *Etymologiarum,* a compendium of ready knowledge widely influential in the Middle Ages.[54] His discussions of prophecy and poetry suggest some of the problems left unsolved by the previous efforts to define a Christian *vates*. Showing men the proper "similitudes" for God, the Holy Spirit inspired the biblical authors. These authors may be called *vates,* for this word applies to poets, priests, and prophets: "Vates a vi mentis appellatos, cuius significatio multiplex est. Nam modo sacerdotum, modo prophetam significatio, modo poetam." [55] But the word is classical and therefore suspect. In the section "De Prophetis," Isidore begins with *vates* but quickly switches to *propheta:*

[53] For a much fuller presentation of these complex metaphors, see Leo Spitzer, *Classical and Christian Ideas of World Harmony* (Baltimore: Johns Hopkins Press, 1963). John Hollander traces the idea of world harmony in renaissance literature in *The Untuning of the Sky* (Princeton: Princeton University Press, 1961).

[54] Smalley, pp. 58–60, discusses the influence of Isidore.

[55] *Etymologiarum* VII.xii.15, ed. W. M. Lindsay (Oxford: Clarendon Press, 1911). All future references are to this edition.

"Quos gentilitas vates appellant, hos nostri prophetas vocant, quasi praefatores, quia porro fantur et de futuris vera praedicunt. Qui autem a nobis prophetae, in Veteri Testamento videntes appellabantur" (VII.viii.1). The section "De Poetis" opens with a quotation from Suetonius describing the origin of poetry in primitive worship: "Id genus quia forma quadam efficitur, quae ποιόιυς dicitur, poema vocitatum est, eiusque fictores poetae" (VIII.vii.2). This maker of organized speech yields immediately to the frenzied *vates*. With no sense of contradiction, Isidore connects the poetic *vates* "a vi mentis" with the same *vates* "quasi vesania": "Vates a vi mentis appellatos Varro auctor est; vel a viendis carminibus, id est flectendis hoc est modulandis: et proinde poetae Latina vates olim, scripta eorum vaticinia dicebantur, quod vi quadam et quasi vesania in scribendo commoverentur. . . . Etiam per furorem divini eodem erant nomine, quia et ipsi quoque pleraque versibus efferebant" (VIII.vii.3). Poetry for Isidore is primarily a classical phenomenon—the section "De Poetis" immediately precedes the section "De Sibyllis"—and he asserts the mistaken but, given his concerns, quite natural derivation of *vates* from *vesania*. *Poeta,* on the other hand, he associates with the Greek word meaning "exquisite speech." Given their differing etymologies, the two words would seem to imply contradictory notions of artistic endeavor. But Isidore assumes that *vates* and *poeta* are harmonious synonyms, as if exquisite speech were the manic creation of insane men.

Here are the seeds of renaissance confusion. In literary contexts the word *vates* connotes insanity, madness, *furor poeticus*. But in theological contexts the same word is a possible synonym for *propheta* and therefore associated with a more complex theory of inspiration. Isidore, speaking of divine frenzy, can say little or nothing about the inspiration of poets. He can say a great deal about the inspiration of biblical prophets:

> Prophetiae autem genera septem sunt. Primum genus ecstasis, quod est mentis excessus; sicut vidit Petrus vas illud summissum de caelo in stupore mentis cum variis animalibus. Secundum genus visio; sicut apud Esaiam dicentem (Esai. 6,1): 'Vidi Dominum sedentem super solium excelsum.' Tertium genus somnium; sicut Iacob subnixam in caelo scalam dormiens vidit. Quartum genus per nubem; sicut ad Moysen et ad Iob post plagam loquitur Deus. Quintum genus vox de caelo; sicut ad Abraham sonuit dicens (Genes. 22,12): 'Ne inicias manum tuam in

puerum.' Et ad Saulum in via (Act. 9,4): 'Saule, Saule, quid me persequeris?' Sextum genus accepta parabola; sicut apud Salomonem in Proverbiis, et apud Balaam, cum evocaretur a Balac. Septimum genus repletio sancti Spiritus; sicut pene apud omnes prophetas. Alii tria genera visionum esse dixerunt. Vnum secundum oculos corporis; sicut Abraham tres viros sub ilice Mambre, et Moyses ignem in rubo, et discipuli transfiguratum Dominum in monte inter Moysen et Heliam, et cetera huiusmodi. Alterum secundum spiritum, quo imaginamur ea quae per corpus sentimus; sicut vidit Petrus discum illum submitti de caelo cum variis animalibus, et sicut Esaias Deum in sede altissima non corporaliter, sed spiritaliter vidit. Non enim Deum forma corporea circumterminat, sed quemadmodum figurate, non proprie multa dicuntur, ita etiam figurate multa monstrantur. Tertium autem genus visionis est, quod neque corporis sensibus, neque illa parte animae qua corporalium rerum imagines capiuntur, sed per intuitum mentis quo intellecta conspicitur veritas sicut Daniel praeditus mente vidit quod Balthasar viderat corpore, sine quo genere illa duo vel infructuosa sunt, vel etiam in errorem mittunt. Omnia tamen Haec genera Spiritus sanctus moderatur. [VII.viii.33–41]

Seven kinds of prophecy, three kinds of vision, the difference between God as He is and God as He is known—the inspiration of prophets can be defined, elaborated, categorized, and made the object of sophisticated rational discourse. But the inspiration of poets remains a vatic mystery, an archaic and savage fury.

In the tradition Isidore represents, prophets and their inspiration were matters of vital concern. It would not be unfair to say that the early church established itself by distinguishing biblical prophets from pagan oracles, unifying the sacred texts with the truth of prophecy, placing this prophetic Word at the center of Christian apologetics, and proving the divinity of Christ with the miraculous foreknowledge of His prophetic watchmen. Prophecy was an instrument of polemic, a winning tactic in important arguments. The poetic *vates,* however, required no such attention. Plato, Aristotle, and Cicero knew best about such matters, and their superiority in the psychology of literary creation could be granted without threatening the faith. To men lacking ironic temperament, all these classical writers could be understood as accepting the theory of *furor poeticus*. Also, any overt effort to comprehend the creation of literature by close analogy with biblical prophecy might inspire heresy. A Christian poet might easily adapt the ancient *furor poeticus* to biblical themes, in which case he would be—at least on the surface—a dangerous Montanist. The language of Isidore illustrates one effect of these historical circumstances. Prophecy has almost (but not quite) divided absolutely between Christian and classical; *propheta* is preferable to *vates* in theological discourse because free from long association with the pagan oracles. But in literary discourse no real effort is made to distinguish sane from insane, art from frenzy. Potentially the literary context is capable of a division similar to the one in theology; a linguistic alternative to *vates* already exists. *Poeta,* associated with craftsmanship, offers a possible escape from *vates* and furious inspiration. This division will appeal to later writers; but to conceive of the poet as a maker of organized speech is either to deny inspiration or to beg the question. Isidore has hardly begun to ask the question. He lavishes sophisticated attention on the biblical *vates*. But the poetic *vates* is dismissed with a Platonic commonplace ironic to Socrates but convenient, unexamined truth to the encyclopaedist. As a theologian Isidore understands the difference between the biblical and the pagan prophet. As a literary critic he understands, or misunderstands, only the pagan *vates*. Isidore and his tradition have yet to consider the inspiration of a Christian poet.

One might argue that, as a result of these and other factors, the development of a sophisticated psychology of literary creation was retarded for centuries. A sophisticated literature certainly developed. One of the fine ironies of our literary history is that so many late medieval and renaissance poets labored in utmost seriousness with an essentially barbaric idea of poetic creation. They paid tribute to the residue of a savage and uncivilized past, great gentlemen imitating the manners of a brute. *Furor poeticus* is no urbane notion. Behind the refined beauty of the invocations in *Paradise Lost* lurks the dark vestige of the tribal priest, the demigod possessed, chanting in frenzy beside the campfire. Actually, a sophisticated idea of creativity did in fact arise. Literary creation was discussed brilliantly in the tradition of humour psychology—the melancholy poet who made his fictional world in response to death, creating in exuberant contradiction to his own despair.[56] The humour tradition was more flexible than prophetic inspiration, better able to account for the range of artistic motives, because it stood relatively free from theological complication. The melancholy poet was in less danger of violating sacred history or official dogma. But in the highest

[56] For the tradition of melancholy genius, consult Raymond Klibansky, Erwin Panofsky, and Fritz Saxl, *Saturn and Melancholy* (London: Nelson, 1964).

literary form, the epic, classical heritage was too unequivocal to be disowned. Imitating the model career of Virgil, renaissance poets moved through the delicate art of pastoral to request, as they began their epic song, vatic possession of the Apollonian Muses. The refined understanding of this request was one long labor of Renaissance literary criticism.

The inspiration of the poetic *vates* became a matter of passionate concern after Christian literature developed in the vernacular. With Dante there appeared a Christian poet who claimed inspiration and whose results were impressive enough, like inspiring like, to excite his humanist readers. In the dedicatory epistle to Can Grande della Scala, Dante explained the necessity of epic invocation for Christian poets: "And this is fitting in their case, for they have need of invocation in a large measure, inasmuch as they have to petition the superior beings [superioribus substantiis] for something beyond the ordinary range of human powers, something almost in the nature of a divine gift [quasi divinum quoddam munus]. Therefore the present prologue is divided into two parts: in the first is given a forecast of what is to follow; in the second is an invocation to Apollo." [57] He went on to define his own visionary experience and to prove, by the authority of Old Testament prophets and the rational arguments of Christian Platonism, that he could not have experienced this vision without the special favors of the Holy Spirit.[58] In the *Commedia* itself, the sightseer often interrupts his narrative to implore aid in the hopeless task of finding words to express an ineffable vision.[59] But the need to invoke a Christian Apollo seems to conflict with the wholly different conception of poetry in the *De Vulgari Eloquentia:* "But it is in the exercise of the needful caution and discernment that the real difficulty lies; for this can never

[57] *Dantis Alagherii, Epistolae,* ed. and trans. Paget Toynbee (Oxford: Clarendon Press, 1920; rev. 1966), p. 203. The authenticity of Epistola X to Can Grande has been questioned by some modern scholars. See Helmut Hatzfield, "Modern Literary Scholarship as Reflected in Dante Criticism," *Comparative Literature,* 3 (1951), 296. But in his 1966 edition, Toynbee accepted the document as "definitely established" (p. 163).

[58] See Joseph A. Mazzeo, "The Letter to Cangrande della Scala," in *Traditio,* 14 (1958), 191–229; *Medieval Cultural Tradition in Dante's Comedy* (Ithaca: Cornell University Press, 1960), pp. 170–71. Karl Vossler also discusses Dante's sense of prophetic inspiration in *Medieval Culture: An Introduction to Dante and His Times,* trans. William Lawton (New York: Harcourt, 1929), II, 96–130.

[59] See especially *Paradiso* XXXIII, 35ff. and 67ff. Allan H. Gilbert treats this subject in *Dante and His Comedy* (New York: New York University Press, 1963), pp. 6–17, 33–60.

be attained to without strenuous efforts of genius, constant practice in the art, and the habit of the sciences. . . . And therefore let those who, innocent of art and science, and trusting to genius alone, rush forward to sing of the highest subjects in the highest style, confess their folly and cease from presumption; and if in their natural sluggishness they are but geese, let them abstain from imitating the eagle soaring to the stars." [60] After ten centuries, the opposition between *furor* and *scientia* emerged in the work of a great poet. The poets and critics who followed Dante were compelled to distinguish the Christian *vates* from the classical *vates* while at the same time admitting a basic affinity between modern poets and their forebears. Since the Christian Dante invoked the pagan Apollo, the question of *furor* and *scientia* tended to dissolve into the question of Apollo and the Holy Spirit. With little attempt at discernment, the early theologians had bequeathed all poets two contradictory names. Literary men of the Renaissance were left with the problem of harmonizing classical and Christian, savage possession and conscious art—reworking in the context of literature what the early Fathers had accomplished in the context of theology. There were distinctions to be drawn. Whereas the Fathers debated over two kinds of prophets, the literary critics of the Renaissance debated over two kinds of poets. The old controversy between the classical and Christian *vates,* its strategies and even its solutions, reappeared in literary criticism.

Addressing the politicians at his Roman coronation, Petrarch agreed with Dante in distinguishing poetry from the rest of the arts: "Whereas in the other arts one may reach one's goal through study and toil it is quite otherwise with the art of poetry, in which nothing is accomplished without a kind of inner power, divinely infused in the poet's spirit." [61] The poet may order and revise, but without infused grace his poetry will fail. In the *De Genealogie Deorum Gentilium,* the theory of vatic inspiration appears alongside the ideals of laborious craftsmanship. Boccaccio presented himself as a laborer who, in order to succeed, must collaborate with God: "I can quite realize this labor to which I am committed—this vast system of gentile gods and their progeny . . . and here I

[60] *Latin Works of Dante Alighieri,* trans. A. G. Ferrers Howell and Philip H. Wicksteed (London: J. M. Dent, 1904), pp. 79–80.

[61] Quoted in Morris Bishop, *Petrarch and His World* (Bloomington: Indiana University Press, 1963), p. 169.

am setting forth to collect these fragments, hither and yon, and fit them together, like another Aesculapius restoring Hippolytus. If I trust my own strength I should stagger under this overload. Wherefore to the most merciful Father, the one true God, maker and Ruler of all things in whom we mortals have our being, I humbly pray that He favor and aid this vast, ambitious work of mind. May he shine upon my way."[62] It seems nothing more remarkable than a prayer. But later, in the Proem to Book XIV, the writer proceeded "With stumbling pace, yet led of the divine way" (p. 14). When Boccaccio came to define poetry itself, this art "ex sinu dei" is in fact a "fervid and exquisite invention." The divine "fervor of poesy" is not, therefore, inerrant. Human invention may fail. A man may be inspired and still write poorly: "Yet if any man who has received the gift of poetic fervor shall imperfectly fulfill its function here described, he is not, in my opinion, a laudable poet. For, however deeply the poetic impulse stirs the mind to which it is granted [quantumcunque urgeat animos, quibus infusus est], it very rarely accomplishes anything commendable if the instruments by which its concepts are to be wrought out are wanting—I mean, for example, the precepts of grammar and rhetoric, an abundant knowledge of which is opportune" (p. 40). The difference between good and bad poetry does not fade into the difference between inspired and uninspired poetry. All true poems are written under the influence of poetic fervor, but the telling factors are rhetoric and decorum, the *plena notitia* of the knowledgeable craftsman. The classical idea of vatic frenzy has been tamed and educated: "Nothing proceeds from this poetic fervor, which sharpens and illuminates the powers of the mind, except that which is wrought out by art" (p. 40). The platonic *vates* was an unconscious "seer," but since Christian epistemology tended to collapse knowing and seeing, it was natural enough for Boccaccio to associate divine "illumination" with artful reason. The word "fervor" here seems to mean little more than an enthusiasm for versifying, the dogged energy to get from the first line through to the last. Boccaccio replaced furor with divine determination.

The Fathers argued that Hebrew prophets were more ancient than pagan philosophers. Following Isidore, Boccaccio

[62] I use the translation of Charles G. Osgood in *Boccaccio on Poetry* (New York: Bobbs-Merrill, 1956), p. 13. I have checked Osgood against *Opere*, X and XI (Bari: Laterza, 1951) and made a few minor adjustments.

contended that the gift of poetry was given first to the Old Testament prophets.[63] Moses wrote in heroic measure:

> For we read that Moses, impelled by what I take to be this poetic longing, at dictation of the Holy Ghost, wrote the largest part of the Pentateuch not in prose but in heroic verse. In like manner others have set forth the great works of God in the metrical garment of letters, which we call poetic. And I think the poets of the Gentiles in their poetry—not without understanding, perhaps—followed in the steps of these prophets; but whereas the holy men were filled with the Holy Ghost, and wrote under this impulse, the others were prompted by mere energy of mind [*vi mentis*], whence such a one is called "vates." Under the fervor of this impulse they composed their poems.[64]

Defending his art, Boccaccio appropriated the biblical prophets for polemic purposes. He put them on the side of poetry—they are the fathers of his art. It is not clear what, if anything, these inspired predecessors who wrote "at dictation of the Holy Ghost" have to do with a Christian poet of the renaissance. He was careful to honor the work of the early Fathers, distinguishing the divine inspiration of the true prophet from the human energy to the pagan *vates*. Indeed, the practice of Boccaccio himself was closer to the classical seer with his *vi mentis* and fervid impulse than to the Old Testament prophet. Taking dictation, the poet could display no art, reveal no learning, construct no fabulous allegory. Although "the writings of the Old Testament and the writings of the poets seem as it were to keep step with each other," this harmony concerns "the outward literary semblance of the visions of Isaiah, Ezekiel, Daniel, and other sacred writers on the one hand, with the outward literary semblance of the fiction of poets on the other" (p. 49). The biblical prophets, like the poets, veiled truth in fiction and allegory; they are more useful as models of artful technique than as examples of necessary inspiration. While preserving a scholarly version of vatic inspiration, Boccaccio escaped into that second view of poetry provided by the word itself: "poetry is generally called an art. Indeed the word poetry has not the origin that many carelessly suppose, namely *poio, pois,* which is but Latin

[63] Osgood, pp. 158–61, treats the influence of Isidore on the conception of poetry in the *Genealogie,* Book XIV.

[64] Osgood, p. 46. Giuseppe Toffanin argues that Boccaccio's sense of the relationship between poet and prophet had its origin in Petrarch (*History of Humanism,* trans. Elio Gianturco [New York: Las Americas, 1954], pp. 134–35).

fingo, fingis; rather it is derived from a very ancient Greek word *poetes,* which means in Latin exquisite discourse (*exquisita locutio*)."[65] Though ennobled by its distant relationship to biblical prophecy, poetry is essentially a human art.

Marsilio Ficino taught a less compromising Platonism. Poets need not be artful, need not even be sane:

> in their madness they sing many admirable things which afterward, when their fury has lessened, they do not well understand themselves, as if they had not themselves made the utterance, but God had announced it through them as through trumpets. Moreover, the great poets were often insane and uneducated. Consequently, poetry is a gift of heaven. In the *Phaedrus* Plato gives as a sign of it that no one was ever outstanding in poetry, though most industrious and erudite in all the arts, if to these qualities there was not added that more ardent excitement of the Soul which we feel when God is in us. We become warm because of His incitement. That impulse contains the germs of the sacred mind.[66]

It would be hasty to conclude from such a passage that Ficino had no use for poetry as an art. However emphatically their allegiances diverged, Boccaccio and Ficino held common assumptions. Both men understood that poets have some special recourse to divine instruction. But whereas in Boccaccio inspiration will fail unless tempered by art, in Ficino art will fail unless exalted by inspiration. Boccaccio tended to heal the distinction between poetry and the rest of the arts, while Ficino gloried in this distinction. Insane and uneducated, poets often achieve what "they do not well understand themselves." Ficino was probably the first man to conflate *furor poeticus* and saturnine melancholy.[67] Poetry was one expression of divine love and love itself was a melancholy *furor.* In a universe animate with love, the ardent soul could become poetic or prophetic. Ficino believed, like Plutarch, that the ability to prophesy resides in human nature: "the souls of men which in some way are separated from the body because of a moderate complexion, purity of life, and rapture of the self, anticipate many things, since they are divine by their nature and

[65] Osgood, p. 40. The translator notes Isidore as the primary source of this passage. See also *Genealogie* XIV.viii, where Boccaccio says that *poetes* refers to the fact of a created poem and not to its mode of creation.

[66] Quoted in Paul Oskar Kristeller, *The Philosophy of Marsilio Ficino,* trans. Virginia Conant (New York: Columbia University Press, 1943), p. 309.

[67] Klibansky *et al.,* pp. 254–74, especially p. 259. See Ficino's *In Platonis Ionem,* in *Opere Omnia* (Bale, 1561), pp. 1281–84.

exercise their divinity when returning into themselves." [68] Both prophecy and poetry, however, were incidental achievements of the contemplative life. One sought a passionate nearness to God. Having attained this *raptus,* the soul might express its knowledge of the divine "Ideas" in poetry or in prophecy. The inspiration of poets and prophets, then, did not differ in kind from any other holy ardor; the psychology of literary creation was simply the psychology of all created beings. Not a remarkable aberration, the inspired poet was in harmony with the rhythms of the universe.

In his exhaustive *History of Literary Criticism in the Italian Renaissance*, Bernard Weinberg has chronicled the effect of the apotheosis of Plato on the critics of the sixteenth century—the long debate between the Platonist defenders of *furor poeticus* and the Aristotelian champions of art.[69] Shouldering the burden of Ficino, most of these critics accepted the Platonic theory of inspiration in one form or another. Not only was Plato a nearly divine authority, but his vatic poet served well in the strategies of polemic. Arguing among themselves, these literary theorists joined together to defend poetry against their common enemies, those stolid zealots who found the whole idea of poetry either trivial or vaguely blasphemous. In this larger debate, the Platonic arguments were invaluable. The historian of ideas who traced poetry back to the inspired *vates* could move immediately to the biblical prophets—an unassailable argument indeed that marshaled both Plato and the Bible to its defense! [70] Surveying the internal quarrel, a historian has remarked: "The suspended op-

[68] Kristeller, p. 312. On pp. 309–12, Kristeller discusses Ficino's belief in his own ability to prophesy.

[69] Chicago: University of Chicago Press, 1961, especially I, 1–348. See also Baxter Hathaway, *The Age of Criticism: The Late Renaissance in Italy* (Ithaca: Cornell University Press, 1962), pp. 399–436.

[70] Among those who claimed that poetry originated in Old Testament prophecy were Pontano, Pomponazzi, Fuscano, Patrizi, Menechini, and Correa. The last seems typical: "In this kind of poetry were active almost all those holy prophets whose works we have in sacred letters, who in part predicted many future things, in part revealed to mortals many things about God and about heavenly matters, in part celebrated excellent deeds, in part exhorted men by divine warnings to religion and to the other virtues, in part deterred them from vices. All these things those men have done, inspired and impelled by a heavenly spirit, and deservedly these things are referred to this first kind of poetry" (Weinberg, I, 320). On this basis Campanella called Tasso a prophetic poet: "Such a poem as Tasso's is very profitable and almost prophetic, because the true prophet is the one who not only says future things, but who scolds princes for their wickedness and cowardice and peoples for their ignorance, for sedition, and for bad behavior" (*ibid.,* II, 1068).

posites of the sixteenth century were not art and nature—that opposition was always readily reconcilable—but art and furor." [71] This furor did not remain imprisoned in the lost moment of creation or in the text that resulted from such furious activity. As Filippo Masini wrote, "These Muses . . . awaken and arouse the souls of poets, and the poets, afflated and inspired, inspire (to use the Platonists' words) their interpreters, and the interpreters move their listeners." [72] Thus inspired, these critics developed the terms of classical rhetoric—invention, imagination, fantasy, memory, imitation—into a civilized psychology of literary creation. One of their enduring problems was the attractive yet reductive claims of *furor poeticus*. Divine afflatus could explain the fitful process of composition, the source of artistic power, the loveliness of the poem itself, and by its absence explain the dull human contrivance of uninspired verse. But the hand of God, explaining so much, threatened to undermine the ancient trivium of grammar, rhetoric, and logic. If poets were inspired from heaven, then poets had no use for the humanism of their audience.

There were many attempts to modify the Platonic *vates* in order to accommodate the endeavors of art. Girolamo Muzio advised poets to invent during their frenzy and to revise when the holy power subsided. Ludovico Castelvetro neatly adapted the *vates* to an Aristotelian theory of imitation and decorum, allowing the poet to claim divine inspiration only for the sake of verisimilitude. When his subject matter offended credulity, the poet might claim special assistance—a remarkably cunning argument, for it assumes that divine inspiration is incredible and, at the same time, conducive to the suspension of disbelief.[73] Bartolomeo Arnigio described the afflatus of the poetic mind as the achievement of internal harmony:

> One can be seized by four holy furors (leaving aside those that come through illness of humors); one is that which is acquired from the rites of meditating on sacred and pious things, that reduces the soul from divided activities to unity; another is that which occurs when the soul, exalted above itself in its fervor, becomes presage of future things; the third is that which is borne into our minds purified and disposed by the celestial Muses when the soul, informed by an obliging and large influx

[71] Hathaway, p. 437.
[72] Quoted, *ibid.,* p. 408.
[73] Hathaway discusses Muzio on p. 404. For Castelvetro, see Weinberg, I, 287.

of poetic light and the turbulent parts quieted by means of harmony, marches with tempered pace toward that unity on which its essence depends; the last is that of love, the most powerful and noblest of all, since the others cannot function well and completely without it.[74]

The strategy here bears an unmistakable resemblance to the descriptions of prophetic calm in Philo and Origen. Poetry results from "furor," from the violation of the mind by a divine power, yet "marches with tempered pace" toward the serene attainments of unity and quiet. Prophecy is one gift of the Spirit, and not the greatest gift. In this strange conjunction of *Phaedrus* and 1 Corinthians, prophecy fails without love.

There is nothing resembling this sophisticated discourse in the literary criticism of England. Claims to the contrary aside, Philip Sidney did not attempt to unify furor and art in the manner of his Italian predecessors. Poets could take pride in their vatic beginnings: "Among the Romans a Poet was called Vates, which is as much a Diviner, Fore-Seer, or Prophet, as by his conioyned wordes *Vaticinium* and *Vaticinari* is manifest: so heauenly a title did that excellent people bestow vpon this hart-rauishing knowledge." [75] In the appeal to prophetic origins, the apologetics of the renaissance poet resemble the apologetics of the early Christian. But the point of this passage has little to do with poets and prophets. The apologist merely offered an implicit contrast between the Romans who honored their poets and the English who had not. As for the vatic inspiration of classical poets, "it were a very vaine and godles superstition, as also it was to think that spirits were commanded by such verses" (I, 154). Sidney however, employed the usual tactic. In its proper context this "very vaine and godles superstition" has a genuine "reasonableness": "And may not I presume a little further, to shew the reasonableness of this word *Vates*? And say that the holy

[74] Quoted in Hathaway, p. 432.

[75] *An Apologie for Poetrie,* in *Elizabethan Critical Essays,* ed. George Gregory Smith (Oxford: Clarendon Press, 1904), I, 154. The idea of divine inspiration in English criticism has been studied by Courtland D. Baker, "Certain Religious Elements in the English Doctrine of the Inspired Poet during the Renaissance," *ELH,* 4 (1939), 300–323. Baker argues with evident justice that references to inspiration are too often dismissed by modern scholars as undigested classicism and rarely studied in relation to Christian theology. But his own attempt is hobbled by a stony sense of tone; whenever a poet or critic referred to inspiration, Baker indiscriminately concludes that he must have thought himself a holy prophet. I am indebted to him for several of the examples cited in the remainder of this chapter.

Dauids Psalmes are a Diuine Poem? If I doo, I shall not do it without the testimonie of great learned men, both auncient and moderne: but euen the name Psalmes will speake for mee, which, being interpreted, is nothing but songes. Then that it is fully written in meeter. . . . Lastly and principally, his handeling his prophecy, which is meerely poetical" (I, 154–55). "If I doo. . . ." It is difficult to assess the hesitation here, for the idea of the Psalms as a "diuine Poem" could not have seemed remarkable to any reader of the *Apology*. Sidney went on to list the poetical aspects of the Psalms—the figures of speech, "the often and free changing of persons." Thinking of Wyatt's lute songs, which were often parodied by divine poets, he added the Davidic convention of "awaking his musical instruments." Sidney delighted in the coincidence of biblical prophecy and poetic convention; by implication, Wyatt had parodied the divinest poet and other godly men had simply returned the stolen convention to its proper dwelling. But David is not discussed in the *Apology* because his inspiration is comparable to that of any other divine poet. Sidney presented the Psalms as a heavenly handbook, a celestial rhetoric of technique; the Psalms comprise an ageless paradigm of poetic success. Surely this "heauenlie poesie" displays its inspired author as "a passionate louer of that vnspeakable and euerlasting beautie to be seene by the eyes of the minde, onely cleered by fayth" (I, 155). David is like later Christian poets only insofar as he loved beauty. All good poets are good Neoplatonists, and their eyes are cleared by "fayth," not by the direct and special action of the Holy Spirit. Sidney probably evaded any precise discussion of vatic inspiration because he did not believe in it.

He wrote in a famous passage that poets "may iustly bee termed *Vates*" who "range, onely rayned with learned discretion, into the diune consideration of what may be, and should be." [76] This particular *vates* deserved his divine name because of what he imitated, because of his subject matter, and not because of his inspiration, his psychological state at the moment of creation. When, as the tradition of poetic apology

[76] I, 159. Sidney had in mind the distinction between icastic and fantastic creation when he wrote that the poet "dooth growe in effect another nature . . . not inclosed within the narrow warrant of her guifts, but freely ranging onely within the zodiack of his owne wit" (I, 156). Such creation could take place with or without inspiration, and the definition of the poet as *vates* implies nothing whatsoever about vatic inspiration.

required, Sidney went forth to unseat the powerful arguments of the *Republic,* he revealed his true position. Plato was a formidable authority "whom the wiser a man is the most iust cause he shall find to have in admiration; especially sith he attributeth vnto Poesie more then my selfe doe, namely, to be a very inspiring of a diuine force, farre aboue mans wit" (I, 192). Terming certain poets *vates,* Sidney distinguished creators of the marvellous and sublime from creators of the historical and quotidian, fantastic from icastic imitation. For a man whose work suggests the influence of Plato and Neoplatonism, he remained far indeed from any genuine endorsement of the poet as a prophet. *Furor poeticus* dissolved into mimesis: "The chiefe both in antiquitie and excellencie were they that did imitate the inconceiuable excellencies of GOD" (I, 158). Imitating an excellent subject, the poet becomes excellent. The correspondence of excellence submerges any possible correspondence of inspiration. Moreover, Sidney understood that "our erected wit maketh us know what perfection is, and yet our infected will keepeth us from reaching unto it." [77] Man is fallen only in will and creates art with the "erected" faculties of his intellect. This unorthodox theological position, closer in spirit to Luther than to Calvin, permits the artist to apprehend and represent the "diuine consideration" of a golden world without special assistance from inspiration.

Placing Sidney in the native tradition, he seems almost as close to the practical George Gascoigne as to the prophetic John Skelton.[78] Though he welcomed divine poetry, he did not expect divine inspiration. English criticism of the sixteenth century offered no extended discussion of *furor poeticus* and no unequivocal identification of the contemporary poet with the biblical prophet. Some fruits of the continental debate appeared in "E. K." 's Italianate notes to *The Sheepheardes Calender* (1579). He introduced the October Eclogue as a

[77] I, 157. The importance of this passage, which allows clear thinking to substitute for inspiration in the mind of the golden poet, has been recognized by Frank B. Evans, "The Concept of the Fall in Sidney's *Apologie,*" in *Renaissance Papers 1969,* ed. George W. Williams, Southeastern Renaissance Conference (Chapel Hill: University of North Carolina Press, 1970), pp. 9–15.

[78] Gascoigne offered sane and sensible advice to the courtly maker in *Certayne Notes of Instruction* (1573), reprinted in Smith, I, 46–57. Laureate and seer, John Skelton defended his divinely inspired art in the second section of his last poem, *A Replycacion* (1528). Stanley Fish discusses the prophetic role of Skelton in *John Skelton's Poetry* (New Haven: Yale University Press, 1965), pp. 8–35, 153–55, 172–75, connecting him with the inspired Alexander Barclay and distinguishing him from the allegorist Stephen Hawes.

treatise on poetry as an art, "or rather no arte, but a diuine gift and heauenly instinct not to be gotten by laboure and learning, but adorned with both: and poured into the witte by . . . celestiall inspiration." [79] Amid learned allusions to Petrarch and Boccaccio, "E. K." distinguished the *vates* from the maker. Poetry was first uttered at a pagan ceremony; but since that first inspired moment, "makers" have formed "lighter music" of "light matter": "At whose wonderful gyft al men being astonied and as it were rauished, with delight, thinking (as it was indeed) that he was inspired from aboue, called him vatem: which kinde of men afterwarde forming their verses to lighter musick . . . found out light matter of Poesie also, some playing with loue, some scorning at mens fashions, some powred out in pleasures, and so well called Poetes or makers" (p. 101). "E. K." did not repeat the traditional chronology that made the biblical prophets the true fathers of poetry. Believing in the classical origin of vatic creation, he avoided consideration of biblical inspiration in relation to poetic inspiration. Though poets have been and might be inspired by God, it was left an open question whether or not such inspiration is comparable to prophetic authority. However, "E. K." certainly favored a return to the beginnings of poetic speech. He associated the renovation of "celestiall inspiration" with the epic, not the pastoral. In the October Eclogue, Cuddie defined his literary ambitions:

> Thou kenst not *Percie* howe the ryme should rage.
> O if my temples were distained with wine,
> And girt in girlonds of wild Yuie twine,
> How I could reare the Muse on stately stage,
> And teach her tread aloft in bus-kin fine,
> With queint *Bellona* in her equipage.
>
> [Ll. 109–14]

"E. K." glossed this passage as a sudden revelation of "Poetical furie": "He seemeth here to be rauished with a Poetical furie. For (if one rightly mark) the numbers rise so ful, and the verse groweth so big, that it seemeth he hath forgot the meanenesse of shepheards state and stile" (p. 100). Rightly marked, the verse "groweth so big" because the lowly pastoral is pregnant with epic aspirations. Masked in the guise of a

[79] *Spenser's Minor Poems,* ed. Ernest de Selincourt (Oxford: Clarendon Press, 1910), p. 96. The quotation is part of the "Argvment" provided by "E. K."

pastoral maker, this poet may one day forget altogether "the meanenesse of shepheards state and stile." *The Shepheardes Calender* was, "E. K." suggested, a preparation for the recovery of vatic art in English literature. Spenser would reverse the course of history: as poetry began with inspiration and progressed to mere making, so this English Virgil would begin with pastoral making and proceed to inspired epic. With his implicit interpretation of Spenser's career, "E. K." provided a framework for Elizabethan criticism. His distinction between *vates* and maker influenced later writers, appearing in *A Discourse of Englishe Poetrie* (1586) by William Webbe and *Palladis Tamia, Wits Treasury* (1598) by Francis Meres.[80] These men followed the anonymous grammarian in emphasizing the classical origins of celestial art. Divine poetry was eclectic indeed. God, who inspired only the prophets of Israel, inspired the poets of many lands—both critics cited Ovid and Spenser as examples of divinely instructed poetry. Equating classical and Christian inspiration, Webbe and Meres seem more like men who delighted in finding the hand of God wherever they looked than men who seriously expected a new *vates* with the inspiration of a holy prophet to appear in contemporary literature. Their concern was less with inspiration than with the religious renovation of secular verse. John Harington, the translator of Ariosto, wrote that "Prophets and Poets have been thought to haue a great affinitie, as the name *Vates* in Latin doth testify." [81] Perpetuating this "great affinitie," English critics hoped to dignify a humble craft and create a favorable audience for the poet of divine intentions. In *The Arte of English Poesie* (1589), George Puttenham (?) discussed *furor poeticus* as one of several alternative ways in which poetry is created. Literary imitation, he wrote, "can not grow but by some diuine instinct—the Platonicks call it furor; or by excellencie of nature and complexion; or by great subtiltie of spirits & wit; or by much experience and obseruation of the world and of course of kinde; or, peradventure, by all or most part of them." [82] For this critic, poetic making in no way contradicted or threatened

[80] For William Webbe, see Smith, I, 230–31. He obviously lifted the distinction from "E. K." Meres followed both "E. K." and Webbe, but his formulation was more radically theological than either of his sources; he was the only one of the three to mention the Old Testament prophets (*ibid.*, II, 313).

[81] From the preface to Harington's translation of *Orlando Furioso* (1591) in Smith, II, 205. Milton owned and annotated this translation.

[82] Smith, II, 3–4.

"diuine instinct." His allusion to celestial inspiration reassured the court ladies to whom he addressed himself that poets were not lascivious men, that an interest in poetry was not a purely secular obsession. Because poets were interested in God and God was interested in poets, the art of poetry was worthy of serious attention. Puttenham, like other sixteenth-century critics, used divine inspiration to dispose his audience toward the wonderful art he was about to expound. The issues raised by Spenser and "E. K." never really took root in England.

One would imagine that the October Eclogue and its pointed notes might easily have inspired a long controversy. After all, "E. K." aligned himself with the fervent literary patriotism of Spenser and his circle. He spoke for men who wished to nationalize the achievements of classical and continental literature, proving to all the world that England had her worthy monarchs, her warriors, saints, and martyrs, her Helicon and her Parnassus. Their aim was no less than the eternal glorification of Queen Elizabeth and the language she spoke. Any statement about the "celestiall inspiration" of poets must have seemed a manifesto worthy of considered response. In his prefatory epistle to Harvey, "E. K." wrote that Spenser had dedicated the "maydenhead" of his poetry "to the Noble and worthy Gentleman, the right worshipfull Ma. Phi. Sidney, a special fauourer and maintainer of all of learning." [83] In the influence of this worthy author lies our best surmise about the failure of the October Eclogue to elicit critical controversy. Writing his *Apology* approximately four years after the publication of *The Shepheardes Calender,* Sidney himself denied the necessity and possibility of "celestial inspiration" for a contemporary poet. Sidney was not only the original dedicatee —he was also a patriot of unimpeachable honor. He believed that English literature could arise without vatic inspiration, and no one could suggest that Sir Philip Sidney had not the glory of his country and his language at heart; his sister was the great patroness of Elizabethan poets. By accepting "E. K." 's distinction between *vates* and maker while denying divine inspiration, Sidney put English criticism on a comfortable course away from the theological whirlpools of inspiration.

This disinterest extended into the seventeenth century. The most influential critic of the Jacobean age quoted Seneca,

[83] *Spenser's Minor Poems,* pp. 8–9.

Plato, Aristotle, Ovid, and Lipsius to affirm his notion of "Poetical Rapture": "First, wee require in our *Poet,* or maker, . . . a goodness of naturall wit. For, whereas all other Arts consist of Doctrine, and Precepts: the Poet must bee able by nature, and instinct, to powre out the Treasure of his minde. . . . Then it riseth higher, as by a diuine Instinct, when it contemnes common, and knowne conceptions. It utters somewhat above a mortall mouth. Then it gets a loft, and flies away with his Ryder, whether, before, it was doubtfull to ascend." [84] For Ben Jonson, the debate really was between nature and art, not inspiration and art. Through "nature" and "Instinct," the poet "utters somewhat above a mortall mouth." But Jonson went on to emphasize practice, study, and diligent application. Nature had to be perfected by art. Let no one think "hee can leape forth suddainely a *Poet,* by dreaming hee hath been in *Parnassus,* or, having washt his lipps (as they say) in Helicon" (VIII, 637). Jonson's distaste for the high style of the classical *genus grande* amounted to a distaste for the claims of inspiration.[85] The mock-epic "On the Famous Voyage" indicates his position with utmost clarity. The man who chooses to write an epic must of course fulfill the conventions of the form; otherwise he will not write an epic. But the conventions of invocation and catalogue require the poet to swell himself beyond recognizably human proportions. Divine afflatus distorts him as a man—and poets (though divine) are men first and last. "And I could wish for their eterniz'd sakes, / My *Muse* had plough'd with his, that sung A-IAX." [86] If the epic poet corresponds with the epic subject of "On the Famous Voyage," then his celestial afflatus is simply an inflation of human flatus. When Ben Jonson reigned at the literary dinners of England he doubtless betrayed his views on this matter; no member in good standing of the Tribe of Ben would, in full seriousness, implore celestial aid

[84] Ben Jonson, *Timber: or, Discoveries* in *Ben Jonson,* ed. C. H. Herford and Percy and Evelyn Simpson (Oxford: Clarendon Press, 1932–47), VIII, 637.

[85] For Jonson's view of the epic—an attitude based primarily on style—see Wesley Trimpi, *Ben Jonson's Poetry* (Stanford: Stanford University Press, 1962), pp. 96–114. Jonson told Drummond that he wished at one time to write "ane Epick Poeme . . . of the Worthies of his Country." This hybrid of Spenser and Drayton never blossomed. Trimpi argues that the epic was not written because of Jonson's intellectual and temperamental objections to the epic form.

[86] "On the Famous Voyage" is the last, longest, and probably most scurrilous poem in *Epigrammes* (1612), the only book of verse Jonson published during his lifetime. The text is in *Ben Jonson,* VIII, 84–89.

for his well-wrought verses. The complete works of Jonson constitute a notable refutation by example of the need for divine inspiration. At his death in 1637, the minimal interest in vatic poetry generated by Spenser and "E. K." was already the history of another age.

On the subject of poetic inspiration, at least, the English critics were unmindful, vague, and often unimpressive. For rhetorical strategy, for purposes of persuasion, the allusions to *vates* and *furor poeticus* were regularly evoked and just as regularly forgotten. The Old Testament prophets helped Sidney, Harington, and Meres apologize for poetry, but their connection with contemporary verse was left undefined. An Englishman of the renaissance could discuss divine poetry without also discussing the precise nature of divine inspiration.[87] No critic attempted to categorize the kinds of celestial instruction or to describe the psychology of the inspired mind. No critic established a firm and detailed distinction between the classical and the Christian *vates*. No critic dealt with the questions of passion and reason, the active creator and the passive secretary. Aside from the pressures of apologetic and the influence of Sidney, I suggest four possible explanations for this startling failure. Perhaps the English critics did not believe in divine inspiration for poets; perhaps they passed on an ancient tradition gone dead at the center, never imagining that a modern poet would shape his creative life around such fanciful notions. Second, a thorough discussion of these matters could easily end in theological confusion or in heresy. The apologists for divine poetry hoped to convince the religious that poetry was worth saving; a precise discussion of poetic inspiration in relation to biblical inspiration might well have had the opposite effect. In any case, such a discussion would have divided and fragmented the audience for divine poetry. Since the sixteenth-century critics were concerned with a national literature, the division of their audience would have social implications; England would suffer disgrace in imitating the literary and political fragmentation of renaissance Italy. Third, no contemporary poet of extraordinary talent wrote a long narrative poem on biblical subjects. The most ambitious literary patriot, Edmund Spenser, chose to work with the knights and ladies of fabulous romance. Had he written a

[87] Lily Bess Campbell considers the movement to convert and purify the secular tradition in *Divine Poetry and Drama in Sixteenth-Century England* (Berkeley: University of California Press), especially pp. 1–138.

biblical epic, he and his audience might have confronted the problems of inspiration more directly. Spenser found the authority to write the *Faerie Queene* in the Virgilian sequence of his career:

> Lo I the man, whose Muse whilome did maske,
> As time her taught, in lowly Shepheards weeds,
> Am now enforst a far vnfitter taske,
> For trumpets sterne to chaunge mine oaten reeds,
> And sing of Knights and Ladies gentle deeds;
> Whose prayses hauing slept in silence long,
> Me, all too meane, the sacred Muse areeds
> To blazon broad emongst her learned throng:
> Fierce warres and faithful loues shall moralize my song.[88]

The invocation is hardly theological at all. As the Muse removes her mask, revealing her sacred nature, she "areeds" the poet for a martial song. In "The Teares of the Mvses," Calliope announces herself as the "golden Trompet of eternitie"; the epic song reshapes the memory of mankind into a moral faculty, doling out eternal fame and eternal rebuke in defiance of temporal flux.[89] The epic poet, taking up his trumpet, implored his sacred Muse to "Lay forth out of thine euerlasting scryne / The antique rolles, which there lye hidden still." Requesting divine aid for his memory and his "dull tong," Spenser closed his invocation with an address to the "Great Lady of the greatest Isle." This epic is dedicated to Elizabeth and England, not to God, and its invocation does not establish a theological relationship between the poet and his source of inspiration. Moreover, Spenser was no heretic, no exile. Glorifying Queen and country and the national "tong," his inspiration could not have threatened the uninspired. When Dante

[88] The opening stanza of the *Faerie Queene,* ed. J. C. Smith (Oxford, 1909), I, 3.

[89] The Muses are the daughters of Memory. In his poem on the woeful Muses (*Spenser's Minor Poems,* pp. 153–71), Spenser stressed the cruel immorality of modern forgetfulness. It was an evil negligence to forget history and heroic example. Note especially the speech of Calliope (11.439–44):

> Ne doo they care to haue the auncestrie
> Of th' old Heroes memorizde anew,
> Ne doo they care that late posteritie
> Should know their names, or speak their praises dew:
> But die forgot from whence at first they sprang,
> As they themselves shalbe forgot ere long.

Milton might have been thinking of Spenser and sacred mneumonics when, in *The Reason of Church Government,* he rejected the invocation to "Dame Memory and her Siren daughters" (CE III, 241).

claimed divine assistance, he provoked nearly three centuries of heated commentary. The fourth explanation for the disinterest of English criticism proceeds from the third. The man who would speak of prophetic inspiration as a genuine possibility for modern poets would require the protection of a nearly invulnerable self-assurance. Raising the question of prophetic authority, he would have to answer understandable doubts about his own authority. England had no man with this inclination and talent enough to make his countrymen attend. In any case, one can understand why Milton went to Italy when he wished to learn how an inspired man created poetry.[90]

In the poetry itself, we find a more diverse and suggestive tradition. For some, divine inspiration was important enough to be desired and preposterous enough to be mocked at the same time. Thus John Davies of Hereford:

The Author, of, and to His Muse

O then, thou great unlimitable *Muse,*
(That rests, in motion, in th' ETERNALS Breast)
Inspire my *Muse,* with *grace* her *pow'r* to use
In nought, but when to thee shall be addrest:
So shall that *Spirit* that made thy *Dauid* sing,
Make *Dauies* too, (a Begger) like a King.[91]

The second line suggests some knowledge of the traditional issues concerning vatic poetry. Should this "unlimitable *Muse*" descend, the poetic mind would presumably experience calm and delight, not frenzy, reposing in the bosom of serene motion. But the tone does not expect any descent. Divine inspira-

90 Even there he would have found little remaining of the Platonist tradition initiated by Ficino and extended in the critical debates of the early sixteenth century. Through the latter half of that century Aristotelian premises gained ascendancy, and inspiration became, as it became in England, a dead tradition evoked in literary apologetics only when comfortably subordinate to the vocabulary of conscious art, careful imitation, and clear reasoning. Tasso, whose commentary on the heroic poem Milton recommends in *Of Education,* argued that the epic poet should not choose a biblical subject because he was not, given the sanctity of his source, free to invent and redispose, making his story appropriately marvellous (*Discourses on the Heroic Poem* in Allan H. Gilbert, *Literary Criticism: Plato to Dryden* [Detroit: Wayne State University Press, 1962], p. 482). The advice assumed that no poet could expect inspiration comparable to that which had aided the composition of the Bible: secular history alone might be transformed by those talents and faculties peculiar to the poet rather than the historian.

Weinberg (vol. II) has documented the increasing influence of Aristotle.

91 *The Muse's Sacrifice, or Divine Meditations* (London, 1612), p. 8.

tion can make David out of Davies, a king out of a beggar; this supplicant promises to write only for eternity and then implores the eternal Muse with an easy pun on his name. Davies playfully indulges the time-serving beggar while begging to become a holy prophet. As he knows himself, his true riches are in the autobiographical puns of sonnets and epigrams. Something of the same tone appears in this poem by Robert Herrick:

Not Every Day Fit for Verse

'Tis not ev'ry day, that I
Fitted am to prophesie:
No, but when the Spirit fils
The fantastick Pannicles:
Full of fier; then I write
As the Godhead doth indite.
Thus inrag'd, my lines are hurl'd,
Like the *Sybells,* through the world.
Look how next the holy fier
Either shakes, or doth retire;
So the Fancie cooles, till when
That brave Spirit comes agen.[92]

Herrick brought together *furor poeticus,* holy prophecy, classical oracles, and the Holy Spirit more overtly than any English critic. But this poem is another of the many cheerful interpentrations of the mundane and the sublime in *Hesperides.* To explain why he does not create a poem every day, Herrick presents himself as a holy prophet. The trivial question evokes a tremendously serious answer, the humble epigram becomes inseparable from a biblical vision, and the category of small things is, as usual in Herrick, pleasantly confused with the category of great things.

Spenser is a more perplexing case and I cannot hope to treat him fully in this regard. Although the invocation to the *Faerie Queene* seems only marginally theoretical, the early translations of Petrarch, du Ballay, and Jan van der Noot suggest his abiding interest in visionary experience and prophetic allegory.[93] The opening of "A Hymne in Honovr of Beavtie" is quite a complex moment in the history of inspired poetry:

[92] *Herrick's Poetical Works,* ed. L. C. Martin (Oxford: Clarendon Press, 1956), p. 242.

[93] See Josephine W. Bennet, *The Evolution of the* Faerie Queene (New York: Ben Franklin, 1960), pp. 109–123.

> Ah wither, Loue, wilt thou now carrie mee?
> What wontlesse fury dost thou now inspire
> Into my feeble breast, too full of thee?
> Whylest seeking to aslake thy raging fyre
> Thou in me kindlest much more great desyre,
> And vp aloft aboue my strength doest rayse
> The wondrous matter of my fyre to prayse.[94]

The passage sustains a double sense. The speaker is a Petrarchan lover, burning with unrequited passion and forced by his lady to praise her cruel fires in a poem. He is also a poet driven by the furious dictates of the divine afflatus. As a lover, he promises to worship the "goodly Pattern" of his lady, divine Venus (l. 32). He hopes for a guerdon:

> That both to thee, to whom I mean it most,
> And eke to her, whose faire immortal beame,
> Hath darted fyre into my feeble ghost,
> That now it wasted is with woes extreame,
> It may so please that she at length will streame
> Some deaw of grace, into my withered hart,
> After long sorrow and consuming smart.
> [Ll. 22–28]

As a poet, his breast was already "too full of thee"—too full of the inspiring force—before beginning these verses. "Whylest seeking to aslake thy raging fyre" by writing a poem, the poet was inspired to write about his inspiration, "the wondrous matter of my fyre to prayse." Whereas the common tactic, familiar to teachers of freshman English and readers of *The Prelude,* is to write about why one cannot write, this poet writes about the force that requires him to write—and does so at the bidding of that force. The psychology of the Petrarchan lover is insepararble from the psychology of the inspired poet. Words such as "fury," "inspire," "raging fyre," and "rayse" have meanings for both Neoplatonic lovers and inspired poets. As in Ficino, there is no difference here between *furor poeticus* and passionate ardor. The pattern of ideal Beauty inspires all lovely things on this earth:

> For through infusion of celestiall powre,
> The duller earth it quickneth with delight,
> And life-full spirits priuily doth powre

[94] *Spenser's Minor Poems,* p. 446. Future references follow the lining of this edition.

> Through all the parts, that to the lookers sight
> They seeme to please.
>
> [Ll. 51–54]

Poets and lovers are both creators. Of necessity, they participate in the continuous renewal and "comely composition" of all beauty (l. 69). Poetic inspiration, then, is only one of the many ardent rhythms that vivify the universe.

To my knowledge, the most uncompromising assertion of prophetic authority in Elizabethan, Jacobean, or Stuart verse appears in the Sylvester translation of Du Bartas. The translator says that he "craveth also the assistance of the Highest." [95] In the section entitled "Urania," his author explains in full detail what such "assistance" means to the divine poet. The theory of inspiration is radical and absolute. He who would write of "th' entercourse of the Celestiall Court" must seemingly take dictation from Urania. The Muse is speaking:

> Each *Art* is learn'd by *Art:* but POESIE
> Is a meer *Heav'nly gift:* and none can taste
> The Deaws we drop from Pindus plenteously,
> If sacred Fire have not his breast imbrac't.
>
> [St. 22]
>
> True *Poets,* right are like Winde-Instruments,
> Which full, do sound; empty, their noise surceases.
> For with their *Fury* lasts their Excellence;
> Their *Muse* is silent, when their *Fury* ceases.
>
> [St. 32]

To be "inspired" is, etymologically, to be breathed into, and poets are therefore "like Winde-Instruments." Urania offers to "conduct thy pen" (st. 17). Divine poets, receiving this favor, are "*Secretaries* of the Heav'nly Court" (st. 47). Urania cites Moses, David, and Jeremiah to bolster this opinion—the theory of poetic dictation rests on a theory of biblical dictation. She seems to be responsible for all poetic speech by, from, and about divinity:

[95] *The Complete Works of Joshua Sylvester,* ed. Alexander B. Grosart (New York: AMS Press, 1967), I, 18. The section entitled "Urania" appears in II, 3–6.

Besides Milton, Urania led one other English poet, William Drummond of Hawthornden, to unsullied knowledge and pure poetry. There was a section called "Vrania, or Spirituall Poems" in Drummond's *Poems* (Edinburgh, 1619); see *The Poetical Works of William Drummond . . . ,* ed. L. E. Kastner, Scotish Text Society (Edinburgh and Manchester: W. Blackwood, 1913), I, 86ff. Lily Campbell overlooks this example in her otherwise authoritative "The Christian Muse," *Huntington Library Bulletin,* 8 (1935), 1–66.

> Thence is't that *Ouid* cannot speak in Prose:
> Thence is't that *Dauid* (Shepheard, turned *Poet*)
> So soon doth learn my *songs*. . . .
> [St. 25]

Indeed, "God, himselfe, the *Delphian* Songs doth teach" (st. 21). Remembering the careful labors of the Fathers to separate Delphi from Israel, the boasting words of Urania may seem crude and imprecise. There is no delicate harmony here, no well-ordered concord of diverse sounds. Zealously displaying her influence over human creations, the Muse goes so far as to cite the devil. Satan himself recognized the importance of poetry: "In's Oracles and Idols speaking wily, / Not common Prose, but curious Verse did use" (st. 51). The somewhat bludgeoning Urania takes care with only one of the traditional difficulties concerning vatic inspiration. She protects the words "Phrenzie" and "Fury" from any human connotations:

> For, as a humane Furie makes a man
> Lesse than a man: so Diuine-Fury makes him
> More then himselfe; and sacred Phrenzie then
> Above the heav'ns' bright flaming arches takes him.
> [St. 30]

The divine poet transmits his inspiration to his best readers, for "oft th' Reader th' Author's form receiveth" (st. 40). Like the poet himself, these readers will be seized "with gentle fury" (st. 40).

Naming her poets "secretaries" and "Winde-Instruments," Urania may not be endorsing the mechanical theory of biblical and poetic inspiration. From the time of Justin Martyr, the metaphors used in speaking about the prophet had always threatened to contradict the nonfigurative descriptions of his activity. Myles Smith, in his preface to the 1611 English Bible, seemingly recommended the secretarial theory to his countrymen: "The author being God, not man; the inditer, the holy Spirit, not the wit of the Apostles or Prophets; the Penmen such as were sanctified from the womb, and ended with a principle portion of God's Spirit." [96] If we emphasize "in-

[96] This preface has been omitted from modern editions, possibly because of this strongly worded passage about biblical authority. See "The Translators to the Reader," in *The King James Bible,* ed. E. J. Goodspeed (Chicago: University of Chicago Press, 1935), p. 40. The word "Penmen" passed into the language. George Rust, for example, spoke of "the *holy spirit* and his Penman *Moses*" in *A Letter of Resolution concerning Origen,* Facsimile Text Society, ser. 3, no. 16 (New York: Columbia University Press, 1933), p. 46.

diter" at the expense of "endued," we can discover the extreme position here at the very heart of Anglicanism. But once again, this kind of paradox emerges naturally from the Bible itself. The Word of God is also the word of the prophet. Sidney did not believe in the divine inspiration of poets, but John Donne wrote these lines in a poem celebrating the Sidney translations of the Psalms:

> A Brother and a Sister, made by thee
> The Organ, where thou art the Harmony.
> Two that make one *John Baptists* holy voyce. . . .
>
> . . . . .
>
> . . . The Organist is hee
> Who hath tun'd God and Man, the Organ we:
> The songs are these, which heavens high holy Muse
> Whisper'd to *David, David* to the Jewes:
> And *Davids* Successors, in holy zeale,
> In formes of joy and art doe re-reveale. . . .[97]

Stressing "re-reveale," the organ conceit, and the reference to John the Baptist, we emerge with the Sidneys as latter-day prophets inspired, if not whispered to, by the "high holy Muse"; their divine translations cry in the wilderness of the native tradition. Stressing "formes of joy and art," we emerge with the Sidneys as rational imitators of an inspired art. Metaphor, particularly metaphor in poetry, offered the witty man some freedom from the rigors of abstract theological discourse. It is important for the modern reader to understand that, with few exceptions, no man of the Renaissance who called prophets or poets "secretaries," "penmen," and "wind instruments" meant to ridicule their office. Obedience to a divine command was the great human freedom.

Through the reign of Charles I, divine furor was never so important to English poets and critics as it was to their Italian counterparts. The critical literature reveals no pressing concern with the relationship between contemporary poets, classical poets, and biblical prophets. Sidney disagreed with "E. K." about poetic inspiration, but no one rushed into the controversy or even recognized it in print. Poets such as Davies and Herrick drew on the vatic tradition as a way of being pious and witty at the same time, ennobling the poetic office without denying the more mundane routines of profes-

[97] *The Divine Poems,* ed. Helen Gardner (Oxford: Clarendon Press, 1952), p. 34.

sional craftsmanship. Other poets, fervently concerned with literary patriotism, served both God and the national language by sanctifying the secular traditions. Spenser invoked a sacred Muse and proceeded to imitate Virgil and Ariosto in the vocabulary of Chaucer. Accepted as an English Virgil, he was adduced as proof positive of the traditional idea that poetry requires divine assistance. Unlike Dante, Petrarch, Boccaccio, Ariosto, and Tasso, his work failed to inspire an extensive interest in vatic creation; but his blend of patriotism and holy zeal continued to impel the work of English poets. The later Donne dedicated himself to the arts of sacred parody and adopted a prophetic stance in some of his poems. He celebrated the English Psalms, paraphrased Jeremiah, and wrote powerfully of the divine and priestly use of language in "The Litany." At the end of *The Progresse of the Soule* he proclaimed himself the herald of God: "I am / The Trumpet, at whose voyce the people came." [98] George Herbert found his metaphors and techniques in the secular brothel, washed them with his tears, dressed them in divinity, and took them to church. He made the dainty devices speak to God.[99] But until 1640 these Christian patriots managed to find a place for divine poetry in the native tradition without raising the issue of vatic inspiration in any devisive way. In England sacred poetry won its battles without suffering a major internal division. An English poet could implore divine aid, even claim divine aid, and offend no eager enemies. As William Browne of Tavistock set out to nationalize the pastoral romance, he invoked his God:

> And thou which through the Desert and the Deepe,
> Didst lead thy Chosen like a flock of sheepe:
> As sometime by a Starre thou guidedst them,
> Which fed vpon the plaines of Bethelem;
> When I shall sing ought of thy Holy hill,
> That times to come, when they my rymes rehearse,

[98] The sense of prophetic authority in the divine poems has received scant attention. It is usually assumed that Donne wrote his early poems to display a fashionable *sprezzatura* and his later poems to provide an outlet for spiritual anguish. But the poem to the Sidneys, "The Lamentations of Jeremy," and the prophetic voice of the *Anniversaries*—bearing the burden of death and Apocalypse—all suggest a far more public motive. See my treatment of the sermons in chapter II, pp. 102–5.

Louis Martz defines sacred parody in *The Poetry of Meditation* (New Haven: Yale University Press, 1954), pp. 179–320.

[99] I use the metaphors of "The Forerunners," in *The Works of George Herbert*, ed. F. E. Hutchinson (Oxford: Clarendon Press, 1941), p. 176.

May wonder at me, and admire my Verse:
For who but one rapt in Coelestiall fire,
Can by his Muse to such a pitch aspire.[100]

This passage shows us one reason why *Paradise Lost* was not written in rhyming couplets. It also shows us that the unremarkable trivia of one age can become the grand passion of another. When Milton wrote his invocations, the meaning of the act had changed significantly.

In 1650 the subject of vatic inspiration aroused the fervid concern of an Englishman for the first time since John Skelton replied to the scholars in 1528. Placing *Gondibert* in the native tradition, William Davenant hoped to sever the long-standing coalition between patriotism and inspired verse: "a wise Poet, like a wise General, will not shew his strengths till they are in exact Government and order; which are not the postures of chance, but proceed from Vigilance and labor. Yet to such painful Poets some upbraid the want of extemporary fury, or rather *inspiration;* a dangerous word; which many have of late successfully us'd." [101] Significantly, this passage was written and first published in Paris. Davenant believed that poets, like the holy politic, must preserve "exact Government and order." Though he did not use the term "Montanist," it is evident that an English critic had finally discovered the devil of heresy concealed in the Christian avatar of the ancient *vates:*

> and *inspiration* is a spiritual Fitt, deriv'd from the antient Ethnick Poets, who then, as they were Priests, were Statesmen too, and probably lov'd dominion; and as their well dissembling of *inspiration* begot them reverence then, equal to that which was paid to Laws; so these who now profess the same fury, may perhaps by such authentick example pretend authority over the people; it being not unreasonable to imagine, they rather imitate the Greek Poets then the Hebrew Prophets, since the later were inspired for the use of others; and these, like the former, prophesie for themselves. [P. 12]

Both the ancient *vates* and the contemporary *vates* were dissemblers. The opposition could not justly claim the Hebrew prophets as their spiritual precedent; true inspiration came only "for the use of others," not for the gratification of the

[100] *The Works of William Browne . . . ,* ed. W. Carew Hazlitt (London, 1868), I, 107. Milton owned and annotated both parts of *Britannia's Pastorals;* his marginalia are reprinted in CE XVIII, 336–40.

[101] *The Works of Sir William Davenant* (London, 1675; rpt. New York: Benjamin Blom, 1968), p. 12.

inspired. Partially a response to Montanus, the patristic distinction between pagan ecstasy and Christian calm had been equally political and theological. With Davenant, the literary tradition returned full circle to the patristic writings. He saw no essential difference between *furor poeticus* and social anarchy, divinely inspired poets and divinely inspired revolutionaries. Every kind of enthusiasm was suspect. Poets, poems, priests, worshippers, statesmen, and subjects should all display "exact Government and order." Beginning with an attack on inspired poetry, Davenant turned immediately to inspired "Statesmen" and, soon after, to inspired "Divines." All three meanings of the word *vates* were equally dangerous to the English nation: "But though the ancient Poets are excus'd, as knowing the weak constitution of those Deities from whom they took their Priesthood; and the frequent necessity of dissembling for the ease of government: yet these, (who also from the chief to the meanest, are Statesmen and Priests, but have not the luck to be Poets) should not assume such fancy familiarity with a true God" (p. 12). But Solomon and the prophets wrote divine poetry, and poetry is beloved of God:

> After this contemplation, how acceptable the voice of Poesy hath been to God, we may (by descending from Heaven to Earth) consider how usefull it is to Men; and among Men, Divines are the chief, because ordain'd to temper the rage of humane power by spirituall menaces, as by sudden and strange threatnings madness is frighted into Reason; and they are sent hither as Liegers from God, to conserve in stedfast motion the slippery joynts of Government; and to perswade an amity in divided Nations: therefore to Divines I first address my self; and presume to ask them, why, ever since their dominion was first allow'd, at the great change of Religions, (though ours more than any inculcates obedience, as an easie Medicine to cool the impatient and raging world into a quiet rest) mankinde hath been more unruly then before? [P. 13]

The implication was that divines had been reading the wrong kind of divine poetry. Like inspiring like, the rage of poets became the rage of priests, and the rage of priests became the rage of congregations. Davenant attacked the quality and not the principle. Like still inspiring like, the cool reason of true poetry should "temper the rage of humane power," "cool the impatient and raging world into a quiet rest." To be truly patriotic, divine poets must drop the conventions of vatic creation.

For Davenant at least, the Puritan Revolution turned an attack on poetic inspiration into a defense of political conservatism. The old vocabulary of *furor poeticus* was no different from the new vocabulary of religious revolution. To describe the psychology of literary creation was automatically to take a position on political and social affairs. Davenant suggested, as forcefully as possible, that the native tradition of literary patriotism needed reexamination. Writing for God and country was a more complicated activity than Spenser had imagined. The true loyalists and the best poets had to remain emphatically uninspired.

Replying to this angry sermon on tranquility, Hobbes maintained a cooler and wittier demeanor:

> In that you make so small account of the example of almost all the approved Poets, ancient and modern, who thought fit in the beginning, and sometimes also in the progress of their Poems, to invoke a Muse, or some other Deity, that should dictate to them, or assist them in their Writings, they that take not the laws of Art, from any reason of their own, but from the fashion of precedent times, will perhaps accuse your singularity. For my part, I neither subscribe to their accusation, nor yet condemn that heathen custom, otherwise than as accessary to their Religion. For their Poets were their Divines; had the name of Prophets, exercised amongst the people a kinde of spiritual Authority; would be thought to speak by a divine spirit; have their works which they writ in Verse (the divine stile) pass for the word of God, and not of man; and to be hearkened to with reverence. Do not our Divines (excepting the Stile) do the same, and by us that are of the same Religion cannot justly be reprehended for it? [102]

Davenant moved without much delicacy from ancient Greece to modern England in his witch-hunt for inspiration. Hobbes kept his sense of history. The classical *vates* was, in his community, a recognized "Authority." Similarly, the contemporary divine properly exercised spiritual authority—Hobbes was reacting to an attack on the "fancy familiarity" with God so vehement as to deny any familiarity at all. This negative proposition would annihilate the difference between divine authorities and their subjects. To have no one claim spiritual authority was just as dangerous as to have everyone claim spiritual authority. But Hobbes of course agreed that "unskillful divines" often "call up such spirits, as they cannot at their pleasure allay again." With respect to poetic inspiration, what Hobbes could allow in the pagan he could not understand in the Christian: "But why a Christian should think it an orna-

[102] "The Answer . . . to . . . D'Avenant's Preface," *ibid.*, p. 23.

ment to his Poem; either to prophane the true God, or invoke a false one, I can imagine no cause, but a reasonless imitation of Custom, of a foolish custom; by which a man enabled to speak wisely from the principles of nature, and his own meditation, loves rather to be thought to speak by inspiration, like a bagpipe" (p. 23). A venerable tradition honored the prophet as the lyre, flute, or wind instrument of a musical God. Here he declined to a bagpipe. Deceiving themselves, inspired poets merely "think it an ornament" or wish "to be thought to speak by inspiration." Hobbes, unlike Davenant, made some attempt to divide the meanings of *vates* and treat them separately. He ridiculed vatic inspiration less as a dire threat to political, religious, and social order than as an affectation patently absurd.

But in the decade following the exchange between Hobbes and Davenant, the claim of divine inspiration was linked with madness, disease, hypocrisy, and political chaos.[103] Meric Casaubon, who declined Cromwell's offer to write the official history of the Puritan Revolution, offered *A Treatise concerning Enthusiasme* in 1655, arguing that mistaken belief in prophetic authority is the great melancholy sickness of Western history, "the occasion of so many evils and mischiefs among men, as no other errour, or delusion of what kind soever, hath ever been of either more, or greater." [104] Casaubon recognized the crucial importance of that issue which other English commentators, living in more harmonious days, had treated with such luxurious indifference. The experiences of the biblical prophets had to be separated, firmly separated, from all other promises of celestial assistance. It was imperative to "distinguish between that *influentia divina,* or that *ignis ardens,* that *burning fire,* that inspired, or inflamed, if

[103] See the classic study by George Williamson, "The Restoration Revolt against Enthusiasm," in *Seventeenth-Century Contexts* (Chicago: University of Chicago Press, 1961; rev. 1969), pp. 202–39, and Truman Steffan, "The Social Argument against Enthusiasm (1650–1660)," *ES,* no. 4126 (1941), pp. 56–70. In *Enthusiasm* (Oxford: Oxford University Press, 1950), Ronald Knox confines his disappointing treatment of the seventeenth century to the Quakers, apparently unaware of the wider implications remarked by contemporary observers such as Davenant, Hobbes, Casaubon, and More. Though he considered this book his masterpiece, many of us enthusiasts will choose to remember Knox as the man who formulated the definitive "rules" of the detective story, and himself produced several masterly examples of this quintessentially rational genre.

[104] Ed. Paul J. Korshin (Gainesville: Scholars' Facsimiles, 1970), p. 4. Korshin reprints the second edition of 1656.

you will, Holy Prophets . . . and that partly naturall, and partly supernaturall . . . *heat,* or *fire,* common or incidentall at least, unto all men by nature" (p. 217). Orpheus was a "mere fanatick" (p. 9). Considering the belief that poets receive divine attention, he asked in a tone midway between exasperation and incredulity: "what more can be said of the truest, and most holy prophets?" (p. 256). A year later Henry More published his *Enthusiasmus Triumphatus,* scornfully expanding the diagnosis of Casaubon. Enthusiasm was "nothing else but a miconceit of being inspired," and the cause was a windy melancholy, "that Flatulency which is in the melancholy complexion." [105] Both men attacked inspiration for being precisely what Plato and his followers had said it to be—irrational. Given the political climate of Cromwell's England, there was no opportunity for a rational man to admire the phenomenon of melancholy genius or to appreciate the aesthetic daring of poetry conflated with prophecy. The Civil War invested the strategies of Christian aesthetics with new meaning and new discipline.

In 1656 Cowley published his collected poems, including the unfinished *Davideis,* and in the preface set forth his understanding of biblical poetry. The Old Testament themes provided countless opportunities for wit, eloquence, and invention: "will not the actions of Sampson afford as plentiful matter as the labors of Hercules?" [106] He saw no need for vatic inspiration in these endeavors:

All the *Books* of the *Bible* are either already most admirable, and exalted pieces of *Poesie,* or are the best Materials in the world for it. . . . None but a good *Artist* will know how to do it: neither must we think to cut and polish *Diamonds* with so little pains and skill as we do *Marble.* For if any man design to compose a *Sacred Poem,* be it onely turning a story of the Scripture . . . into Rhyme; He is so far from elevating of Poesie, that he onely abases *Divinity.* In brief, he who can write a *prophane Poem well,* may write a *Divine one better;* but he who can do that but ill, will do this much worse. The same fertility of *Invention,* the same wisdom of *Disposition;* the same *Judgement* in observance of *Decencies,* the same lustre and vigor of *Elocution;* the same modesty and majestie of *Number;* briefly the same kinde of *Habit,* is required to both. . . . But sure I am, that there is nothing yet in our *Language* (nor perhaps in *any*) that is in any degree answerable to the *Idea* that I conceive of it.

[105] Augustan Reprint Society, no. 118 (Los Angeles, 1966), pp. 2, 12.
[106] "Preface" to *Poems* (London, 1656), n. pag.

The sacred poet who wished to retell the Bible could not find his authority in vatic inspiration. He had to be a good diamond cutter who, perhaps, had proved his skill in marble. Whether of diamond or of marble, cutting was cutting; the sacred poet required the same skills as the secular poet. Cowley was unconcerned about the presumption of exercising "fertility of *Invention*" on biblical subjects. These remarks about biblical epic represent an application of Jonsonian practicality—art, labor, and craft—to the subject of sacred poetry.

Davideis began with an invocation to Christ in which the poet offered himself as a new "Apostle" for the conversion of "Muses-lands" (p. 4). But in the fascinating notes that accompany the poem, Cowley disowned any efforts toward divine inspiration. He first defended the passage as a practical and conventional gesture:

> I hope this kind of boast (which I have been taught by almost all the old *Poets*) will not seem immodest; for though some in other Language have attempted the writing of a *Divine Poem;* yet none, that I know of, hath in English. . . . The custom of beginning all *Poems,* with a *Proposition* of the whole work, and an Invocation of some God for his assistance to go through with it, is so Solemnly and religiously observed by all the ancient *Poets,* that though I could have found out a better way, I should not (I think) have ventured upon it. But there can be, I believe, none better; and that part, of the Invocation, if it became a Heathen, is no less then necessary for a *Christian Poet. A Jove principium, Musae;* and it follows then very naturally, *Jovis omnia plena.* The whole work may reasonably hope to be filled with a *Divine Spirit,* when it begins with a Prayer to be so.[107]

It is significant that Cowley apologized for "this kind of boast." Surely his Royalist friends, including Davenant and Hobbes, were among those to whom the invocation might have "seemed immodest." The defense itself was as weak as possible. Until the last sentence, the convention appears to be desirable simply because it is conventional. Then we learn that the work "may reasonably hope" to express "a" Spirit—Cowley made no connection between the need for divine assistance and the justification of "invention," of presuming to

[107] P. 24. See also Cowley's notes to "The Muse" in *Literary Criticism of Seventeenth-Century England,* ed. Edward W. Tayler (New York: Knopf, 1967), p. 313. Here Cowley glosses an extravagant conceit about inspired creation with the old distinction between creating what is not and recreating what already is. Again, it is as if he were apologizing for the imaginative license he permitted himself in the act of composing his poem.

rewrite the Word of God. Like Jove, God was everywhere. And if He were not, Cowley would have followed tradition anyway. The invocation, despite its hyperboles, was a "*Prayer* to be so" and not a claim to be so. Requesting divine inspiration, Cowley took issue with the literary dictates of Davenant and Hobbes. But his defense of this practice conceded the major point. The stillborn Royalist epic required a note to subdue its immodesty.

Announcing the unrealized intentions of *Davideis,* Cowley also announced his artistic death. "The Poet dies before the *Man,*" and his sad Muse must now be "assisting at her own funeral." [108] Unable to finish Davideis, Cowley began a long patriotic poem on the Civil War. There was no hope at all for this second endeavor: "it is so uncustomary, as to become almost *ridiculous,* to make *Lawrels* for the *Conquered.*" Having sunk so low in spirit, he could not return to the biblical epic: "But I have had neither *Leisure* hitherto, nor have *Appetite* at present to finish the work, or so much as to revise that part which is done with that care which I resolved to bestow upon it, and which the *Dignity* of the *Matter* well deserves." Still, the preface bristled with the remnants of fervid ambition. We recognize the old righteous zeal of the divine poet. Though the devil has usurped many human activities, "there is none that he so universally, and so long usurpt, as *Poetry.*" If poets were obedient to the Word and wrote about biblical subjects, they would find "the bonds and fetters of it" to be "the truest and greatest *liberty.*" We recognize the old literary nationalism in the unfinished war poem and, more familiarly, in the unfinished sacred epic. Now dead, this English Apostle once hoped to convert the native Muse.

The historian of literary psychology finds in Cowley a uniquely interesting figure. He began by separating literary patriotism and religious zeal from vatic inspiration. A great epic both English and Christian could be written without much attention to divine assistance. That left him with patriotism and zeal. Then he discovered that, after the Civil War, he had no country to write for. That left him with a proselytizing zeal which proved too weak to see him through the project. In Cowley the traditional identity of the English poet fell apart, motive by motive, stance by stance, until nothing re-

108 "Preface" to *Poems.* All remaining quotations from Cowley in this chapter are from the unnumbered preface.

mained except what he called "the Art of Oblivion." He vowed to retire into country solitude. "And I think *Doctor Donnes Sun Dyal in a grave* is not more useless and ridiculous then Poetry would be in that *retirement*."

The disintegration of Cowley suggests that, after the revolution, the traditional and traditionally unexamined synthesis of God, country, and inspiration was difficult for an English poet to sustain. Royalist or Puritan, anyone hoping to write patriotic verse with divine assistance must have found the situation unfavorable. If the poet had fought for the winning side, his triumph was, by 1656, already dissolving into a defeat. When the king returned four years later, it was obvious that neither side could claim an unambiguous victory—a poet with allegiances would have to write patriotic verse for one section of a divided nation. Of course, this poet might take comfort in the fact that Cowley had written without divine aid. He had attempted to create sacred art with the workmanlike outlook of a secular poet. Though he had implored the Spirit, he had done so primarily to fulfill a conventional expectation. Genuine inspiration might protect another poet against all human weakness:

> O! that I may thus be perfected by feebleness, and irradiated by obscurity! And, indeed, in my blindness, I enjoy in no inconsiderable degree the favor of the Deity, who regards me with more tenderness and compassion in proportion as I am able to behold nothing but himself. Alas! for him who insults me; who maligns me merits public execration! For the divine law not only shields me from injury, but almost renders me too sacred to attack; not indeed so much from the privation of my sight, as from the overshadowing of those heavenly wings which seem to have occasioned this obscurity; and which, when occasioned, he is wont to illuminate with an interior light, more precious and more pure. [CE VIII, 73]

A student of history is never comfortable in asserting the uniqueness of an idea, an emotion, a psychological event. Renaissance poets continually mentioned their great affinity with the inspired prophets of Israel. Their tone was often grave—but in its gravity marked by a sense of knowing excess. To one degree or another, they disowned full responsibility for their claims. Measured against this passage, the conceptions of prophetic inspiration in "E. K.," Spenser, Sidney, Puttenham, Webbe, Meres, Harington, Davies, Donne, Jonson, and Herrick fall to ashes like paintings in a fire. Milton required the convention of vatic inspiration to live his life as well as his life in art. Divine instruction guarded him against the humiliations of incompletion:

> higher Argument
> Remains, sufficient of itself to raise
> That name, unless an age too late, or cold
> Climate, or Years damp my intended wing
> Deprest; and much they may, if all be mine,
> Not Hers who brings it nightly to my Ear.[109]

Cowley fit perfectly the negative image of the poet of *Paradise Lost.* All was his, and the poetic man died without completing his poem. As Cowley himself said, cold climate had damped his intended wing:

> And if in quiet and flourishing times they [poets] meet with so small encouragement, what are they to expect in rough and troubled ones? if *wit* be such a *Plant,* that it scarce receives heat enough to preserve it alive even in the *Summer* of our cold *Clymate,* how can it choose but wither in a long and a sharp *Winter?* a warlike, various, and a tragical age is best to *write* of, but worst to *write in.*

> The truth is, for a man to write well, it is necessary to be in good humor; neither is *Wit* less eclypsed with the unquietness of *Mind,* then *Beauty* with the *Indisposition* of *Body.*

Urania protected her poet from "barbarous dissonance" (VII.32), from cold, senility, and death. She preserved the tranquillity of a poet who had once intended to write a poem doctrinal and exemplary to the nation. Though his nation failed, his God could not.

But what did the inspired poet mean by "an age too late"? Merritt Hughes has glossed this phrase as a reference to the old age of the world, the decay of human genius (p. 379). The doctrine appears nowhere else in the epic. As evidence Hughes cites Prolusion VII and "Naturam Non Pati Senium," both schoolboy exercises, one of which argues precisely the opposite case. Why would Milton, closing the final invocation of his epic, speak with such anxiety of a possibility which had not concerned him for thirty years? The Reverend Henry Todd, compiler of the variorum edition of the early nine-

[109] *Paradise Lost* X.42–47, in *Complete Poetry and Major Prose,* ed. Merritt Y. Hughes (New York: Odyssey, 1957), p. 379. Following the recent practice in Milton criticism, all future references to the poetry use the Hughes text.

Milton's third wife, Elizabeth Minshull, remembered that his favorite English poets were Spenser, Shakespeare, and Cowley (see W. R. Parker, *Milton: A Biography,* I, 600).

teenth century, quoted from *The Reason of Church Government*[110] a passage about the conditions favorable for an epic poem based on English history: "if to the instinct of nature and the imboldning of art ought may be trusted, and that there be nothing advers in our climat, or the fate of this age, it haply would be no rashnesse from an equal diligence and inclination to present the like offer in our own ancient stories" (CE III, 137). In the event, there was indeed something adverse waiting in the fate of this age; the phrase "an age too late" should be understood as a comment, poignant but unsentimental, about the effect of the Civil War on an attempt to write a Christian, English, and inspired poem. The ambitious young poet, whose literary pilgrimage to Italy had been interrupted by political disputes at home, recognized that his art could not survive amid these divisive passions: "were I ready to my wishes, it were a folly to commit any thing elaborately compos'd to the carelesse and interrupted listening of these tumultuous times" (CE III, 234). The same poet, in *An Apology against a Pamphlet . . . against Smectymnuus,* promised to write a poem which "might be worth your listening, Readers, as I may one day hope to have ye in a still time, when there shall be no chiding; not in these noises, the adversary as ye know, barking at the doore" (CE III, 305). Twenty years later the tumult had not subsided, the enemy had not retired. Perhaps an Englishman of this time could not enjoy the tranquillity necessary for poetic creation of the highest order and, rather than raise his voice against the hoarse shouts of controversy, would be wise to remain silent. Cowley thought so. Certainly it was "an age too late" for the unqualified patriotism of another Spenser. As he took up the composition of *Paradise Lost* in the years before the Restoration, Milton was in close association with Andrew Marvell.[111] Here was another negative example:

[110] *The Poetical Works of John Milton* (London, 1809), VII, 11–12. The gloss originated with Newton.

[111] Aubrey said that *Paradise Lost* was begun "about 2 yeares before the King came in, and finished about three yeares after the King's restauracion" (*Aubrey's Brief Lives,* ed. Oliver Lawson Dick [Ann Arbor: University of Michigan Press, 1957], p. 202). The authority for this statement was Edward Phillips, who remained vague about the time of composition in his own biography (see J. H. Hanford and James G. Taaffe, *A Milton Handbook* [New York: Appleton-Century-Crofts, 1970], pp. 158–59).

Milton first requested the services of Andrew Marvell in 1653. The request was not granted until 1657, about the time when, according to our only concrete source, Milton began work on his epic.

The forward Youth that would appear
Must now forsake his *Muses* dear,
  Nor in the Shadows sing
  His Numbers languishing.[112]

Soon after writing these lines, Marvell himself all but abandoned his muses or, rather, put them in the service of topical dispute. Tranquillity was the dearest luxury of this age. And if the disharmonies of war threatened all poetic creation, they were particularly dangerous to inspired creation.

Milton, like the early Fathers, associated prophetic inspiration with mental calm. One could not prepare to make "devout prayer" when distracted by the barbarous dissonance of a noisy age:

Neither doe I think it shame to covnant with any knowing reader, that for some few years yet I may go on trust with him toward the payment of what I am now indebted, as being a work not to be rays'd from the heat of youth, or the vapours of wine, like that which flows at wast from the pen of some vulgar Amorist, or the trencher fury of a riming parasite, nor to be obtain'd by the invocation of Dame Memory and her Siren daughters, but by devout prayer to that eternall Spirit who can enrich with all utterance and knowledge, and sends out his Seraphim with the hallow'd fire of his Altar to touch and purify the lips of whom he pleases. . . . Although it nothing content me to have disclos'd thus much before hand, but that I trust hereby to make it manifest with what small willingnesse I endure to interrupt the pursuit of no lesse hopes than these, and leave a calme and pleasing solitarynes fed with cherful and confident thoughts, to imbark in a troubl'd sea of noises and hoars disputes, put from beholding the bright countenance of truth in the quiet and still air of delightful studies. [CE III, 240–41]

The heats of youth and wine and lust, vulgar forms of *furor poeticus,* are transformed into the "hallow'd fire" that touched the lips of Isaiah. The "pursuit of no lesse hopes than these" properly takes place in "a calme and pleasing solitarynes fed with cherful and confident thoughts." Years later when he pursued these hopes again, Milton found solitude readily enough. But calm and cheer were undeniably more remote:

But cloud instead, and ever-during dark
Surrounds me, from the cheerful ways of men
Cut off. . . .

[III.45–47]

[112] *The Poems and Letters of Andrew Marvell,* ed. H. M. Margoliouth, rev. Pierre Legouis and E. E. Duncan-Jones (Oxford: Clarendon Press, 1971), I, 91. The few poems we know certainly to have been written after the Horatian Ode are either (like the Ode itself) occasional or satirical.

though fall'n on evil days,
On evil days though fall'n, and evil tongues;
In darkness, and with dangers compast round,
And solitude. . . .

[VII.25–28]

The inspired narrator of Paradise Lost feared "an age too late," feared nothing less than the death of true poetry.

In ages past true poetry had been closely identified with true prophecy and therefore with true religion. The patristic writers established their faith with a series of distinctions between classical and Christian prophecy. The greatest prophets in the Bible exercised free will, experienced divine serenity, understood their parabolic visions, and lived exemplary lives. Concerned almost exclusively with one meaning of *vates,* the Fathers defined their *propheta* and left to the Italian renaissance the labor of distinguishing between classical and Christian poetry—a labor which inevitably raised questions about poetic inspiration, especially if the ancient connection between poetry and prophecy were to be preserved. But in English literature the question of divine inspiration was subordinate to the larger issue of divine literature itself. As the Fathers slighted the poet to clarify the prophet, so English critics slighted the prophet to clarify the poet. The divine poet of England—learned, zealous, patriotic—depended for his existence on the essential unity of a literary audience which in turn depended on the essential unity of English culture. Typically, the divine poet raised his harp to glorify his language, honor his monarch, and dignify his national religion. Though he often scorned the secular tradition, he promoted a kind of unity by parodying its conventions. After the English Revolution, however, this complex of typical motives collapsed. The political and religious division of the nation inevitably meant a divided national literature. Examining the past for seeds of present anarchy, Royalists such as Davenant and Hobbes discovered that poetry was not without blame. Contemporary life had imitated ancient art: the postures of divine inspiration had helped to create a general tolerance for unsubdued enthusiasm of all kinds. Another Royalist apologized for the excessive invocation of an unfinished epic. Abraham Cowley, with no one country and no national religion, found himself with no sense of purpose—it was not enough to defy the secular poets. That he felt no divine presence to sustain his epic in the absence of church, king, and country was probably a matter of individual temperament. But the absence of a creative Spirit was also rooted in history: English literature had not provided the sacred poet with a forceful tradition of inspired creation. After the Civil War, the divine poet who could not identify his purposes with the purposes of God was in danger of oblivion. The continuity of English literature was in danger of fundamental disruption.

When Milton composed the bulk of his epic, the native tradition of sacred verse stood in a shambles. Literary patriotism was, like political patriotism, divided and sectarian. Vatic creation had been identified with social revolt. Poets were writing of love with insouciant wit or developing a new satire not dissimilar from the "noises and hoars disputes" of political pamphleteers. Since the inspired revolutionaries had failed, the divine poet who claimed inspiration might easily become the object of gloating ridicule. He might fail as Cowley had failed, once more depriving the English language of a sacred epic. Worse still, his failure would be a failure of inspiration, questioning the premise of his religious and political beliefs as well as his literary theory. And worse still for a committed Puritan, England had abandoned God and might expect God to abandon England, refusing to inspire a poet of this nation with a doctrinal and exemplary poem. It is in such a context that we must understand the prophetic verse of John Milton, his generation of a literary identity at once political and divine. To understand this context—especially the equation between inspired poets and Puritan revolutionaries—we must return to the history of prophetic inspiration as a theological and not a literary idea.

CHAPTER II

Prophets and Protestants

DESPITE the unceasing effort of rationalists, whether philosophers or scientists or men of common sense, prophecy has stubbornly refused to disappear from popular mythology and the literature that embodies this mythology. Though divine foresight was, in the late Middle Ages, a distant phenomenon no longer vital to the people of the new dispensation, authors of romance preserved the classical arts of divination, supplying their readers with auguries and portents, wise old men who stood at the crossroads to advise errant heroes about adventures still to come. It would be hazardous to conclude that the world of fiction bore any immediate relationship to actual belief. Characters with the gift of prophecy might be acceptable as a literary convention to people who would retreat with disgust from a prophet in real life. Prophetic characters tacitly admit the artifice of the fictional world. Like the author, they know what is going to happen next. They remind us of the existence of a planner and a plot. As we enter a fictional world, the future of that world already exists—indeed, we hold it in our hands.

But considering the theological prophecies of Joachim and the folklore oracles of Merlin, foresight was probably more than a fictional device in the Middle Ages. Intelligent men such as Geoffrey of Monmouth attended seriously to this form of knowledge. Theologians, however, remained generally oblivious to such movements, and most of the theorizing about prophecy concerned itself with a biblical past safely removed from contemporary affairs.[1]

[1] Norman Cohn (pp. 99–107) discusses the relationship of Joachim to medieval apocalyptism. Frank Kermode, in *Continuities* (New York: Random House, 1968), pp. 122–51, demonstrates the remarkable flexibility of this medieval prophetic scheme by suggesting that D. H. Lawrence appropriated Joachite doctrine to organize his major fiction. For the prophecies of Merlin, see Geoffrey of Monmouth, *History of the Kings of Britain,* trans. Sebastian Evans, rev. Charles W. Dunn (New York: Dutton, 1958), pp. 133–53.

I have excluded folklore prophets, astronomical prognosticators, and practitioners of the occult from this study. Although some persist in reading

This biblical past could be drawn on as a way of justifying new endeavors, lending a sense of continuity to the intellectual history of the religion. The early Fathers tended to change Old Testament prophecy into Christian exegesis. Continuing this transformation, the scholastic theologians of the Middle Ages found in prophecy an attractive precedent for their own various activities. Roger Bacon, for example, contended that all philosophy requires divine illumination. The "possible" human intellect receives knowledge from the senses, but the "active" intellect organizes empirical knowledge when inspired by God:

> And although angels may cleanse, illumine and arouse our minds in many ways, and though they may be to our minds like stars to the eyes of the body, yet Augustine ascribes to God the principle influence, just as to the sun is ascribed the flow of light falling through the window, and the angel is compared to one opening the window according to Augustine in his gloss on the Psalm, "Give me understanding." . . . All this is evidence of the fact that the active principle illuminating and influencing the possible intellect is a separate substance, that is God himself.[2]

The study of Scripture is not different in kind from the study of the book of creatures. The scientist, like the exegete, understands the object of his knowledge by virtue of divine illumination. About to examine the geometry and mathematics of visual experience, Roger Bacon claimed prophetic authority for his science. He returned to the rabbinical idea that prophets concealed all wisdom in their parabolic narratives. There-

---

"L'Allegro" and *Comus* as expert anthologies of English fairy legends, I cannot imagine that Milton was much concerned with such things. He never mentioned the notorious Nostradamus or the famous English prophets, such as Cunningham, Forster, and Dee. Furthermore, he seems to have been oblivious to the passionate controversy over witchcraft—a subject which Ralegh, Bacon, Browne, More, and many others found worthy of serious consideration. Milton was no Joseph Glanvill.

As one might expect, prophecy and fortune-telling appear often in the literature of witchcraft. In *A Most Certain, Strange, and True Discovery of a Witch* (London, 1643), a group of Parliamentary troops chance to see a woman walking upon a river. Horrified at this *imitatio Christi,* they immediately recognize the lady for a witch—a conclusion which not even the discovery of a submerged log beneath her can weaken. They proceed to murder her. Before she dies, the supposed witch admits the justice of their sentence by uttering a dark prophecy concerning the house of Essex. On these subjects, see Don Cameron Allen, *The Star-Crossed Renaissance* (Durham: Duke University Press, 1941); Katherine M. Briggs, *Pale Hecate's Team* (New York: Humanities Press, 1962), especially pp. 16–58.

[2] *The Opus Majus of Roger Bacon,* trans. Robert Belle Burke (London: Oxford University Press, 1928), I, 47.

fore all philosophy is divine: "This general proposition can be proved finally by the fact that the full measure of philosophy was given to the same men to whom also the law of God was given, namely, the holy patriarchs and prophets from the beginning of the world. . . . For the patriarchs and prophets alone were true philosophers, knowing all things, to wit, not only the law of God, but all the parts of philosophy" (I, 52). A contemporary philosopher might experience the illumination of the prophets, but he would express his divine knowledge through ordered discourse and rational demonstration.

The prophets had become examples of visionary apprehension. Isidore of Seville concluded his differentiation of the prophetic experience with a definition of three kinds of vision —the physical vision of the eyes, the spiritual vision "quo imaginamur ea quae per corpus sentimus," and the highest vision "per intuitum mente," which dispenses with corporeal images altogether. Bacon adapted this framework to his investigation of optics, repeating the old distinction in a new context:

> A comparison can be drawn here in many ways; for directness of vision belongs to God; deviation from the straight lines through refraction, which is weaker, befits the angelic nature; reflected vision, which is weakest, may be assigned to man. For just as a mirror because of its suitability aids vision, and gives to the species an opportunity of multiplying itself to the eye, so that vision may be effected, so does the body animated by the sensitive soul by its own nature and fitness aid the intellectual soul in its perception, and give it perception in those matters in which the intellect is dependent on the corporeal sense. . . . Man has a three-fold vision; one perfect, which will come in a state of glory after the resurrection; the second in the soul separated from the body in heaven until the resurrection, which is weaker; the third in this life, which is the weakest, and this is correctly said to be by reflection. As the apostle says, "We now see by means of a glass darkly, but in glory face to face," and after the resurrection in perfect directness, and before it in a deviation from the directness of vision in our soul. . . . Moreover, in our present state is vision threefold, namely, direct in those that are perfect; refracted in those that are imperfect; and in the evil and in those who neglect the commandments of God by reflection, according to the Apostle James; for it is compared to a man beholding his natural face in a glass. [II, 579–80]

There are three kinds of vision in the universe—the direct seeing of God, the refracted seeing of angels, and the reflected seeing of man. But in its journey back to God, the soul of man sees in three ways—one in this life, one between death and resurrection, one after the resurrection. And in this life itself a man may see in three ways. This final triad corresponds to the distinction in Isidore: we see by reflection with our physical eyes, by refraction with our mental eyes, and by direct vision with our powers of divine intuition. Bacon's excellently sturdy, fastidious elaboration represents the scholastic tendency toward categorization at its best. But prophecy has been absorbed into a systematic theory of illumination. The Old Testament prophets "saw" in the same way that any godly and knowledgeable man may "see." Prophetic vision is subordinate to a broad conception of knowledge based on an analogy with visual experience.

So theologians of more mystical inclination characterized the prophets as exemplary followers of the *via contemplativa*. Prophets were interesting because of their exquisite privilege, their nearness to God. The accounts of prophetic experience in the Bible showed the aspiring mystic his goal and his possible reward in this life. The theory of prophetic calm in the early Fathers yielded to the theory of beatific ascent in the thirteenth-century Platonists. Bernard of Clairvaux turned the correspondence theory of knowledge, which the early Fathers had used to ennoble exegesis, into a ladder of mystical contemplation. Knowledge was love to St. Bernard, and whatever Plotinus and Augustine had argued about knowing, he argued about feeling: "But sick sympathize with sick, and hungry with hungry, the more clearly they are alike. For just as pure truth is seen only with a pure heart, so a brother's misery is truly felt with a miserable heart." [3] Similarly, one can know God only insofar as he becomes godlike. To know God is to become one with Him:

> When the iniquity which causes that unlikeness which is in part has been put away, there will be a union of the spirit, there will be a mutual vision and a mutual love. When that which is perfect is come, then that which is in part shall be done away; and there will be a chaste and consummate love between them, a full comprehension, a clear vision, a firm union, an inseparable association, a perfect likeness. Then the soul will know even as also it is known; then it will love even as also it is loved; and the Bridegroom will rejoice over the bride, being himself both knower and known, lover and beloved.[4]

[3] Bernard of Clairvaux, *The Steps of Humility* iii.6, trans. George Bosworth Burch (Cambridge: Harvard University Press, 1940), pp. 133–35.

[4] Sermon 82 on Canticles 8, *ibid.*, p. 92.

The scholastic scientist Roger Bacon bolstered his optical theories with the metaphor of 1 Cor. 13.12. In the theory of knowledge which resulted, prophetic visions could be assimilated by rank and category. St. Bernard adapted the same text to his theory of mystical union. Yet he understood no significant difference between the Pauline definition of knowing and the parable of the bridegrooms. What resulted was a theory of love based on the same visual analogy as the old theory of knowledge. As seeing became loving and *scientia* became *caritas,* St. Paul replaced the prophets both as theoretician and as example of the inspired man.

Isidore ranked the conversion of Paul as an example of fifth-level prophetic experience—"Quintum genus vox de caelo." For Bernard, the mystical *raptus* on the road to Damascus was perhaps the most important human event (excluding the gospel narratives) in the entire Bible. The description that most appealed was the one in 2 Corinthians: "Scio hominem in Christo ante annos quattuordecim, siue in corpore nescio, siue extra corpus nescio, Deus scit: raptum euismodi usque ad tertium caelum. Et scio huiusmodi hominem, siue in corpore siue extra corpus nescio, Deus scit: quoniam raptus est in Paradisum: et audiuit arcana uerba, quae non licet homini loqui" (12.2–4). About this passage Bernard erected a theory of contemplative ascent. Through the office of the Son, a soul arrives at the first heaven of humility. Through the office of the Spirit, a soul arrives at the second heaven of mercy. Bernard argued that the journey to the first two heavens is not, properly speaking, a rapture. Though aided by a divine guide, the soul cooperates fully. There is no seizure. Transition to the third heaven reached by Paul demands that the active Father seize a passive soul. Only this last movement is genuinely a rapture, is genuinely a seeing.[5] Bernard conflated the three kinds of vision with the three heavens of contemplation:

Great is he whose business is to distribute the use of the senses, like public funds, dispensing it for the salvation of himself and of many. And no less great is he who has made the use of the senses a step toward those things which are invisible, by philosophizing. . . . But greatest of all is he who spurns all use of things and of the senses, so far as is permitted to human weakness, and is accustomed to fly to those heights by contemplating, not by ascending steps but by unexpected raptures. To this last class, I think Paul's raptures belong.

[5] *Steps of Humility* viii.22, *ibid.,* pp. 167–71.

> Raptures, not ascents; for he himself asserts that he was caught up, rather than ascended. . . . Do you wish those species of consideration to be distinguished by different names? The first, if you please, let us call dispensative, the second estimative, the third speculative.[6]

Along with Paul, several Old Testament prophets exemplified the "speculative" experience: "Raptus est Paulus, raptus est Elias, translatus est Enoch."[7] Yet this conflation of seeing, knowing, and loving shifted the emphasis in discourse about the biblical prophets. Those who achieved the most perfect "vision" were the most perfect prophets. This tendency is barely detectable in Isidore. By the time of Bonaventure and Bernard, Moses was exalted as a greater prophet than David because he achieved the *visio dei*.[8] But the vision of Moses had little to do with history, with the burden of foreknowing. In elevating the *visio dei* above other prophetic experiences, the medieval theologians devalued the comprehension of time, the terrors of foresight, the bitter burdens of lamentation. To the mystic, the prophetic books were valuable as a kind of psychological data—and even as data, they were less informative than St. Paul. Though no contemporary man could receive direct knowledge about history without becoming a heretic, contemplative monks could strive for the beatific vision. Prophecy shifted from exegesis to mystical knowing.

I suggested in the last chapter that the creative psychology of the divine poet did not become sophisticated until the Italian renaissance. In fact, the new psychology of literary creation was an application of the old psychology of divine contemplation. The concept of spiritual vision outlined for Can Grande derived from Christian mysticism; significantly, it is St. Bernard himself who leads the sightseer to his ultimate *visio dei* in the last cantos of the *Paradiso*. All knowing assumes the infused *caritas* of God; poetry, as a form of knowing, naturally requires a similar illumination. The *Commedia* moves inevitably toward its loving vision and is, in this sense, a prophetic poem. Given the Platonism of the time, it would be impossible for a critic to separate this extended *raptus* from theories of prophetic inspiration. There simply was no theory

[6] *Consideration* V.ii.3, *ibid.*, pp. 28–29.

[7] *Steps of Humility* viii.25, *ibid.*, p. 168.

[8] James Preus, *From Shadow to Promise: Old Testament Interpretation from Augustine to the Young Luther* (Cambridge: Belknap Press, 1969), pp. 65–66, 98. See also Heiko Augustinus Oberman, *The Harvest of Medieval Theology* (Cambridge: Harvard University Press, 1963), p. 374.

of prophetic inspiration wholly distinct from a theory of divine contemplation. In seeking the same *visio dei,* the same illumination, poets were related (however indirectly) to the biblical prophets. Appropriating the fruits of the mystical tradition from Augustine to Bernard, Dante worked with one of the most complex and sophisticated psychologies ever developed.

Aquinas followed the early Fathers and the Christian mystics in granting the extraordinary virtue of the prophetic gift while implying that such gifts, at least as they are manifested in the Old Testament, can have no great influence on the continuing history of the church. Prophecy was knowledge in the form of divine enlightenment. Since all human minds are to some extent imperfect, prophets saw only in part. They were not always able to distinguish the issue of their own spirit from the infused knowledge of the Holy Spirit. The occasional failure of conscious knowing was a flaw in prophecy as a mode of apprehension. Prophecy represented only an imperfect likeness of divine foreknowledge.[9]

Augustine had argued that the biblical prophets saw types of future events in God, mirror of eternity. In the *Summa Theologica,* Aquinas reversed this metaphor:

> And these images illumined by the Divine light have more of the nature of a mirror than the Divine essence: since in a mirror images are formed from other things, and this cannot be said of God. Yet the prophet's mind thus enlightened may be called a mirror, in so far as a likeness of the truth of the Divine foreknowledge is formed therein, for which reason it is called the *mirror of eternity,* as representing God's foreknowledge, for God in His eternity sees all things as present before Him. . . . The prophets are said to read the book of God's foreknowledge, inasmuch as the truth is reflected from God's foreknowledge on the prophet's mind. [II–II.clxxiii.1]

Here Aquinas insisted on the first of Roger Bacon's three triads—all human "seeing" occurs by reflection. Unlike Bacon and Bernard, Aquinas obviously realized that "illumination" was in fact a metaphor and chose to apply this metaphor with precision, doing no violence to other, non-figurative distinctions.[10] The prophetic mind was like a mirror. In this mirror the prophet beheld an image of the divine present. Thus

[9] Aquinas treats prophetic knowledge in the *Summa Theologica* II–II.clxxi–clxxvi, trans. Fathers of the English Dominican Province (London: Burnes, Oates, and Washburne, 1916–25), XIV, 1–85 (hereafter cited as *S.T.*).

[10] Etienne Gilson, *The Christian Philosophy of St. Augustine,* pp. 75–111, compares "illumination" in Augustine and Aquinas.

prophecy might include knowledge of the past and present as well as the future. Moses was a prophet when he wrote, "In the beginning. . . ."[11] Aquinas moved toward a tentative reaffirmation of prophecy as an understanding of history.

But he graded prophecy according to the mode of inspired seeing. Waking visions are superior to dreams; direct visions are superior to visions of a divine speaker. The highest degree of prophecy transcends our normal sense of corporeal vision: "But it is evident that the manifestation of divine truth by means of the bare contemplation of the truth itself, is more effective than that which is conveyed under the similitude of corporeal things, for it approaches nearer to the heavenly vision whereby the truth is seen in God's essence. Hence it follows that the prophecy whereby a supernatural truth is seen by intellectual vision, is more excellent than that in which a supernatural truth is manifested by means of the similitudes of corporeal things in the vision of the imagination" (II–II.clxxiv.2). In St. Thomas, the evaluative distinction among kinds of vision followed from his acceptance of the earlier notion of prophetic calm. He argued that "a man might be hindered from the act of prophesying by some very strong passion, whether of anger, or of concupiscence as in coition, or by any other passion" (II–II.clxxii.3). Since prophecy is, as a mode of knowing, antagonistic to passion, the superior prophet receives his visions through the intellect and not the excitable imagination. On this basis Moses was a greater prophet than David, although David admittedly spoke more of the future: "The prophecy of David approaches near to the vision of Moses, as regards the intellectual vision, because both received a revelation of intelligible and supernatural truth, without any imaginary vision. Yet the vision of Moses was more excellent as regards the knowledge of the Godhead; while David more fully knew and expressed the mysteries of Christ's incarnation" (II–II.clxiv.4). On this basis Samson, moved to passionate action, exemplifies the lowest grade of prophetic inspiration: "Now knowledge is more proper to prophecy than is action; wherefore the lowest degree of prophecy is when a man, by an inward instinct, is moved to perform some outward action. Thus it is related of Samson

[11] *S.T.* II–II.clxxi.3. Aquinas quotes Gregory to show how the knowledge of future events belongs most properly to prophecy. Since prophecy is not, for Aquinas, a natural faculty or a natural medium for accumulating knowledge, he emphasizes the "remoteness" of prophetic knowledge: we need no prophets to tell us that the tide will come in or that Christ will return.

that 'the Spirit of the Lord came strongly upon him, and as the flax is wont to be consumed at the approach of fire, so the bands with which he was bound were broken and loosed' " (II–II.clxxiv.3). Aquinas graded prophecy a second time according to content. But this second categorization was implicit in the first—prophecy that contains knowledge beyond natural wisdom was superior, for example, to prophecy that recreates natural wisdom.

Preferring contemplation to action, Moses to David, and knowledge of God to knowledge of history, St. Thomas accepted in large measure the emphasis of his Platonist contemporaries. His section on prophecy immediately precedes a discussion of rapture; this exceptional vision is a "degree of prophecy" and, in fact, the highest degree (II–II.clxxiii–clxxiv). St. Paul on the way to Damascus exceeded the imperfect limits of prophetic knowledge. As he was abstracted from the sensible world, his ineffable vision was not really a vision at all but an intellectual apprehension beyond metaphors and riddles. The degrees of rapture follow closely the degrees of prophecy. In the first heaven, visions are received through the senses. In the second heaven, reached by the major prophets, visions are received through the imagination. In the third heaven, the visionary receives direct intellectual knowledge of divine essence, the secret knowledge and secret words of Paul. When Aquinas wrote of prophecy, he stated that "Moses was simply the greatest of all" (II–II.clxxiv.4). But when he wrote of rapture, St. Paul was clearly the best authority and the greatest example. Moses appears only once in the whole section—in a quotation from St. Augustine (II–II.clxxv.3). The brotherly division between "prophecy" and "rapture" in medieval theology reflected the brotherly division between Israel and Christendom. Defined and experienced by St. Paul, rapture could be sought by the orthodox Christian. Old Testament prophecy, however, was the great gift of another age.

Under the guidance of the church, in the period of Christian grace, the extraordinary had become ordinary. Aquinas remarked that through the study of causes men can duplicate the knowledge of the divinely inspired; in some cases, then, science replaced prophecy as a way of knowing the future (II–III.clxxii.1). Although "at all times there have not been lacking persons having the spirit of prophecy," this gift now served "not indeed for the declaration of any new doctrine of faith, but for the direction of human acts" (II–II.clxxiv.6).

Moreover, prophecy had yielded in these late days to the interpretation of speeches:

> The interpretation of speeches is reducible to the gift of prophecy, inasmuch as the mind is enlightened so as to understand and explain any obscurities of speech arising either from a difficulty in the things signified, or from the words uttered being unknown, or from the figures of speech employed, according to Dan. 5.15, "I have heard of thee, that thou canst interpret obscure things, and resolve difficult things." Hence the interpretation of speeches is more excellent than the gift of tongues, as appears from the saying of the Apostle, "Greater is he that prophesieth than he that speaketh with tongues; unless perhaps he interpret." Yet the interpretation of speeches is placed after the gift of tongues, because the interpretation of speeches extends even to the interpretation of diverse kinds of tongues. [II–II.clxxvi.2]

So Aquinas ranked the gifts of God, prophecy including interpretation, interpretation including knowledge of languages—the response of a scholarly man to an intractably irrational subject. In the Reformation to come, it was argued that the gift of prophecy degenerated among the scholastics into the quibbling of arrogant tongues, and the great principle of correspondence inherited and preserved by Aquinas was turned against his church with the fiery vengeance of prophecy reborn.

All revolutionary rhetoric is in one way or another apocalyptic. Things are coming to an end, the center cannot hold. Revolutionary leaders usually assume a prophetic role, denouncing the present while envisioning a more perfect future. The early career of Martin Luther, who wondered if the world would end before he finished translating the Bible, was no exception. His personal identification with the Old Testament prophets is clear from the early prefaces. For the traditional "letter" and "spirit," he substituted *sensus historicus* and *sensus propheticus* as the two meanings of Scripture, reemphasizing the old connection between prophecy and exegesis.[12] Dividing the prophets into comforters and threateners, he never failed to mention the hazards of their office, the hostility of their audience: "For it was the habit of the people to mock the prophets and hold them madmen; and this has happened to all servants of God and preachers; it happens every day and will continue."[13] Isaiah was sawn

[12] Preus, pp. 144–49.

[13] *Works of Martin Luther,* ed. Andrew Spaeth *et al.* (Philadelphia: Muhlenberg, 1930–43), VI, 407–8.

asunder, Jeremiah stoned, Daniel persecuted, Hosea branded a heretic, and Amos beaten to death with a rod. Luther himself lived in a wicked time "even worse than that of Jeremiah" (VI, 410). His hermeneutic studies reveal a new interest in the penitent man, the man without grace and waiting for grace. The Old Testament Israelites living under the promise of redemption provided a ready historical parallel to this unredeemed penitent. In Catholic theology, it had usually been assumed that the prophets spoke to Christians: men of the new dispensation were the true audience of the Hebrew prophets. But Luther turned to the Old Testament with a reawakened sense of history. The original audiences of prophecy were more interesting as men adjusting to a promise than as ironic misinterpreters of the full truth concealed to all except the prophets. The prophets were more interesting as courageous men denouncing universal corruption than as contemplative men privileged with the *visio dei.*[14]

Curiously, Luther's apocalyptic disposition did not extend, at first, to the Book of Revelation. In 1522 he wrote, "my spirit cannot fit itself into this book" and can "nohow detect that the Holy Spirit produced it." There were too many "visions and figures," too few of them pointing to the Savior.[15] By 1545, however, he found Revelation perfectly acceptable—acceptable because of and not in spite of its relative obscurity. The later preface distinguishes three kinds of prophecy:

> This prophecy is of three sorts. The first does it in express words, without symbols and figures. So Moses, David, and most of the prophets prophesy of Christ, and Christ and the apostles prophesy of Antichrist, false teachers, etc. The second sort does this with symbols, but sets alongside them their interpretation in express words. So Joseph interprets dreams and Daniel both dreams and symbols. The third sort of prophecy does it without either words or interpretations, like this book of Revelation. . . . So long as this kind of prophecy remains without explanation and gets no sure interpretation, it is a concealed and dumb prophecy, and has not yet come to the profit and fruit which it is to give to Christendom. [VI, 480]

This distinction implies no hierarchy of value. It is based on how the prophecies can be understood by a reader of the Bible, not on the mode of vision or the quality of knowing. The third kind of prophecy requires prophetic exegesis: "There are many kinds of prophecy in the church. One is

[14] Preus, pp. 123–32, 160–75.

[15] VI, 488–89. Skepticism about the authenticity of Revelation may be traced to Eusebius, *Historica Ecclesiastica* III.xxv.

prophecy which interprets the writings of the prophets. Paul speaks of it in I Corinthians xii and xiv, and in other places. This is the most necessary kind and we must have it every day, because it teaches the Word of God, lays the foundation of the Church, and defends the faith; in a word, it rules, preserves, establishes, and administers the preaching-office" (VI, 478–80). The rhetoric here is, on the surface, traditional and unremarkable. But Luther has adapted the old idea of prophetic exegesis to support his evangelistic conception of preaching. The Word can be spoken anew, and spoken with the authority of the Old Testament prophets. Armed with this authority, Luther went on to identify the beasts in Revelation with the temporal kingdom of the Pope (VI, 482–86). Osiander, his follower, revived the Joachite prophecies with Luther in the role of the messianic *homo spiritualis* who would inaugurate the triumphant age of the Holy Spirit. Luther approved his efforts.[16] Arguing that the interpretation of prophetic writing might itself be prophetic, the Fathers had intended to strengthen the scholarly exegete and weaken the ecstatic denouncer. Now that same idea emerged as an instrument of religious polemic. Luther turned tradition against itself.

On the subject of prophecy, at least, Calvin was the most interesting and influential of the early reformers. He held extreme views about the nature of prophetic utterance. The prophets spoke only the divine word, never their own:

> The holy men spoke as they were moved by the Spirit of God; that is, they did not babble out fables, moved by their own impulse and as they willed. In short, the first step in right understanding is that we believe the holy prophets of God as we do him. The apostle calls them *holy men of God* because they performed faithfully the task which was laid upon them; and in this service, they were surrogates for the person of God. Peter says they were *moved,* not because they were bereft of their own minds (as the Gentiles imagined their prophets to have been during their enthusiasm), but because they did not dare to say anything of their own. They followed the Spirit as their guide and obeyed him to such an extent that their mouths became his temple, and he ruled in them.[17]

[16] Roland Bainton describes the Lutheran revival of Joachite doctrine in *Studies on the Reformation* (Boston: Beacon Press, 1963), pp. 62–66.

[17] *Commentaries,* ed. Louise P. Smith, trans. Joseph Haroutunian, Library of Christian Classics, 23 (Philadelphia: Westminster Press, 1958), p. 89. Hereafter the Library of Christian Classics will be cited as LCC.

Calvin insisted on this point. Unaided human nature is incapable of producing anything of value: "What could come forth from the defiled mouth of Isaiah and the foolish mouth of Jeremiah but filth and folly, if they spoke their own word?" The prophets were "forbidden to invent anything of their own." [18] Calvin referred to these obedient men, perhaps metaphorically, as "amanuenses." [19] But in recompense for their restraint the prophets received tremendous power. "When the prophets are bound by this reverence not to deliver anything but what they have received, then they are adorned with extraordinary power and excellent titles." [20] Once again, the rhetoric is familiar enough. But Calvin, like Luther, approached the traditional paradox of strength through weakness with a sense of imaginative identification. When a prophet stood alone against the unrighteous, he commanded measureless force. Calvin expanded magnificently on Mic. 3.8:

> Therefore, when Micah says that he is "filled with power," it is evident that he is taking his stand before the eyes of the whole nation, and that alone, by himself, he is challenging a great throng. False teachers were running around everywhere. The devil always has seed enough, when God lets him loose. Therefore their number was not small; yet Micah did not hesitate to come forward. "I myself," he said (for the pronoun *anoki* is emphatic); "you despise *me* as only one man (or with a few others); you may imagine that I who serve God am alone. But I myself am enough for a thousand, or rather for numbers beyond counting, because God stands on my side, and approves of my ministry because it is his service. For I offer you nothing except what he has commanded." [21]

The tone of this passage crossed over from biblical commentary to European politics despite the efforts of its author.

Calvin argued, in a lecture on Jeremiah, that prophets were sent to admonish kings, and he himself read Daniel with the French monarch in mind.[22] The reformer was certainly

[18] *Institutes* IV.viii.3, ed. John T. McNeill, trans. F. L. Battles, LCC, 20 and 21 (Philadelphia: Westminster Press, 1960), pp. 1152, 1151.

[19] Modern scholars have debated the meaning of this metaphor in Calvin. For a review of this debate, see Rupert E. Davies, *The Problem of Authority in the Continental Reformers: A Study in Luther, Zwingli, and Calvin* (London: Epworth, 1946), pp. 114–19. Cf. Kenneth Kantzer, "Calvin and the Holy Scriptures," in Walvoord, pp. 115–55.

[20] *Institutes,* IV.viii.3.

[21] *Commentaries,* pp. 380–81.

[22] See Michael Walzer, *The Revolution of the Saints* (Cambridge: Harvard University Press, 1965), pp. 63–64.

aware of the radical implications of his theology. These implications appear most clearly in his discussion of how to understand the inspired Bible. Calvin accepted the old theory of inspired exegesis, yet he stated this traditional position without the slightest equivocation. Only the elect can read the Scriptures with profit. "But the truth is that without the good sense we receive from the Spirit, it helps us little or nothing to have the Word of God in our hands." [23] Calvin's extreme view of prophetic inspiration matched an equally extreme view of the inspiration necessary to interpret the words of God. "The same Spirit, therefore, who had spoken through the mouths of the prophets must penetrate into our hearts to persuade us that they faithfully proclaimed what had been divinely commanded." [24] Fidelity to Scripture is not the only principle of correct interpretation. The Word of God must echo in the Word within—even the devil quotes Scripture. As the mouth of the prophet became the temple of the Spirit, so the heart of the interpreter becomes the temple of the same Spirit. Exegetes, like prophets, obey the Spirit and add nothing of their own.

But how can we know who possesses the Spirit? How can we know the Bible is inspired? One must have the Spirit to recognize the Spirit, be inspired to recognize inspiration, but such formulations are, in practice, unlikely to solve ideological disputes. "Since not everyone who calls himself a prophet is one," Calvin asked, "where do we get our discernment?" [25] To answer this dangerous question, Calvin confronted the epistemological difficulties that have divided his followers ever since: "But here comes a difficult question. If everyone has a right to be a judge and arbiter in this matter, nothing can be set down as certain; and our whole religion will be full of uncertainty. I reply that we must test doctrines in a twofold way: private and public. By private testing, each one establishes his own faith, and accepts only the teaching which he knows to be from God. . . . Public testing of doctrine has to do with the common consent and polity of the church." [26] Calvin was the first man to recognize fully the implications

[23] *Commentaries*, p. 87.

[24] *Institutes*, I.viii.1. For the persistence of this epistemological assumption in the Lutheran tradition, see Robert Preus, *The Inspiration of Scripture: a Study of the Theology of the Seventeenth-Century Lutheran Dogmaticians* (Edinburgh: Oliver and Boyd, 1957).

[25] *Commentaries*, p. 87. [26] *Ibid.*

of inspired exegesis. Though he placed this principle at the center of his theology, he understood the possible consequences: this radical epistemology, this radical doctrine of biblical authority could dissolve the community into anarchy. The "private testing" of one man might not correspond with the testing of another. If all hearts discovered their own Spirit, who was to arbitrate "the common consent"? Upon this potential anarchy Calvin imposed a church. To resist the possible fragmentation of the Spirit, this church required doctrine. Calvin labored over his *Institutes*. In the words of a modern commentator, "it is not surprising that, having propounded to his great credit the doctrine of the inner testimony of the Holy Spirit, he circumscribed it as narrowly as possible, lest he should find himself where he did not want to be." [27] One of the places he did not want to be was at the ideological center of political revolt.

The emphasis had shifted once again. Prophecy was no longer mystic vision and not primarily exegesis. For the early reformers, biblical prophecy authorized evangelical preaching. Commenting on St. Paul's list of ministerial offices in Ephesians 4, Calvin stated that only pastors and teachers have "an ordinary office" in the church. As for prophets, "this class either does not exist today or is less commonly seen." [28] Calvin expanded this point in his Christology, in the doctrine of the *triplex munus*. Augustine had formulated a twofold office which divided the ministry of Christ between priesthood and kingship.[29] To this orthodox position Calvin added a third, the prophetic office.

The origins of this idea are somewhat obscure. Luther and Melanchthon restated the traditional doctrine. However, Luther argued implicitly that the prophetic authority of Christ passed to the church as prophetic interpretation—and indeed, this argument had been implicit throughout the theological history of Christianity. Melanchthon defined the priestly office as Christ's preaching, praying, blessing, and His sacrifice. Bullinger retained the twofold scheme but added the sanctification of the people with the Holy Spirit to the priestly office. So the two offices already contained the third. But only Osiander, of all the reformers, made this

[27] R. E. Davies, p. 146. [28] *Institutes,* IV.iii.4.

[29] See *De Trinitate* I and IV, where Augustine defines Christ as a king and as the priest at His own sacrifice.

separation explicit and taught the *triplex munus* before Calvin.[30]

In Calvin's *Genevan Catechism*, the master asks, "In what sense do you call Christ a prophet?" Destined for the ministry, his well-trained scholar has a ready answer: "Because on coming into the world he declared himself an ambassador to men, and an interpreter, and that for the purpose of putting an end to all revelations and prophecies by giving a full exposition of his Father's will." [31] This interpretive work was, for Calvin, one of the three forms of voluntary obedience by which Christ redeemed the disobedience of the first Adam. As a prophet, Christ concealed his absolute knowledge and accommodated himself to his audience. He spoke in such a way that the true Israel, but not the false, might comprehend him. It was part of his humility.[32] The church maintained this gift as an educational office—preaching, teaching, and interpreting.

In his study of *Calvin's Doctrine of the Work of Christ*, J. F. Jansen has argued that the addition of the prophetic office was a relatively unimportant doctrine, of little interest in the history of theology (pp. 51–54). Considering the implicit presence of this idea in earlier theology, there is much justice in this attitude. But the doctrine was of some interest to Calvin himself. The 1536 *Institutes* appeared with a twofold office. Thereafter, in 1545 and 1559, Christ was a prophet as well as a priest and king.[33] Calvin was notorious for his meticulous care with the *Institutes*. The new doctrine also interested his followers. Many of them, equally careful with their beliefs, accepted the *triplex munus* as the christological essence of reformed dogmatics. In the history of ideas, the prophetic office merely renamed an old belief. In the history of imagination, not ideas, the prophetic office symbolized a new fervor in the dissemination of the Word.

[30] E. David Willis, *Calvin's Catholic Christology* (Leiden: E. Brill, 1967), pp. 85–87; J. F. Jansen, *Calvin's Doctrine of the Work of Christ* (London: J. Clark, 1956), pp. 23–38; *English Reformers*, ed. T. H. L. Parker, LCC, 26 (Philadelphia: Westminster Press, 1966), pp. 187–88.

[31] John Calvin, *Tracts and Treatises*, trans. Henry Beveridge (Grand Rapids: Erdmans, 1958; rpt. of Edinburgh, 1844–51), II, 42.

[32] Willis, pp. 85–86.

[33] The prophetic office was mentioned, but not expanded, in 1536. J. I. Packer has said that Calvin never changed his mind about a single theological issue of any importance ("Calvin the Theologian," in *John Calvin: A Collection of Essays*, ed. Gervase E. Duffield [Grand Rapids: Erdmans, 1966], p. 152).

Examining the connection between theology and politics in medieval jurisprudence, Ernst Kantorowicz has shown that the notion of the king as *persona gemina* is intimately related to the double nature of Christ, both man and God. Moreover, "since the divine model is at once King and Priest, the kingship and priesthood of Christ have to be reflected in his vicars as well, that is, in the King and the Bishop, who are at the same time *persona mixtae* (spiritual and secular) and *personae geminatae* (human by nature and divine by grace)." [34] If the medieval state can be understood as a secular embodiment of the two offices of Christ, one may speculate that the political upheavals inspired by the Reformation—including the Puritan Revolution—represent an attempt somehow to accommodate within the civil order the new christological office appended by Calvin. It was somewhere near the heart of the argument. For Calvinist Christology assumed a definition of the church and its proper activities. His "prophetic office" associated the Christian preacher with those solitary, persecuted, angry divines of Israel. The term itself authorized a furious zeal in the workers of the Spirit. New prophets might appear, with voices like fire, to rage against institutional corruption. The *triplex munus* appeared in the *Corpus Doctrinae Christianae* of the Paraeus group and the *Compendium Theologiae Christianae* of Johannes Wollebius. In England, John Hooper published *A Declaracion of Christe and of his offyce* in 1547 with a twofold theory and then in 1550, apparently having read the 1545 *Institutes,* expounded the threefold office in *A briefe and clear confession of the Christian faith.* The doctrine proved popular enough to attract Anglican preachers like John Donne and Puritan poets like John Milton.[35] Calvin probably believed that his *triplex munus* had established yet another public institution or "common consent" to restrain the private anarchy generated by his epistemology. But the Anabaptist Thomas Muntzer sermonized before the princes as if he were Micah before

[34] *The King's Two Bodies* (Princeton: Princeton University Press, 1957), pp. 58–59. See especially pp. 42–86.

[35] See the *Corpus Doctrinae Christianae* (Geneva, 1621), pp. 171–74, for Paraeus on the prophetic office. Wollebius has been reprinted in *Reformed Dogmatics,* trans. John W. Beardslee (New York: Oxford University Press, 1965); the prophetic office is expounded on pp. 99, 113. T. H. L. Parker reprints Hooper's first treatise in *English Reformers,* pp. 185–220. Donne develops the *triplex munus* about the text of John 1.8 in *Sermons,* ed. George Potter and Evelyn Simpson (Berkeley: University of California Press, 1953–62), III, 349–50. Milton treats the subject in *De Doctrina Christiana* (CE XV, 287–301).

the unholy: "For the pitiable corruption of holy Christendom has become so great that at the present time no tongue can tell it all. Therefore a new Daniel must arise and interpret for you your vision and this prophet, as Moses teaches, must go in front of an army." [36] John Foxe and his friend John Bale wrote antipapist commentaries on Revelation–a practice which Puritans would find increasingly more effective, particularly when the dreaded beasts turned out to be Anglicans as well.[37] Genevan exiles such as Miles Coverdale, John Rogers, John Knox, and Christopher Goodman returned to England burning with prophetic evangelism. Spiritual outcasts of all varieties found comfort in their interpretation of biblical prophecy and strength in their identification with the men who wrote these prophecies.

The career of John Knox illustrates the anarchic potential of this identification. Calvin had allowed a single exception to his defense of temporal authority: "But in the obedience which we have decided to be due to the commands of our rulers, we must always make this exception–or rather, this must be our primary consideration–that it may not lead us away from our obedience to Him, to whose will the wishes of all kings must be subject, to whose decrees their commands must give way, to whose majesty the emblems of their majesty must submit." [38] Through this crack in the *Institutes* Knox grew strong. "The prophet of God," he wrote, "sometimes may teach treason against kings, and yet neither he, nor such as obey the word spoken in the Lord's name by him, offends God." [39] In his history of the Scottish Reformation, Knox told of how one congregation answered a proclamation of the French queen regent attacking the revolutionary content of Protestant preaching:

[36] "A Sermon before the Princes" in *Spriritual and Anabaptist Writers,* ed. George Huntston Williams, LCC, 25 (Philadelphia: Westminster Press, 1957), p. 64.

[37] John Bale, *The Image of Bothe Churches after the Moste Wonderfull and Heavenly Reuelacion of Sainct John the Evangelist* (London, ca. 1550); John Foxe, *Eicosmi, seu meditationes, in sacram Apocalypsin* (London, 1587). Foxe's work is unfinished.

William Monter offers a readable account of Geneva and its many refugees in *Calvin's Geneva* (New York: Wiley, 1967), esp. pp. 165–92.

For the effect of reformation apocalyptism on the English Puritans, see Ernest Lee Tuveson, *Millenium and Utopia* (Berkeley: University of California Press, 1949), pp. 1–112; Cohn, pp. 315–74.

[38] *Institutes,* IV.xx.32.

[39] Quoted in Walzer, p. 100.

the same God who plagued Pharaoh, repulsed Sennacherib, struck Herod with worms, and made the bellies of dogs the grave and sepulchre of despiteful Jezebel, will not spare the cruel Princes, murderers of Christ's members in this our time. . . . Where her Grace declares, "It will not be suffered that our preachers mell with policy, nor speak of her nor of other Princes but with reverence," we answer, "That as we will justify and defend nothing in our preachers, which we find not God to have justified and allowed in his messengers before them. Elijah did personally reprove Ahab and Jezebel of idolatry, of avarice, of murder; and siclike Isaiah the Prophet called the magistrates of Jerusalem in his times companions to thieves, princes of Sodom, bribe-takers, and murderers: He complained that their silver was turned into dross, that their wine was mingled with water, and that justice was bought and sold. Jeremiah said, 'That the bones of King Jehoiakim should wither with the sun.' Christ Jesus called Herod a fox; and Paul called the High Priest a painted wall, and prayed unto God that he should strike him, because that against justice he commanded him to be smitten. Now if the like or greater corruptions be in the world this day, who dare enterprise to put silence to the Spirit of God, which will not be subject to the appetites of wicked Princes?" [40]

The most subjective of historians, Knox probably wrote the entire passage. He once replied to a similar charge: "Better it were unto you plainly to renounce Christ Jesus, than thus to expose his blessed Evangel to mockage. If God punish you not, that this same age shall see and behold your punishment, the Spirit of righteous judgment guides me not" (II, 65). The rearrangement of Calvin is striking. The prophetic office of preaching and teaching, derived from Christ, has become a political office derived from the Old Testament prophets–Christ remains only as the man who called Herod a fox. Evangelical preachers bear the burden of denunciation more emphatically than the burden of salvation. Their divine authority, springing from the "Spirit of righteous judgment," precedes the authority of temporal institutions; their God is the Old Testament God of renunciation, war, and vengeance. Calvinist theology made this posture inevitable. The Spirit was finally in the righteous believer and not in the institution. Biblical prophecy, summarized by Christ, passed to the holy as their authority to speak the Word, tend the Spirit. The difference between Calvin and Knox was more a matter of temperament than belief. Calvin had opened the seals, instituted and inspired a new age of prophetic revelation.

[40] *John Knox's History of the Reformation in Scotland,* ed. William Croft Dickinson (London: Nelson, 1949), I, 227–28.

One great event of this age, the English Revolution, can be viewed as a kind of epistemological allegory. The Elizabethan Settlement rested uneasily on the ability of both Anglicans and Puritans to derive their theological beliefs from John Calvin. This fundamental argreement was threatened but not destroyed by men like Richard Hooker and Lancelot Andrewes. The coalition began to erode in a public way when the Calvinist King James, recognizing the rebellious tendencies of reformed theology, forbade the teaching of Calvin at Oxford. Under Archbishop Laud the Calvinist divines were actively persecuted. If the resulting conflict proceeded from an intellectual division, the English Revolution demonstrated the final incompatibility of the public institution and the private Spirit. What Calvin labored to harmonize ultimately split in two: the institutional conformity of Laud and his bishops could not contain the private motions of the Word. After the Puritan triumph, Calvinism was officially reinstated in the Westminster Confession. Yet by 1650 the Spirit had taken hold. Even the new institutions of Oliver Cromwell could hardly restrain the fragmentation. In the pamphlet literature of the time, writer after writer dwelled on the question of sect, schism, disunity and division. Whether they approved or not, most were shocked at the extent of social fragmentation. More than one Spirit was loose in revolutionary England. The nation divided and the division itself divided. Become a country of warring prophets, England discovered the implications of Calvinist epistemology.[41]

Rather than elaborate and qualify this brief allegory, I have chosen to discuss three men who responded to the traditional conceptions of prophecy in a particularly imaginative way. Two of them were preachers. Their appeal to the prophetic calling, interesting in and of itself, displays the special importance of prophecy for servants of God in the seventeenth century. The other man—wily and skeptical and quite a rationalist—would probably never have treated prophecy at all had not most intellectuals of his time been seriously concerned with the nature and function of divine inspiration.

John Donne accepted the *triplex munus* and found, in the prophetic office of Christ, the source of his authority as a preacher of the Word. He elaborated this office with visual and auditory metaphors derived from the Bible. The Hebrew

[41] This paragraph is most indebted to Herschel Baker's admirable *The Wars of Truth* (Cambridge: Harvard University Press, 1952).

prophets "saw" the Word; the visionary accounts in the Bible suggested a kind of divine synesthesia. Donne spoke of John the Baptist as a "burning and shining lamp" and also as a prophet who chose for himself, among all the great names, the title *vox clamantis*.[42] As Christ is both Word and Light, the prophet of Christ is both voice and lamp, foreseer and forth-speaker, visionary and orator. In this passage Donne connected these two metaphorical attributes: "First, God will send them prophets that shall be *Tubae,* Trumpets; and not onely that, but *speculatores;* not onely Trumpets which sound according to the measure of breath that is blown into them, but they themselves are the watchmen that are to sound them: not Trumpets to sound out what airs the occasions of the present time, or what airs the affections of great persons infuse into them; for so they are onely Trumpets, and not Trumpetors; but God hath made them both." [43] Here Donne defined precisely the role of the prophetic speaker of the *Anniversaries,* who is both the watchman to a dying world and the trumpet at whose call its people came. He speaks in order that we may learn to see. The narrator of *Paradise Lost* receives inspiration through the eye and the ear, just as Adam learns from Michael with first his eyes and then his ears. It is Satan who treats his prophets like *tubae* and bagpipes; the devil enters through the mouth and turns the vessel of his word into a mere instrument.[44] I mention these matters out of season because Donne provided such a rare moment of lucidity in the history of metaphorical names for the prophet. He made the traditional metaphors complex enough to convey a paradoxical definition—the prophet as *speculator,* as rational

[42] *Sermons,* II, 264, 172.

[43] *Ibid.,* II, 168. Donne was more moderate on this point than his fellow churchman Richard Hooker, who accepted a position closer to Calvin: "This is that which the prophets mean by those books written full within and without; which books were so often delivered them to eat, not because God fed them with ink and paper, but to teach us, that so oft as he employed them in this heavenly work, they neither spake nor wrote any word of their own, but uttered syllable by syllable as the Spirit put it into their mouths, no otherwise than the harp or the lute doth give a sound according to the discretion of his hands that holdeth and striketh it with skill" (*The Works of That Learned and Judicious Divine, Mr. Richard Hooker* [Oxford, 1865], II, 756). While Donne carefully distinguished the prophets from mere musical instruments, Hooker carefully defined them as precisely that. The case of Hooker suggests that defenders of reason could embrace, with no awareness of contradiction, an extreme view of biblical inspiration.

[44] IX.179–91. Satan "inspir'd" the snake literally—that is, he spoke inside its body, treating the snake precisely as God was supposed to have treated the Philonic prophet.

knower, and at the same time as *tuba,* as passive instrument. The narrator of *Paradise Lost,* we will see, worked with the same polarities.

Donne, like all orthodox Christians, used prophecy as a way of harmonizing the two Testaments. His God loved renovations, not innovations. The minister of the New found authority in the prophet of the Old. *"Prophecy,"* Donne preached, "is but antidated *Gospell,* and *Gospell* but postdated *prophecy."* [45] God "is a God of harmony, and not of discord" (II, 173–74). But God composed his harmonies with diverse sounds, creating concord out of discord, and Donne followed Calvin in emphasizing the differences between Hebrew prophets and Christian preachers. The one voice of Scripture spoke in two tones. To be sure, Jeremiah had a commission from God "to root out, and to pull down, to destroy and throw down," and the Christian minister "does not his duty that speakes not as boldly, and as publiquely too, and of Kings, and great persons, as the Prophets did" (II, 303). But Donne's sermon *in quintus novembris* commemorated the Gunpowder Plot by contending that revolution had no sanction in the Old Testament prophets, since they "were extraordinarily raised to denounce, and to execute Gods Judgements" (IV, 257). Ordinary ministers have no such authority. In another sermon Donne divided the office of Christ from the activities of his forerunners: "Compare the Prophets with the Son, and even the promises of God, in them, are faint and dilute things. Elishaes staffe in the hand of Gahazi his servant, would not recover the Shunamites dead child; but when Elisha himselfe came, and put his mouth upon the childs mouth, that did: In the mouth of Christs former servants there was a preparation, but effect and consummation in his own mouth" (III, 320). Insofar as ministerial authority proceeds from Christ, this division of Christ from his prophets served to inhibit the sense of identification experienced by a John Knox. Moses was a partial exception to the limited success of the prophets. Following Aquinas, Donne said that men know God "by reflexion" in a glass of "darke similitude, and comparison" (VIII, 220, 225). Moses, however, knew God without reflection or similitude, "by a more immediate working, then either sense, or understanding, or faith" (VIII, 226). Here Donne accepted the mystical tradition, disowning

[45] *Sermons,* IV, 176.

prophets as political denouncers and commending them as examples of extraordinary knowing. The Old Testament is too treacherous to be imitated by the careless Christian: "It is a true, and an usefull Rule, that ill men have been Types of Christ, and ill actions figures of good" (III, 318).

Donne believed the prophetic office of Christ to reside in the order of grace: "The office of a *Prophet* was *Naturall* to none; none was *born* a prophet" (III, 350). Christ inherited both his kingship and his priesthood by virtue of his descent, his blood. As the seed of David, he possessed these two offices in the order of nature as well. Dividing the three offices between nature and grace allowed Donne to move away from the extreme Calvinist theories about the comprehensibility of Scripture. To divide the ministry of Christ is in effect to divide His Word. Interpretation remains a prophetic activity, but only in certain cases. Often the natural light of reason suffices: "that which I cannot understand by reason, but by especiall assistance from God, all that is Prophecy; no Scripture is of private interpretation" (III, 210). Donne attempted to minimize, even abolish the anarchic community of private interpreters. Rational men can debate the truth, or much of the truth, apart from the conflicting claims of the Spirit.

Thomas Hobbes devoted fully one half of his *Leviathan* (1651) to biblical exegesis, and these chapters are, in fact, a long commentary on the nature and function of prophecy. The trappings are more or less familiar. Hobbes offered a graded scale ranging from the Spiritus Sanctus of Onthoniel, Gideon, Jephtha, and Samson, "an extraordinary Zeal, and Courage in the defence of Gods people," to the consummate inspiration of Moses (p. 431). He distinguished between the ecstasy of Delphi and the rational calm of the true prophets (p. 461). He accepted the *triplex munus*. Like Donne, he divided the Word of God into "Naturall" and "Propheticall" meanings (p. 409). He presented a comprehensive survey of the significance of the word "prophet" in Scripture:

> The name of PROPHET, signifieth in Scripture sometimes Prolocutor; that is, he that speaketh from God to Man, or from man to God: And sometimes Praedictor, or a foreteller of things to come: And sometimes one that speaketh incoherently, as men that are distracted. It is most frequently used in the sense of speaking from God to the people. So Moses, Samuel, Elijah, Jeremiah and others were Prophets. And in this sense the High Priest was a Prophet, for he only went into the Sanctum Sanctorum, to enquire of God; and was to declare his answer

to the people. . . . Also they that in Christian congregations taught the people are said to prophecy. . . . For Prophecy . . . signifieth . . . praising God in Psalmes, and Holy Songs. And in this signification it is, that the Poets of the Heathen, that composed Hymnes and other sorts of Poems in the honor of their God, were called *Vates* (Prophets) as is well enough known by all that are versed in the Books of the Gentiles, and as is evident where St. Paul saith of the Cretans, that a Prophet of their owne said, they were Liars; not that St. Paul held their Poets for Prophets, but acknowledgeth that the word Prophet was commonly used to signifie them that celebrated the honour of God in Verse. [Pp. 456–57]

The very fact that Hobbes examined prophecy so thoroughly suggests the extent to which the Puritans appropriated the tone, manner, and authority of the Old Testament prophets. No one has ever doubted that the *Leviathan* is a refutation of the English Revolution. In his chapters on prophecy, Hobbes struck at the heart of this event—brilliantly, deftly, swiftly. The surface was traditional: but if his Puritan readers did not attend to each premise, marking with care the direction of the argument, they surely found themselves condemning themselves.

He asked the usual question. How does a prophet convince us of his authority? How do we know the prophet from the pretender? No divine commandment obligates the Christian to accept the claims of any man. "So that though God Almighty can speak to a man, by Dreams, Visions, Voices and Inspiration; yet he obliges no man to beleeve he hath so done to him that pretends it; who (being a man), and (which is more) may lie" (p. 411). In biblical times a prophet performed miracles and taught nothing contrary to the Mosaic Law—he could be tested against these criteria. But miracles have ceased, and so has Old Testament prophecy:

Seeing therefore Miracles now cease, we have no sign left, whereby to acknowledge the pretended Revelations, or Inspirations of any private man; nor obligation to give ear to any Doctrine, farther than it is conformable to the Holy Scriptures, which since the time of our Saviour, supply the place, and sufficiently recompense the want of all other Prophecy; and from which, by wise and learned interpretation, and careful ratiocination, all rules and precepts necessary to the knowledge of our duty both to God and man, without Enthusiasme, or supernaturall Inspiration, may easily be deduced. [P. 414]

But one epistemological difficulty has dissolved into another. For how do we know the Holy Scriptures are the words of

God? Characteristically, Hobbes argued that this question has nothing to do with knowledge: "Again, it is manifest, that none can know they are Gods Word, (though all true Christians beleeve it,) but those to whom God himself hath revealed it supernaturally; and therefore the question is not rightly moved, of our *Knowledge* of it" (p. 425). Epistemology has been annihilated. The question is rightly moved of authority—that is, of power.

The problem of biblical authority led Calvin to the circular correspondences of the Spirit. The same problem led Hobbes not to the inspired heart of the interpreter but to the larger question of authority in general. He was a brilliantly literal man: if we must ask about authority, then he would talk about authority. To decide this question, Hobbes forged a lethal version of the *triplex munus*. The Levellers had used this doctrine to sanctify the individual with complete sovereignty.[46] But Hobbes used the *triplex munus* to sanctify his Leviathan.

His approach was historical. During the period from Moses to Christ, authority was divided among kings, priests, and prophets. Christ gathered the strands: "For hee was the Messiah, that is, the Christ, that is, the Anointed Priest, the Soveraign Prophet of God; that is to say, he was to have all the Power that was in Moses the Prophet, in the High Priests that succeeded Moses, and in the Kings that succeeded the Priests" (p. 515). In his prophetic office Christ was a teacher. And, as in Calvin, this function passed to the Apostles. But it passed to them only by virtue of the kingly office: Christ delegated authority to the Apostles just as Moses delegated authority to Aaron and to the seventy elders. The kingly office passed, of course, to kings. Hobbes reminded his readers that the phrase "kingdom of God" is no metaphor. Christ was, literally, the sovereign prophet. Rather than redistribute his offices, Christ restored the unity of the Mosaic era. Only a king is now a pastor *de juro divino*. All other officers of the church speak and teach *de juro civile* (pp. 489–501).

In any other system of prophetic authority there is no authority, only that chaotic community of private spirits which so horrified Calvin. "For when Christian men, take not their Christian Soveraign, for Gods Prophet; they must either take their owne dreams, for the Prophecy they mean to bee gov-

[46] See Arthur Barker, *Milton and the Puritan Dilemma* (Toronto: University of Toronto Press, 1942), pp. 153–54.

erned by, and the tumour of their own hearts for the spirit of God" (p. 469). Either every man is a prophet or one man is a prophet—the alternatives are chaos or kingship. Hobbes himself understood the revolution as a demonstration of epistemological failure. The stirring in the Calvinist heart was actually a tumor. Hobbes cut it out; he divided Calvinist theology, saving the public institution by excising the private Spirit, just as Puritan extremists saved the Spirit by excising the institution. Having defended monarchy with natural laws, Hobbes went on to defend monarchy with prophetic laws. Never was the divine right of kings proved so elegantly.

The finest theoretical study of prophecy in the seventeenth century was John Smith's long essay "Of Prophecy," printed in *Select Discourses* (1660). The introduction to this volume compared Smith to Moses on the basis that both understood "Mysterious Hieroglyphical learning"—natural philosophy, music, physic, and mathematics. Smith had worked on his essay for a considerable time, confronting a topic "not commonly treated of." [47] This praise was not unwarranted. Previous theologians had categorized the kinds of vision and the kinds of prophetic mission, but prophetic experience itself had rarely been treated in any detail, with any sense of imaginative complicity. The actual moments of contact with God remained as secret as the words of Paul. Rapture aside, prophecy is not an ineffable experience. It is one mystical event that does not, by definition, transcend language; the prophet is a speaker as well as a seer. So we cannot account for the absence of detailed examination by remarking that prophetic experience is unknowable. The most probable explanation is that few had or expected to have a direct prophetic revelation; there are countless descriptions of how the Spirit flames in the heart of the prophetic exegete. "Of Prophecy" is the fullest treatment of the prophetic experience I have been able to discover. Smith also discussed the intellectual issues concerning prophecy, and discussed them brilliantly. Gathering and ordering many scattered sources, Smith was a great historian of ideas.

But the essay has its eccentricities. Smith rarely cited Thomas Aquinas, although he arrived at a theory of degrees of inspiration which recapitulates Aquinas almost perfectly. There are few references to any Christian authority. Instead,

[47] For reasons of convenience I have used the second edition, Cambridge, 1673. The introduction, by John Worthington, is unpaginated.

Smith chose to cite rabbinical material. Perhaps he attempted a scholarly *tour de force:* he would show his readers the exact similarities between the Jewish Platonist Maimonides and the Christian Aristotelian Aquinas without even mentioning these similarities. For the Cambridge Platonist, all rational knowledge, whatever its source, agreed.[48]

Smith began by collapsing natural and revealed theology, certainly a fine arrogant way to open an essay on prophecy: "For so we may call as well that Historical Truth of Corporeal and Material things, which we are informed of by our Senses, *Truth of Revelation,* as that Divine Truth which we now speak of: and therefore we may have as certain and infallible a way of being acquainted with this one, as with the other" (p. 163). All men are naturally capable of receiving knowledge *lumine prophetico.* Though all be ready, few are chosen. Abolishing the difference between supernatural illumination and natural reason, between grace and nature, Smith proceeded to an extremist view of biblical accommodation. God desired to be understood: "If he should speak in the language of Eternity, who could understand Him, or interpret his meaning?" So God spoke rationally—or worse. "Truth speaks with the most Idiotical sort of men in the most Idiotical way, and becomes all things to all men" (p. 165). It was probably this tendency to denigrate the Word which led Smith to examine the prophetic experience. He was more interested in psychology than in dogma.

Prophecy is rational, a heightening of intelligence. Thus Smith reiterated the strictures of the Fathers against ecstatic prophecy. During a vision, the mind of the prophet always remains serene and calm. The biblical prophets often spoke in musical verses because music soothes the mind. Although the human soul is naturally disposed toward prophecy, still it is not probable that "those who were any way of crazed Minds,

[48] I have in mind the syncretistic attitudes of a work like Ralph Cudworth's *True Intellectual System of the Universe* (Cambridge, 1678). Cudworth glossed the Osiris myth as a manifesto for the unification of all religious beliefs: "In which words, Plutarch intimates, that the Egyptian Fable, of Osiris being mangled and cut in pieces by Typhon, did allegorically signifie the Dispertion and Distraction of the Simple Deity, by reason of the Weakness and Ignorance of vulgar minds (not able to comprehend it altogether at once) into severall Names and Partial Notions, which yet True Knowledge and Understanding, that is, Isis, makes up whole again and unites into One" (p. 355). The passage resembles the famous myth of *Areopagitica,* but Milton's friends of Truth are more discerning collectors than Cudworth's Isis. Like Smith, Cudworth believed that all men are by nature prophetic (pp. 710–15).

or who were inwardly of inconsistent tempers by reason of any perturbation, could be very fit for these serene impressions" (p. 237). Plato, "no careless observer of these matters," rightly condemned the ecstatic diviners of his time. And for this same reason Smith himself roundly censured "the Enthusiastical Imposters of our Age" (pp. 185, 187). Donne divided biblical texts into those fit to be interpreted by reason and those fit to be interpreted by prophetic inspiration. In Smith's epistemology, the two ways of knowing became interchangeable alternatives:

> an Inspiration abstractly considered can only satisfie the mind of him to whom it is made, of its own Authority and Authenticalness (as we have shewed before:) and therefore that one man may know that another hath that Doctrine revealed to him by a Prophetical spirit which he delivers, he must also either be inspired, and so be *in gradus prophetico* in a true sense, or be confirmed in the belief of it by some Miracle. . . . Or else there must be so much Reasonableness in the thing it self, as that by Moral Arguments it may be sufficient to beget a belief in the Minds of sober and good men. [P. 259]

Unlike Hobbes, Smith believed that the question of authority is rightly moved of knowledge.

It may seem as if Smith eluded altogether the circularities of inspired interpretation. If prophecy is rational, then one need not be a prophet to understand a prophet. Actually, Smith substituted one correspondence for another. Reason itself is illumination. Like his colleague Nathaniel Culverwel, Smith based his epistemology on a metaphor not understood as a metaphor. Reason is the candle of the Lord: "There is a clear and bright heaven in mans Soul, in which Lucifer himself cannot subsist, but is tumbled down from thence as often as he assayes to climb up into it." [49] The divine illumination of prophecy must correspond to the inner illumination of the interpreter. Only sober and good men understand the revelations of sober and good prophets. Plato defined the relationship of the soul to God as that of vision to light. Plutarch applied this same proportion to the prophet and his God. The metaphor is probably as old as language itself, and even today we can hardly speak of a mental action without using a visual metaphor. A prophet who has visions is a seer, and to see is to understand, and to understand is to have insight: we are

[49] P. 196. Culverwel's *Discourse of the Light of Nature* (1669) has been reprinted in *The Cambridge Platonists,* ed. Ernest Trafford Campagnac (Oxford: Clarendon Press, 1901), pp. 211–321.

always shedding light on the things we view. But the Puritans with their inner light and the Platonists with their candle of the Lord often used this ancient metaphor as if it were not a metaphor. Inspecting the diagrams of Ramist logic, an anti-scholastic Puritan could literally see his way to a solution.[50] Because something seen was something known, Smith made no distinction between the vision of prophecy and the vision of reason.

Smith ranked the prophets according to the relative proportion of rational understanding to imaginative sensation. His scheme is based on the three kinds of vision defined in medieval philosophy—sensual, imaginative, and intellectual. If no fanciful pageantry intervenes between the prophet and his intellectual perception, then the prophet sees only incorporeal essences and achieves *gradus Mosaicus,* the highest experience available to a rational man. There are three more degrees which, as they descend from *gradus Mosaicus,* involve a greater accommodation on the part of God. In the lowest of these, the turbulence of the imagination impairs the intellect. Receiving parables, visions, similitudes, and allegories, the prophet cannot understand them himself. Finally, the lowest degree of revelation is the "Spiritus Sanctus" or "Filia Vocis" of a man like Samson. Jacob's ladder symbolizes this *scala prophetica* (p. 211).

The finest prophets understood the typological meaning of their visions. Though confronted with imaginary apparitions, the prophet was also a rational interpreter: "the Understandings of the Prophets were alwaies kept awake and strongly acted on by God in the midst of these apparitions, to see the intelligible Mysteries in them, and so in these Types and Shadows, which were Symbols of some spiritual things, to behold the Antitypes themselves: which is the meaning of that old Maxime of the Jew which we formerly cited out of Maimonides, Magna est virtue seu fortitudo prophetarum qui assimilant formas cum formante eam" (p. 172). Connecting type with antitype, representation with fact, the prophets removed themselves from sequential time. They spoke of the future in the past tense, the past in the present tense. "We must not seek for any Methodical concatenation of things in

[50] For the development of spatial or visual logic, see Walter J. Ong, *Ramus: Method, and the Decay of Dialogue* (Cambridge: Harvard University Press, 1958). Ong views the decay of "aural culture" more speculatively in *The Presence of the Word* (New Haven: Yale University Press, 1967).

the Law, or indeed in any other part of Prophetical writ; it being a most usual thing with them many times . . . to knit the Beginning and End of Time together" (p. 271). The prophets, refusing logical method, expressed their sense of time in a poetic style. Though all poets were not prophets, all prophets were poets: " 'Tis true, the poets are anciently called Vates, but that is no good argument why a singer should be called a Prophet: for it is to be considered that a Poet was a Composer, and upon that account by the Ancients called Vates or a Prophet" (p. 232). Never merely singers, the prophets composed as well. They translated their visions into words, words that the reader of the Bible must trust absolutely.

To explain the relationship between the prophet and his vision, the active interpreter and the passive receptor, Smith developed a complex, ancient metaphor: the prophetic experience took place on a stage. Both dreams and visions "are perpetually attended with those Visa and Simulacra Sensibilia, as must needs be impressed upon Common sense or Fansie, whereby the Prophets seemed to have all their Senses waking and exercising their several functions, though indeed all was but Scenicall or Dramatical" (p. 174). Metaphorically, then, a prophetic vision is a drama produced by God, sometimes acted in by angels, and viewed by a privileged spectator. The comparison was hardly unusual. Many writers had defined the imagination as a theatre, imaginings as plays.[51] Naturally enough, this figure often appears with regard to prophetic vision: "Now because the imagination, whether when we are transported in our thoughts being awake, or in dreams, is capable of having those scenes acted upon it, and of being so excited by them, as to utter them with pompous figures, and in a due rapidity; this is another way of inspiration that is strictly called *prophecy* in the Old Testament."[52] The metaphor evoked rich associations for the renaissance Christian. The world itself was a stage, and had been for centuries.[53]

Plotinus was the classical writer who developed this figure

[51] Prophecy was often treated in discussions of the imagination. See, for example, Pico's *On the Imagination,* ed. Harry Caplan, Cornell Studies in English, vol. 16 (New Haven: Yale University Press, 1930), pp. 56–57.

[52] Thomas Burnet, *An Exposition of the Thirty-Nine Articles of the Church of England,* ed. James Page (New York, 1850), p. 110.

[53] Ernst Robert Curtius, in *European Literature and the Latin Middle Ages,* trans. Willard Trask (New York: Harper and Row, 1963), pp. 138–44, traces the history of the *theatrum mundi.*

most impressively: "Murders, death in all its shapes, the capture and sacking of towns, all must be considered as so much stage-show, so many shiftings of scenes, the horror and outcry of a play; for here, too, in all the changing doom of life, it is not the true man, the inner Soul, that grieves and laments but merely the phantasm of the man, the outer man, playing his part on the boards of the world." [54] For the Neoplatonist, the drama of life suggested the unreality of the world. Nothing really "is" in time and flux. Tertullian used the same metaphor to define a Christian theatre in his *De Spectaculis*. Attacking the Roman games and drama, their lewd "spectacles," he offered a Christian spectacle to take their place. All the world is a spectacle, and God its spectator. He looks "at brigandage, . . . at cheating, adultery, fraud, idolatry, yes, and the spectacles, too." [55] God is the only true "seer" in the universe. A famous passage from 1 Corinthians enriched this conception. "For I think that God hath set forth us the apostles last, as it were appointed to death: for we are made a spectacle unto the world, and to angels, and to men" (4.9). Though the world watches the righteous man, angels watch the world—as the eyes of God, they join with Him to form a celestial audience. God searches all hearts. The *theatrum mundi,* popular throughout the Middle Ages, was not discarded by the reformers. This universe, Calvin said, "was founded as a spectacle of God's glory." [56] Poets were as attracted as theologians. Ralegh knew that heaven "the Iudicious sharpe spectator is, / That sits and markes still who doth act amisse." [57] At the end of his polemic Tertullian considered the Christian who, recognizing himself as a spectacle, wishes to enjoy an entertainment nonetheless. That man should imagine the spectacle of the Last Judgment, the triumph of good and the correction of injustice. Only at the Apocalypse can the righteous share the theatrical perspective of heaven, the consummate knowledge of God. This imaginative theatre proved equally popular. Jeremy Taylor wrote: "O how great and delightful a theater shall it be to see God as he is, with all his infinite perfections, and the perfections of all creatures, which are eminently con-

[54] *Enneads* III.2.15, in *Plotinus* III, 31.

[55] *De Spectaculis* XX, in *Tertullian,* trans. T. R. Glover, LCL (London, 1931), p. 281.

[56] *Institutes,* I.v.5.

[57] *The Poems of Sir Walter Ralegh,* ed. Agnes Latham (Cambridge: Harvard University Press, 1951), pp. 51–52.

tained in the Deity! How admirable were that spectacle, where were represented all that are, or have been, pleasant or admirable in the world!"[58] Though actors before their God, Christians created a theatre in the imagination. The fiercely righteous might watch in comfort the torments of the damned. The gently righteous, like Taylor, could contemplate the perfections of God revealed.

But prophets were allowed to see the future before its time. Whereas all men provide a spectacle for God, God provided a spectacle for the prophets. Both Donne and Aquinas called the prophets *spectatores,* and theatrical metaphors were customarily associated with prophetic vision. Spenser translated a few poems for Jan van der Noot's *Theatre for Worldlings* (1569) and Thomas Beard discussed the providential fall of the wicked in *Theatre of Gods Judgements* (1597).[59] Ben Jonson distinguished the "Players" of this world from those few men chosen to be spectators:

> *I have* considered, our whole life is like a *Play:* wherein every man, forgetfull of himselfe, is in travaile with expression of another. Nay, wee so insist in imitating others, as wee cannot (when it is necessary) returne to our selves: like Children, that imitate the vices of *Stammerers* so long, till at last they become such; and make the habit to another nature, as it is never forgotten.
>
> *Good men* are the Stars, the Planets of the Ages wherein they live, and illustrate the times. *God* did never let them be wanting to the world: as *Abel,* for an example, of Innocency; *Enoch* of Purity, *Noah* of Trust in Gods mercies, *Abraham* of Faith, and so of the rest. These, sensuall men thought mad, because they would not be partakers, or practisers of their madnesse. But they, plac'd high on the top of all vertue, look'd downe on the Stage of the world, and contemned the Play of *Fortune.* For though the most be Players, some must be *Spectators.* [VIII, 597]

Because the Last Judgment is to be the true Christian spectacle, the time when righteous actors join the heavenly audience, theatrical metaphors often appear in commentaries on the Book of Revelation. Joseph Mede, whose *Clavis Apoca-*

[58] *Contemplations of the State of Man* II.iv, in *The Whole Works of Jeremy Taylor* (London, 1835), I, 381.

[59] Roy W. Battenhouse considers the theological uses of the *theatrum mundi* in "The Doctrine of Man in Calvin and the Renaissance," *JHI,* 9 (1948), 447–71. See also his *Marlowe's* Tamburlaine: *A Study in Renaissance Moral Philosophy* (Nashville: Vanderbilt University Press, 1941), pp. 123–26. Battenhouse argues that the concept of God as a tragic dramatist influenced the character of Elizabethan tragedy.

lyptica (1627) was translated in 1643, defined St. John as a celestial spectator: "The Apocalyptique Theatre, I call that Empericall session of God and of the Church described in the fourth chapter: and exactly framed according to the forme, of that ancient encamping of God with Israel in the wildernesse" (p. 30). Mede suggested that John and "other beholders" viewed a "rehersall" of the Apocalypse, "not much unlike to our Academical interludes, where the prompters stand neere the Actors, with their books in their hands" (p. 61). The great book contains the plot of all remaining history, and as the seals opened, John watched the future in rehearsal.

The Paraeus *Commentary upon the Divine Revelation,* translated in 1644, used the traditional metaphor to defend the Book of Revelation against charges of undue repetition and confused development. John was merely following "Dramaticall decorum." Many "Writers of Tragedies" often "mingle feigned things with serious, both for preparation, as for delights sake, and to distinguish their *Dramaes,* or Interludes into *Acts, Scenes,* and *Chores,*" and the same is true of this "Dramaticall Prophesie."[60] Choirs, musicians, and harpists perform between the acts of this divine spectacle. But unlike earthly interludes, these celestial songs are "not so much to lessen the wearisomenesse of the Spectators, as to infuse holy meditations into the mindes of the Readers, and to lift them up to Heavenly matters" (p. 20). As this statement indicates, Paraeus was rather confused about whether or not John was a spectator. God exhibited "Typical Speeches and Actions . . . to Iohns sight or hearing . . . in the Heavenly Theatre," but John was also an actor. The Dramatis Personae for the Prologue (p. 20) reads:

Iohn the Evangelist, Actor, and interlocutor throughout

Christ in a glorious form walking amongst the Seven Candlesticks: The Authour of the Revelation, and maker of the prologue

John was the spectator at this theatrical vision. But to the reader of the tragedy, he is inevitably an actor in the spectacle. Christ the "maker" wrote his lines and directed his performance.

The *theatrum mundi* would seem to exclude most Christians

[60] David Paraeus, *A Commentary upon the Divine Revelation of the Apostle and the Evangelist,* trans. Elias Arnold (London, 1644), p. 26.

from the pleasures of the spectator. However, the metaphor often received another formulation. Calvin defined the world as a divine spectacle—with no awareness of contradiction, he also said that man "has been placed in this most glorious theatre to be a spectator."[61] Once again, the source was St. Paul. Another famous passage in 1 Corinthians reads, in the version of Beza, "Cernimus enim nunc per speculum at per aenigma, tunc autem coram cernemus: nunc cognosco ex parte, tunc vero cognoscam prout cognitus fuero." Preaching on this text, Donne conflated the *spectaculum* of 1 Cor. 4.9 with the *speculum* of 1 Cor. 13.12, that dark mirror or dark window or dim watchtower which opens out on the dark sayings of God: "*Spectaculum sumus,* sayes the Apostle; *We are made a spectacle to man and angels.* The word is there *Theatrum,* and so S. Hierom reads it: And therefore let us be careful to play these parts well, which the Angels desire to see well acted."[62] Yet man sees as well. Like Tertullian, Donne believed the purest Christian spectacle, the seeing face to face, to be "the day of resurrection, the day of Judgement, the day of the actuall possession of the next life." There is no true spectacle but God: "All other sight is blindnesse, all other knowledge is ignorance" (III, 219). But now we see in part. Donne allegorized the dark glass of 1 Corinthians as the theatre of the world:

> For our sight of God here, our Theatre, the place where we sit and see him, is the whole world, the whole house and frame of nature, and our *medium,* our *glasse,* is the Booke of Creatures, and our light by which we see him, is the light of Naturall Reason. . . . [III, 220]

> Aquinas calls this Theatre, where we sit and see God, the whole world; And *David* compasses the world, and findes God every where, and sayes at last, *Whither shall I flie from thy presence: If I ascend up into heaven, thou art there.* . . . [III, 220]

> The whole frame of the world is the Theatre, and every creature the stage, the *medium,* the glasse in which we may see God. [III, 223]

These metaphors reverse the roles of the normal *theatrum mundi.* Here man is the spectator, the rest of the world a play,

[61] Institutes, I.vi.2.

[62] *Sermons,* III, 218. In Beza, the word is *spectaculum:* "Deus enim, puto, nos, ultimos apostolos, spectandos proposuit, ut morti addictors: nam spectaculum facti sumus mundo, et angelis, et hominibus" (*Novum Testamentum* [London, n.d.], p. 167).

and God the content of this play. Man must view the drama properly in order to know its creator. Thus reversed, the figure becomes profoundly epistemological. Calvin compared God's other revelation, the Bible, to both a mirror and a pair of spectacles: "In short, let us remember that the invisible God, whose wisdom, power, and righteousness are incomprehensible, sets before us Moses' history as a mirror in which his living likeness glows. For just as eyes, when dimmed with age or weakness or by some other defect, unless aided by spectacles, discern nothing distinctly; so, such is our feebleness, unless Scripture guides us in seeking God, we are immediately confused." [63] Through these clear spectacles we view the spectacle of the world. The other formulation of the *theatrum mundi,* with God as the spectator and man the spectacle, concerns divine and not human epistemology. God sees all things, we are always on His stage. So the notion of a spectator encompasses both knowing and being known. As spectators we know; as actors we are known.

Smith applied this metaphor to prophetic vision and extended it with great care. The prophet was a spectator at a drama. The numerous shifts in speaking voice and the abrupt transitions of prophetic writing could be subsumed within this comparison, "Exits and Intrats upon this Prophetical stage being made as it were in an invisible manner" (p. 271). The metaphor seems to collapse when we consider that the prophets performed actions, that the Bible contains the lives of the prophets as well as their visions. But Smith refused to separate historical narrative from prophetic vision. Everything in the prophetic books is drama. Hosea married a harlot at the command of God: "But we shall not here doubt to conclude both of that and all other actions of the Prophets which they were enjoined upon the Stage of Prophecie, that they were only Scenical and Imaginary" (p. 213). The prophets were both spectators and spectacles, interpreters and actors. In a passage of great imaginative compression, Smith turned his metaphor one final time:

> But for a more distinct understanding of this business, we must remember what hath been often suggested, That the Prophetical Scene or Stage upon which all apparitions were made to the Prophet, was his Imagination; and there all those things which God would have revealed

[63] *Institutes* I.xiv.1. The Latin *specilla* is sometimes synonymous with *specula,* lenses with mirrors (see Pico, pp. 50–51).

> unto him were acted over Symbolically, as in a Masque, in which divers persons are brought in, amongst which the Prophet himself bears a part: and therefore he, according to the exigency of this Dramaticall apparatus, must, as the other Actors, perform his part . . . and so not only by Speaking, but by Gestures and Actions come in his due place among the rest. [P. 215]

Perhaps something along these lines was already implicit in Paraeus, who defined John as actor and viewer. But this passage achieves a remarkable unification of the two formulations of the *theatrum mundi*. Prophecy, a divine masque, annihilates the distinction between the watcher and the watched. The entertainers at the heavenly court mingled interchangeably with the audience. As human masquerades confused art and life, divine masquerades confused allegory and history. The prophet was part of the design he envisioned. Given a revelation, he simultaneously revealed himself. He knew even as he was known. Smith discovered the lucid metaphor, the definitive genre.

It is virtually impossible that John Smith had any influence on the author of *Paradise Lost*. His *Discourses* were not published until 1660, well after the epic was underway. The rationalist contempt for accommodation and mystical disregard for history would not in any case have appealed to Milton. But I do suggest that during the period from his retirement at Horton through the early pamphlets, from about 1635 to 1645, Milton was evolving a conception of masque and drama not dissimilar from the metaphorical masque and drama in "Of Prophecy." Like Smith, Milton tried to achieve "a more distinct understanding of this business."

Several passages in the early prose indicate that Milton was, as he began to write political pamphlets, a millenarian.[64] Without doubt he was well-read in apocalyptic commentary. When Milton entered Christ's College in 1625, one of the Fellows was Joseph Mede, who published *Clavis Apocalyptica* in 1627. It is likely that bright undergraduates of the seventeenth century, like their counterparts today, studied the writings of their faculty with particular attention. Milton referred to David Paraeus in *The Reason of Church Government* (CE III, 238), and since the English translation was not published until 1644, he must have been interested enough

[64] In *Animadversions,* for example, Christ is ready at the door to begin his reign (CE III, 148). See Michael Fixler, *Milton and the Kingdoms of God* (Evanston: Northwestern University Press, 1964).

to read the weighty Paraeus in Latin. This "grave authority" was in fact an active opponent of the millenarians.[65] He attracted Milton, not because his interpretation was definitive, but because he developed the *theatrum prophetiae* in such a literal way. We know from Milton's Commonplace Book that he was interested in the problem of dramatic spectacle:

> Spectacula
>
> In the work entitled *De Spectaculis* Tertullian condemns their vogue and excludes Christians from them. In fact, it is not only with arguments (which excoriate the pagan games only) that he supports his obligation to bind with religious scruples the mind of a wary and prudent Christian from venturing to witness a dramatic poem, artistically composed by a poet no wise lacking in skill. Still, in the epilogue of the work he very finely with all the flowers of rhetoric directs the mind of a Christian to better spectacles, namely, those of a divine and heavenly character, such as, in great number and grandeur, a Christian can anticipate in connection with the coming of Christ and the Last Judgment. Cyprian, or whoever wrote the book that deals with the same subject, rolls exactly the same stone. And Lactantius with arguments by no means stronger puts a stigma upon the whole dramatic art. He does not even once seem to have reflected that, while the corrupting influences of the theatre ought to be eliminated, it does not follow that it is necessary to abolish altogether the performance of plays. This on the contrary is quite senseless; for what in the whole of philosophy is more impressive, purer, or more uplifting than a noble tragedy, what more helpful to a survey at a single glance of the hazards and changes of human life [quid utilius ad humanae vitae casus et conversiones uno intuitu spectandos]? [CE XVIII, 206–7]

Man, having so much to learn, is properly a spectator. Admitting the "corrupting influences of the theatre," Milton defended the potential of drama as a better teacher than philosophy. Yet he was taken with the last section of *De Spectaculis* —Tertullian wrote "very finely" when he offered the apocalyptic imagination as an alternative to corrupt secular theatre. In *The Reason of Church Government,* the prophetic theatre of Revelation promises that drama can be divine, didactic, spectacular, and apocalyptic:

> Or whether those Dramatick constitutions, wherein *Sophocles* and *Euripides* raign shall be found more doctrinal and exemplary to a Nation, the Scripture also affords us a divine pastoral Drama in the Song of

[65] The title page of the Arnold translation informed the buyer that this book contained matter "against the Millenarians" in chapter 20. See also *A Commentary upon the Divine Revelation,* pp. 524–30, refuting the Chiliasts.

Salomon consisting of two persons and a double *Chorus*, as *Origen* rightly judges. And the Apocalyps of Saint *John* is the majestick image of a high and stately Tragedy, shutting up and intermingling her solemn Scenes and Acts with a sevenfold *Chorus* of halleluja's and harping symphonies: and this my opinion the grave authority of Paraeus commenting that booke is sufficient to confirm. [CE III, 237–38]

Author of *Arcades* and *Comus*, the young poet had already experimented with "pastoral Drama" in the secular tradition. Now that he wished to begin a divine poem, the poet was no longer so young. It was time to leave the shady groves. He wondered whether divinity could be taught "not only in Pulpits, but after another persuasive method, at set and solemn Paneguries, in Theaters, porches, or what other place" (CE III, 240). With these ideas in mind, Milton was planning a tragedy on the Fall at about the same time he wrote both *The Reason of Church Government* and the "Spectacula" entries in his Commonplace Book.[66]

The four drafts of this tragedy in the Trinity College Manuscript all project allegorical characters from the tradition of Jonsonian masque. In the first three drafts these characters are to appear throughout the drama, but in the fourth projection, "Adam unparadiz'd," the first allegorical figure, Justice, would not appear until after the Fall. The four outlines, then, move progressively away from the masque and toward a recognizable tragedy. In the third draft, entitled

[66] All modern attempts to date the entries in the Commonplace Book are indebted to J. H. Hanford's "The Chronology of Milton's Private Studies," *PMLA*, 36 (1921), 251–314. Following his guidelines, the Yale editor, Ruth Mohl, dates the three entries under "Spectacula" as follows: Tertullian was copied 1637–38, and Cyprian during the same period; the entry on Lactantius, including the refutation, was copied 1639–41 (*Complete Prose Works*, I, 489–90). This dating associates the Lactantius entry with the writing of *The Reason of Church Government*, which contains several suggestive remarks about drama. See W. R. Parker, *Milton: A Biography*, I, 218.

The four drafts have usually been assigned to 1640–42. Fresh from his Italian journey, Milton planned his tragedy under the influence of *sacre rappresentazione*—see Grant McColley, *Paradise Lost: An Account of Its Growth and Major Origins* (Chicago: Packard, 1940), pp. 290–93. The drafts also reflect the influence of the Jonsonian masque.

I think the drafts are interesting as attempts to discover the proper form for an inspired poem. Other than discussing the nature of this form, I make no elaborate connections between this project—little more than inspired doodling, really—and *Paradise Lost*. Parker cautions against attributing great importance to the echo of "Paradise Lost" and *Paradise Lost* in "The Trinity Manuscript and Milton's Plans for a Tragedy," *JEGP*, 34 (1935), 225–32. Still and all, Edward Phillips claimed to have seen *Paradise Lost* IV.32–113 as a soliloquy in an unfinished tragedy.

"Paradise Lost," Act I would consist of Justice, Mercie, and Wisdome debating "what should become of man if he fall" (CE XVIII, 229). Act II would present characters named "Heavenly love" and "Evening starre," both holdovers from the two earlier drafts. But in "Adam unparadiz'd" all this clutter has been discarded. With the exception of Justice, all the masque characters of the early scenes disappear—and Justice seems to function as nothing more than a representation of Adam's conscience. After the Fall, Justice "cites him to the place whither Jehova call'd for him" and later "appeares" and "convinces him" not to blame Eve for his loss (CE XVIII, 231). Only one masquerade remains in "Adam unparadiz'd." The fifth act of "Paradise Lost" would consist of Adam and Eve "praesented by an angel with" a series of "mutes to whome he gives thire names." Similarly, the angel of "Adam unparadiz'd" would cause "to passe before his eyes in Shapes a mask of all the evills of this life & world . . . at last appeares Mercy, comforts him, promises the Messiah, then calls in faith, hope, & charity" (CE XVIII, 232). Since Adam has not yet been expelled from the garden, this masque "of all the evills" would be a prophetic masque. The hypothetical audience at this unwritten tragedy would watch the theatre of the mind, the vision of a prophet. They would join with Adam as spectators in the *theatrum prophetiae;* the Adam before them on the stage would be at once a spectator and an actor. The four drafts show that Milton tended more and more to eliminate the elements of masque except with respect to the prophetic vision. The devices of masquerade would slow and diffuse a tragic drama. But in a drama of foreseeing, the masque would be decorous and proper.

The outlines also suggest that another problem with this divine tragedy was the character of the prologue. "Michael" heads the first list of dramatis personae. Presumably, the angel would have spoken a prologue directly to the audience: the "Genius of the Wood" in *Arcades* and the Attendant Spirit in *Comus,* both sent from Jove, would metamorphose into an angel sent from the Christian God. But in the next two drafts Michael is replaced by Moses.[67] The divine prophet of "Paradise Lost" recounts "how he assum'd his true bodie, that it corrupts not because of his [being] with god in the mount"

[67] In the second draft Milton first wrote "Michael," then "Moses or Michael," then finally "Moses" (see Hanford, "That Shepherd Who First Taught the Chosen Seed," p. 403).

(CE XVIII, 229). Having narrated his miraculous *visio dei,* Moses "exhorts to the sight of God, tells they cannot se Adam in this state of innocence by reason of thire sin." [68] If ever presented, the prologue would have disoriented the innocent spectators. Seated comfortably in their earthly theatre, the human audience would learn that they were too impure to sit in the celestial theatre. The prologue would define the absolute difference between human and divine spectators. "Paradise Lost" is the most suggestive of the outlines, for the audience would not in fact have seen Adam until Act IV, after the Fall. They would not have seen paradise lost.

This plan, though fairly hopeless as drama, suggests that Milton was weighing two opposite conceptions of his divine tragedy. The angel, an agent of vision and accommodation, could offer the pleasures of celestial theatre to earthly spectators. In the first draft, where Michael speaks the prologue, Adam and Eve appear "with the serpent"—the Fall, then, would have occurred on stage and in full view of the human audience. This conception emphasizes the privileged position of the audience—listening to an angel, they would stand in relation to this ambassador as prophets stand in relation to divine beings. They would be cast in the role of prophets, *spectatores;* the tragedy would be a spectacle for men. But when Moses speaks the prologue in "Paradise Lost," he insists on the difference between his ineffable vision and the impure vision of the audience. This conception emphasizes the privileged position of heaven, not earth. As the audience watched the spectacle on stage, they would be reminded of the greater spectacle off stage. The tragedy of the Fall would be a spectacle only for God, His angels, and His prophets. Men would see the consequences but not the tragic deed. In "Adam unparadiz'd," the angel is back again: "The angel Gabriel, either descending or entring, shewing since this globe was created, his frequency as much on earth, as in heaven, describes Paradise" (CE XVIII, 231). But though the angel returns, the Fall still takes place off stage. Adam and Eve do not enter until "seduc't by the serpent." No prophet gloats over his superior vision; yet no human audience can watch the prelapsa-

[68] Hanford (*ibid.*) corrects "hasts to the sight of god," the mistaken reading of the Columbia Edition. For a discussion of the spectacle implicit in these drafts, see F. T. Prince, "Milton and the Theatrical Sublime," in *Approaches to* Paradise Lost, ed. C. A. Patrides (London: Edward Arnold, 1968), pp. 53–63. Prince quotes a suggestive passage from Andreini about the "Theatre of the Soul" that makes "your heart the spectator of all" (p. 62).

rian spectacle. Milton ended "Adam unparadiz'd" with the words "compare this with the former draught." Doing so, we discover an uneasy reconciliation. The fourth draft was a tentative compromise between the first and the third. One good reason why Milton never wrote this tragedy was his inability to imagine anyone pure enough to see it.[69]

The convention of addressing the audience caused the difficulty. As the projected characterization of Moses suggests, the young poet was drawn to Neoplatonist theories of mystical rapture and divine vision.[70] Such experiences were not for the impure. The Spiritual "Genius" of *Arcades* heard the music "which none can hear / Of human mold with gross unpurged ear" (ll. 72–73). In *Ad Patrem,* the poet looked forward to escaping the mortal sight of vulgar men:

> Iamque nec obscurus populo miscebor inerti,
> Vitabuntque oculos vestigia nostra profanos.
> [Ll. 103–4]

> [I shall no longer mingle unknown with the dull rabble
> and my walk shall be far from the sight of profane eyes.]

About to recount his sacred ambitions in *An Apology* (1642), Milton protected himself with the parenthetical injunction, "let rude ears be absent" (CE III, 303). Elitist and defensive, this view of inspired knowledge conflicted with the patriotic ambitions of the Protestant tragedian. He could not become a literary evangelist, writing to inspire his countrymen, unless already assured of their purity. Speaking to a theatre of men, the divine agent of the prologue had to adopt a posture with respect to these men—either elevate them as fellow prophets or insult them as fallen mortals. The problem was to find a stage which the prophet and the angel could share together. Then neither character would have to acknowledge the audience. The vision could be simultaneously given and withheld. Human spectators could watch the prophet in dialogue with his source of inspiration, watch the prophetic masque glide by in the theatre of his vision. Such a stage might satisfy both the elitist Neoplatonist and the evangelical Protestant, al-

[69] Marianna Woodhull reached conclusions similar to my own in *The Epic of Paradise Lost* (New York, 1907; rpt. New York: Gordian, 1968), pp. 108–26.

[70] Given sanction by the Epistle of Jude, the preservation of the body of Moses became a favorite allusion in manuals of Neoplatonist magic such as the *De occulta philosophia* of Cornelius Agrippa. See *Three Books of Occult Philosophy,* trans. J. F. (London, 1651), pp. 574–75.

lowing Milton to dramatize the illuminations and ascending raptures of medieval theology and, in the content of these revelations, to figure forth the moral significance of Christian history. Moses with his private vision, David with his sense of history, and Samson with his mission of political action might all receive their due emphasis in this *theatrum prophetiae*. The grace would be to represent, not an action, but the inspiring of a prophet with the vision of an action.

With some adjustment, the necessary form was already there: as the audience looked on, a masque was to pass before the eyes of Adam. Milton had discovered this form in the Nativity Ode, and he would discover this form again for the pure readers of *Paradise Lost*.

CHAPTER III

Visionary Song, Zealous Prose

> For there are some "secreta theologiae," which are only to be understood by persons very holy and spiritual; which are rather to be felt than discoursed of; and, therefore, if peradventure they be offered to public consideration, they will therefore be opposed, because they run the same fortune with many other questions; that is, not to be understood, and so much the rather because their understanding, that is, the feeling, such secrets of the kingdom, are not the results of logic and philosophy, nor yet of public revelation, but of the public spirit privately working; and in no man is a duty, but in all that have it is a reward,—and is not necessary for all, but given to some; producing its operations, not regularly, but upon occasions, personal necessities, and new emergencies. Of this nature are the Spirit of obsignation, belief of particular salvation, special influences, and comforts coming from a sense of the spirit of adoption, actual fervours, and great complacencies in devotion, spiritual joys,—which are little drawings aside of the curtains of peace and eternity, and antepasts of immortality.
>
> Jeremy Taylor, *The Liberty of Prophesying*

THERE can be no mistaking the lordly certitude of Milton's pages. The prose writer continually calls upon God to witness his righteousness, gloating over the broken spirit and subsequent death of his opponent Salmasius: "I am he, who . . . with this stylus, the weapon of his choice, stabbed the reviler to the heart" (CE VIII, 15). The poet transcribes without premeditation an entire epic brought to him visit after visit by a divine messenger. For three hundred years readers have absorbed these fancies of self-importance and have tended to strike an imaginative balance between Milton and the other great English poet. Shakespeare appears in the history of criticism as a writer unique in his facelessness, both all artist and no artist, a mystery and not a man, while Milton emerges as a poet of the ego, a legend of hubris. Shakespeare is so perfectly human that he is no longer an individual, Milton so perfectly an individual that he is no longer human.

But conceptions of the self, like most conceptions, have

histories too difficult and elusive to accommodate such easy prejudice. What we might call lordly pride in Milton, the man himself would have considered a form of humility and obedience to God. Yet the invocations of *Paradise Lost* are dangerously ambitious in any context, contemporary or historical. This fearful presumption has rarely been the object of scholarly examination, the learned having found abundant opportunity to exercise their skills without confronting the naked claims of these passages. In particular, the identity of the Heavenly Muse has been an evasive pursuit for Milton criticism, distracting attention from the more important suggestions of the invocations and insulating readers from their surface complexities. Attempts to identify the Muse have often lusted after strange esoterica in the *Zohar* and the Orphic Hymns or relied too heavily on the *De Doctrina Christiana*. The power invoked is simply more complicated than any single one of the divine names defined in the theological treatise. The invocations represent, as Merritt Hughes has remarked, a kind of serious play with the many names of God.[1] The epic narrator carefully distinguishes himself from the magician, for whom names have an independent existence and power. He calls forth "The Meaning, not the Name" (VII.5), the essence that his language can only symbolize. This statement alone should caution readers against the pursuit of theological names and definitions for their own sake. Urania, divine light, sister of Wisdom, spectator and participant at the Creation, inspirer of Moses, the healing power of Christ—these diverse names gather together the attributes of God. His name, including all, is the only one large enough to contain them all. We do the invocations more justice by considering the "Meaning" of the act of speaking these names at a particular moment in a particular poem.

The epic opens with a list of the powers necessary for its successful completion. Through a sequence of biblical places, the poet alludes to sources of inspiration progressively more perfect. The sequence follows the chronology of biblical history and summarizes the progressive revelation of God to His people. Thus Moses first saw God in the burning bush "on the secret top / Of *Oreb*" and later was allowed a fuller vision on Sinai (ll. 7–10). The Word was fully revealed when

[1] *Ten Perspectives on Milton* (New Haven: Yale University Press, 1965), p. 94. Hughes compares the solemn play of the invocations with the linguistic inquiries of Socrates in the *Cratylus*.

the incarnate Christ healed the blind man at "*Siloa's* Brook that flow'd / Fast by the Oracle of God" (ll. 11–12). The allusions move from the Old to the New Testament, from Moses to his fulfillment in Christ, for the poet is here recounting the history by which the story of Fall and redemption, the Word of God, reached him. Choosing the name "Oracle of God" for the temple of Jerusalem, he emphasizes prophetic rather than institutional Christianity. No priest, Milton wishes to participate in the prophetic history of the private motions of God. He hopes to continue the sequence, becoming a new vessel for the Word. The Muse invoked is a Spirit of the new dispensation: "And chiefly Thou O Spirit, that dost prefer / Before all Temples th' upright heart and pure" (ll. 17–18). The truest church is the inspired heart. Old Testament prophets were concerned with the building of an external temple, but at the coming of Christ, *summa propheta,* the heart of man became an inner temple and an inward "Oracle of God" for the Spirit—these lines recapitulate the earlier movement from the Old Testament to the New. Since the epic will retell the events of Genesis, the Spirit who aids the singer must be the Spirit of Creation:

> Instruct me, for thou know'st; Thou from the first
> Wast present, and with mighty wings outspread
> Dove-like satst brooding on the vast Abyss
> and mad'st it pregnant. . . .
>
> [I.19–22]

Milton once wrote that the true poet "ought him selfe to bee a true Poem," and not presume to speak of heroic deeds "unless he have in himselfe the experience and the practice of all that which is praise-worthy" (CE III, 303–4). What is true of mortal poets is also true of immortal poets. The Spirit "know'st" and can therefore properly inspire a literary creation about Creation, whether by Moses or by Milton.

We understand that the narrator intends to imitate Homer and Virgil while also competing with these pagan poets. This epic will attempt to soar "Above th' Aonian Mount" (l. 15). But the relationship between *Paradise Lost* and the Bible is more difficult to define. The poet invokes the same Spirit which inspired Moses to write Genesis. Indeed, the first words of the Bible, "In the beginning," are repeated in *Paradise Lost* (l. 9). The invocation proceeds from Moses to Christ, Sinai to Siloa, because the poet will sing of restoration as well as the Fall. Does the epic assimilate Genesis only to exceed that account? Is the poet imitating and yet competing with Moses? What are we to make of "Things unattempted yet in Prose or Rhyme" (l. 16)? The line is often explained as a paraphrase of Ariosto, but in context the meaning of this paraphrase far transcends its source. Not so long ago a critic remarked that none of the many commentaries on the opening of the epic offer a convincing explanation of this puzzling line.[2] Other poets had imitated the Bible in heroic verse. The Bible itself had surely been "attempted."

Andrew Marvell recorded his initial reaction to the epic. In the beginning, this poem left him deeply uncomfortable:

> When I beheld the Poet blind, yet bold,
> In slender Book his vast Design unfold,
> Messiah Crown'd, God's Reconcil'd Decree,
> Rebelling Angels, the Forbidden Tree,
> Heav'n, Hell, Earth, Chaos, All; the Argument
> Held me a while misdoubting his Intent,
> That he would ruin (for I saw him strong)
> The sacred Truth to Fable and old Song
> (So Sampson grop'd the Tample's posts in spite)
> The World o'erwhelming to revenge his sight.[3]

As if to insist upon a point, Marvell wrote his dedicatory poem in rhyme; he alluded to the well-known anecdote about Dryden's plans to "tag" the blank verse of the epic in a rhyming opera. But this passage seems to present a more serious fear. The first invocation of *Paradise Lost,* if experienced at all, cannot help but force us into "misdoubting his

[2] Allen R. Benham, "Things Unattempted Yet in Prose or Rime," *MLQ,* 14 (1955), 341–47. Benham contends that the line refers to a nonchronological retelling of Genesis, using the narrative patterns of Greek and Latin epic. Perhaps so, but a reader who apprehends the line so particularly must suppress his immediate response—a far broader, more interesting one, which Milton could easily have avoided had he so desired.

The standard commentary on the first invocation is David Daiches, "The Opening of *Paradise Lost,*" in *The Living Milton,* ed. Frank Kermode (London: Routledge, 1960), pp. 55–69. "Is he going to overgo Moses as Spenser intended to overgo Aristo?" Daiches asks. He concludes that the epic is "a complete retelling, under new plenary inspiration deriving from the same divine source as Moses' inspiration, of the whole story of the mutual relations of God and man" (p. 63). But Milton would not have understood the term "plenary inspiration" and the line does not suggest that what is here attempted has ever been attempted before, even in the Bible. The progression of the sources of inspiration indicates that the narrator writes with greater authority than Moses. He has access to the cumulative wisdom of the entire prophetic tradition.

[3] "On Paradise Lost," ll. 1–10.

Intent"–into wondering whether this poet will "ruin" the "sacred Truth." An awesome conclusion hovers between the narrator of the epic and his reader, for if the poet claims higher inspiration than Moses, it seems distressingly easy to conclude (let rude ears be absent) that the epic intends to be a document superior to a portion of Holy Scripture. Inspired on Sinai, Moses sang of Creation and Fall. But this poem requires both the inspiration of Sinai and the inspiration of Siloa: the poet will sing of Creation, Fall, and with full clarity, of redemption. Attempting the unattempted, the poet will sing an adventurous song of the "beginning" more perfect than Genesis. Marvell went on: "At once delight and horror on us seize, / Thou sing'st with so much gravity and ease." "Delight and horror" is, I think, absolutely right. The sheer ambition of the poem–if only a hovering inference–dazzles. The spectacle of a man presuming so much both excites and terrifies. If successful, who could imagine the reward? But if a failure, who could calculate the punishment? If the narrator is deluded, if he has no God in his mind, if the Muse he invokes is in reality a devil of presumption and soaring arrogance, who could measure the wrath of God? Who could justify the ways of this man to God?

The narrator further explores his relationship to Moses in the invocation of Book III. His address to light depends on the old definition of three kinds of vision–a definition which, as we have seen, often appeared in discussions of prophecy, rapture, and mystical contemplation. Blind, the narrator cannot see with his physical eyes. Limited to intellectual vision, he requests the "Bright effluence of bright essence increate" (l. 6) to "Shine inward" (l. 52). The vision requested would transcend corporeal images altogether, allowing the favored poet to "see" essences. He asks for the *viso dei* itself:

> Hail holy Light, offspring of Heav'n first-born,
> Or of th' Eternal Coeternal beam
> May I express thee unblam'd? since God is light
> And never but in unapproached Light
> Dwelt from Eternity, dwelt then in thee. . . .
>
> [Ll. 1–5]

The poet seems to fear that he has violated a mystery, broken a taboo. "May I express thee unblamed?" He proceeds to call the roll of blind classical prophets–Thamyris, Maeonides, Tiresias, Phineus. But the narrator suggests, through allusion and metaphor, that his genuine hope is to repeat and even exceed the experience of Moses on Sinai. The proper biblical context for this invocation is Exod. 33.12–13, where the prophet of Israel asks God if he may see Him plainly: "Yet thou hast said, I know thee by name, and thou hast also found grace in my sight. Now therefore, I pray thee, if I have found grace in thy sight, show me now thy way, that I may know thee, and I may find grace in thy sight." The narrator expresses the "name" of God, "since God is Light," and hopes that "unapproached Light" may shine within him. Whereas Moses asked the unapproachable God for an external vision, the blind poet requests an internal vision. Inside his head, the narrator recreates the situation on Sinai. Moses spoke to "the cloudy pillar." The blind eyes of the narrator are with "dim suffusion veil'd" (l. 26), like the veiled face of Moses. This phrase results in the metaphor of a cloud:

> But cloud instead and ever-during dark
> Surrounds me, from the cheerful ways of men
> Cut off, and, for the book of knowledge fair,
> Presented with a universal blank. . . .
>
> [III.45–48]

His address to light concludes with the hope that this "cloud" may be dispersed:

> Shine inward, and the mind through all her powers
> Irradiate; there plant eyes, all mist from thence
> Purge and disperse, that I may see and tell
> Of things invisible to mortal sight.
>
> [III.51–55]

But no man can see and tell of the face of God.[4] In the *De Trinitate,* Augustine discussed the spiritual education of Moses in Exodus 33. The prophet asked to see his Lord plainly, but this vision could not be granted to him. Instead, Moses saw only the "back parts" of God. These "back parts," Augustine said, prefigure Christ, for only in the Son is the Father visible to men.[5]

[4] Cornelius Agrippa, in *The Vanity of Arts and Sciences,* XCIX (London, 1676), pp. 340–44, distinguishes between the "Morning-vision" of seeing God in His creatures and the "Meridional Understanding" of seeing God face to face. The second, granted to Paul, "no tongue of men or angels can express" (p. 341). Milton recognizes full well the daring of his request, for he has the examples of Moses who was denied, and Paul, who was silent, before him. "May I express thee unblamed?" surely means more than "Have I named you properly, Lord?"

[5] *De Trinitate* II.xvi–xvii.

In the course of Book III, the poet relives this spiritual education. As the Father announces the obedient Sacrifice of the Son, angels take "thir gold'n Harps" and "introduce / Thir sacred Song, and waken raptures high" (ll. 365–69). A spectator at this ceremony, the narrator proceeds to participate in the joyous singing. His descriptive narrative becomes inseparable from the event described:

> Thee Father first they sung Omnipotent,
> Immutable, Immortal, Infinite,
> Eternal King; thee Author of all being,
> Fountain of Light, thyself invisible
> Amidst the glorious brightness where thou sit'st
> Thron'd inaccessible, but when thou shad'st
> The full blaze of thy beams, and through a cloud
> Drawn round about thee like a radiant Shrine,
> Dark with excessive bright thy skirts appear,
> Yet dazzle Heav'n. . . .
>
> [III.372–81]

The *visio dei* is withheld. Though the "dim suffusion" has been pierced to allow a vision of heaven, the vision itself is of a "cloud" both bright and dark. Christ is the light of this world. The narrator sees only the "back parts" of God:

> Thee next they sang of all Creation first,
> Begotten Son, Divine Similitude,
> In whose conspicuous count'nance, without cloud
> Made visible, th' Almighty Father shines,
> Whom else no Creature can behold; on thee
> Impresst th'effulgence of his Glory abides,
> Transfus'd on thee his ample Spirit rests.
>
> [III.383–89]

Here the prayers are answered, the narrator has gained his entrance. The invocation began, "Hail holy Light, offspring of Heav'n first-born," then offered an alternative conception of light as the "coeternal" essence of divinity. Now by his own experience the narrator has discovered the true names of holy light, separating the light of the Son, "of Heav'n first-born," from the eternal light of the Father. Seeing Christ, "of all Creation first," he sees through the cloud to "Divine Similitude." He undergoes, that is, the experience of Moses with the understanding of Augustine. Blind, he perfects the shadowy sight of his great predecessor. Having achieved this vision, the poet may now "express thee unblam'd":

> Hail Son of God, Savior of Men, thy Name
> Shall be the copious matter of my Song
> Henceforth, and never shall my Harp thy praise
> Forget, nor from thy Father's praise disjoin.
> [III.412–15]

At the beginning of Book III, the words "Hail holy light" elicited fears of presumption and excess. But now the poet tunes his harp with the angelic harps, hailing the Son of God and using "thy Name" with divine approval. His songs of praise, including the song he is singing now, will join their mortal notes to the heavenly anthem. The harp—traditional symbol of David and sacred song—is the emblem of his achievement, for the poet of *Paradise Lost* has entered the company of those Old Testament prophets granted the *visio Christi*. Having found grace in the sight of God, he may express the divine mysteries unblamed.

The angelic song wakens "raptures high." In the invocation to Book VII, the poet tells us that he has been seized, "rapt above the Pole" (l. 23). Following the definitions of rapture in Bernard and Aquinas, the narrator has not reached the third heaven of the *visio dei*. This extraordinary translation requires absolute passivity of the rapt soul. The epic narrator, however, cooperates with his divine guide. In Book III he revisits the guide "with bolder wing" (l. 13). Unlike those in a genuine rapture, he visits Sion and actively feeds on thoughts "that voluntary move / Harmonious numbers" (ll. 37–38). Nor is he distracted from the sensible world, remaining ever conscious of his literal blindness. The narrator, though seized, participates in his own rapture.

The invocation to Book VII continues to unfold what is perhaps the most striking aspect of these addresses—the paradox of an action both voluntary and involuntary. The narrator says that Urania visits either his dreams or his waking hours, whereas in the previous invocation he himself was the nighttime visitor. "Nightly I visit" (III.23) becomes "thou / Visit'st my slumbers Nightly" (VII.28–29). This passive receiver and active seeker, this dreamer whose thoughts feed while his body sleeps, bids Urania to "govern thou my Song" (VII.30). The Heavenly Muse must "fit audience find, though few" (l. 31). This famous line should probably be understood in relation to the theory of inspired interpretation. Milton cannot sing of Creation unless the Spirit who presided over Creation also presides over the creation of his song. Similarly, the reader cannont understand the song unless the presiding Spirit also governs him. Thus Urania, source of all inspiration, must "find" the appropriate audience for the inspired epic.

This invocation also expands previous statements about the relative efficacy of classical and Christian inspiration. In Book I the poet announced his epic flight "Above th' *Aonian* Mount." In Book III he wandered by night to both Helicon and Sion, "Smit with the love of sacred Song" (l. 29)—a love embracing the pagan epic and the Christian Bible. Here he divides Helicon from Sion, one sacred song from another:

> But drive far off the barbarous dissonance
> Of *Bacchus* and his Revellers, the Race
> Of that wild Rout that tore the *Thracian* Bard
> In *Rhodope,* where Woods and Rocks had Ears
> To rapture, till the savage clamor drown'd
> Both Harp and Voice; nor could the Muse defend
> Her Son. So fail not thou, who thee implores:
> For thou art Heavn'ly, shee an empty dream.
> [VII.33–39]

The harp is also the symbol of Orpheus. Milton indicates his brotherhood with the classical *vates* even as he distinguishes himself from this forebear. The passage alludes to the distinction of the early Fathers between manic and serene prophecy, but here the distinction is made within the classical tradition itself—the "barbarous dissonance" of the ecstatic bacchantes contrasting with the harmonious rapture of Orpheus—and not between classical and Christian oracles; the pagan myths already contained this distinction. But having told the story, the poet immediately claims that the story is false. There was no Muse, only "an empty dream." The empty dream, which appears to be metaphorical, is a literally empty dream to be compared with the inspired dreams brought by the Heavenly Muse. In this invocation, Milton gives the classical name "Urania" to his source of inspiration. But as a result of the efforts of Du Bartas, the Muse is fully Christian —"The meaning, not the Name I call." As the Christian "meaning" is to the classical name "Urania," so the narrator of *Paradise Lost* is to Orpheus. His significance fills the empty words.

Milton invokes the aid of Urania in excluding the dangerously unfit from the privilege of reading his poem. An evil audience tore Orpheus to pieces, greeting his inspired song with a "barbarous dissonance" opposed to the rapturous attention of innocent nature. Milton emphasizes the physical power of their antisong—the phrase "savage clamor" stands for the murderous violence of the bacchantnes. Disordered sound is a mortal danger. Though commanding power over nature with his inspired song, Orpheus was vulnerable to the unnatural song of "savage clamor": an inspired poet can be "drown'd," the language assumes, in dissonance. Certain readers are, in their barbaric disharmony, intrinsically unpoetic. Urania must drive such readers from the epic; there are some ears too rude to hear a sacred song. Since the "wild Rout" is the unfit audience of *Paradise Lost,* this passage must equate the body of Orpheus with the epic itself. As the murderous audience becomes "savage clamor," people represented as sound, so the inspired poem turns into the inspired poet, sound represented as a person. *Paradise Lost* is indistinguishable from the author of *Paradise Lost.* Milton was never one to abide impure speech; the blind pamphleteer believed himself "almost too sacred to attack" (CE VIII, 73). His inspired poem is militantly inviolate, terrible in its integrity like a pure person almost too sacred to touch. Evil readers may dismember both the body of the singer and the body of his song.

At certain moments in *Paradise Lost* we recognize that Milton is enacting the moral drawn from the story of Orpheus, guarding himself against dismemberment, finding the harmonious audience and driving off the dissonant. Here the epic poet bids farewell to false love, not to sexual love:

> into thir inmost bower
> Handed they went; and eas'd the putting off
> These troublesome disguises which wee wear,
> Straight side by side were laid, nor turn'd I ween
> Adam from his fair Spouse, nor *Eve* the Rites
> Mysterious of connubial Love refus'd:
> Whatever Hypocrites austerely talk
> Of purity and place and innocence,
> Defaming as impure what God declares
> Pure, and commands to some, leaves free to all.
> Our Maker bids increase, who bids abstain
> But our Destroyer, foe to God and Man?
> Hail wedded Love, mysterious Law, true source
> Of human offspring, sole propriety

In Paradise of all things common else.
By thee adulterous lust was driv'n from men. . . .
[IV.738–53]

Appropriately enough, this passage is the most intimate one in the epic, the only extended passage during which the narrator speaks as a man to other men; Urania understands his superiority in this matter, just as Raphael acknowledges in Adam the proper authority of human love. The definition of innocent sexuality becomes a way of narrowing the fit audience, excluding from this inspired poem both the austere hypocrites and the men from whom "adulterous lust" has not been driven. Improper readers, recoiling in offended purity or snickering in compulsive delight, are agents of "our Destroyer"–Milton would not have them follow him into the inmost bower. Proper readers join with the inspired poet by choosing to participate in phrases such as "our Destroyer" and "disguises which we wear." Having shed two kinds of "barbarous dissonance," the epic poet deliberately evokes another literary tradition:

Here Love his golden shafts imploys, here lights
His constant Lamp, and waves his purple wings,
Reigns here and revels; not in the bought smile
Of Harlots, loveless, joyless, unindear'd,
Casual fruition, nor in Court Amours,
Mixt Dance, or wanton Mask, or Midnight Ball,
Or Serenate, which the starv'd Lover sings
To his proud fair, best quitted with disdain.
These lull'd by Nightingales imbracing slept. . . .
[IV.763–70]

At this moment the fit reader, "handed" with his inspired guide, enjoys the renovation of a poetic style. After isolating two improper responses to prelapsarian love, Milton offers the triumphant Cupid of the sonneteers waving his purple wings, the reigning god of the traditional secular lyric from Wyatt to the Cavaliers. Still more careful with his audience, the narrator interrupts his unfinished epithalamium in order to purge all fallen associations from the word "revels." To "revel" in Eden has nothing to do with the familiar "revels" of the Renaissance aristocracy–nothing to do with masques, dances, serenades, and the entertainments of the palace courtiers. The explicit contrast is between the court setting of the lustful secular lyric and the garden setting of this innocent divine lyric. Milton regenerates and restores the word "revels" as a way of sanctifying the lyric tradition. "Barbarous dissonance" is in the language, in the poetic language—in the very fabric of verse. But inspired language protects itself from disharmony. As he drives off the fallen connotations of "revels," Milton quite literally drives far off the savage clamor "Of *Bacchus* and his Revellers." Purging the tradition of secular verse from his sacred language, he banishes the audience of this tradition from his vision of prelapsarian innocence. The fallen love lyric is the creation and the joy of "the Race / Of that wild Rout."

In this passage, as in others, Milton "finds" the ideal reader by placing familiar literary language in an unfamiliar context. He uses the resonant situations of the epic to create a unique kind of sacred parody, adapting for his own purposes the old technique of the divine poet. Satan is also a parodist. The negative poet of *Paradise Lost,* he too evokes the secular love lyric:

> Wonder not, sovran Mistress, if perhaps
> Thou canst, who art sole Wonder, much less arm
> Thy looks, the Heav'n of mildness, with disdain,
> Displeas'd that I approach thee thus, and gaze
> Insatiate, I thus single, nor have fear'd
> Thy awful brow, more awful thus retir'd.
> [IX.532–37]

The "starv'd Lover" who serenaded "his proud fair" was "best quitted with disdain." Poetic Satan tries to disarm this guardian "disdain." He speaks as the typical aristocratic lover of the renaissance lyric, making his "sovran" lady into a god and flattering her with witty puns on "Wonder" and "one"—Eve cannot "Wonder" because she is "sole Wonder" to "single" Satan. Satan draws on these literary conventions in their familiar context of seduction. The world of the narrator, including the literary world of the English language, belongs to Satan. He is the father of human evil and evil human literature. The sacred poet lives among latter-day "Revellers," compassed round with evil tongues. Urania must purge the dissonance of the secular "Revellers" from his answerable style—and in the process she drives far away the intrinsically unpoetic audience of this secular tradition. Satan, however, is a proper lyricist. From the vantage point of the barbarous reader, he is really no parodist: he uses literary conventions in the decorous tone with familiar intent at the appropriate occasion. Satan speaks for seducers to those who would be seduced. The audience of "barbarous dissonance," banished from the verse of God, can exalt the devil as their own true poet. The destructive speaker inherits the murderous audience. *Paradise Lost* solves the difficulty of the unfinished tragedy by dividing its audience into those fit to understand inspired song and those fit to revel in their own sophisticated savagery.

Hobbes could not understand why any poet would wish to be a bagpipe for God to blow through, but George Herbert labored to build an altar untouched by human tools.[6] In the work of Milton, the paradox of an artless art is nowhere more clearly examined than in the last invocation of *Paradise Lost:*

> If answerable style I can obtain
> Of my Celestial Patroness, who deigns
> Her nightly visitation unimplor'd,
> And dictates to me slumb'ring, or inspires
> Easy my unpremeditated Verse:
> Since first this Subject for Heroic Song
> Pleas'd me long choosing, and beginning late. . . .
> [IX.20–26]

The Celestial Patroness of this passage, who makes "Her nightly visitation unimplor'd," was earlier implored to drive off the barbarous dissonance and bring no empty dreams: "So fail not thou, who thee implores" (VII.38). Within the passage itself, "If . . . I can obtain" seems rather at odds with "unimplor'd." The matter of the poem "Pleas'd me long choosing," but the verse is "unpremeditated." How can the poem be both chosen and dictated? The poet goes on to say that he is "not sedulous by Nature to indite" classical and romance heroes, as if his "Nature" and predisposition do not in any way conflict with unpremeditated, dictated verse. The invocation presents a remarkable conjunction of voluntary choice and blind dictation.

We can resolve some of these difficulties by arguing that the nightly dreams are unimplored, artless, while the translation of these dream visions into poetry requires effort, choice, and art. But the distinction is, measured against the

[6] I refer of course to "The Altar" (*Works,* p. 26), one of Herbert's many intricate artifices in praise of artlessness.

text, a false one. The poet himself indicates that part of the epic is dictated and part of the epic inspired. In Book VII, Urania comes either at night or in the early morning:

> yet not alone, while thou
> Visit'st my slumbers Nightly, or when Morn
> Purples the East. . . .
>
> [VII.28–30]

This separation of the dream from the waking reappears in Book IX: "And dictates to me slumb'ring, or inspires. . . ." Sometimes the passive poet receives dictation in his sleep; other times the Muse "inspires" the poet in the act of composition. In either case, the narrator is an agent through which a greater poet realizes himself. He reminds us of those mystics who hit the target by not aiming, of those biblical prophets who wrote the words of God in books that bear their own names. Milton is both author and amanuensis. He has both everything to do and nothing to do with *Paradise Lost.*

The narrator exemplifies the radical form of prophetic inspiration defined in Calvin. He must add nothing of his own to what he speaks:

> Mee of these
> Nor skill'd nor studious, higher Argument
> Remains, sufficient of itself to raise
> That name, unless an age too late, or cold
> Climate, or Years damp my intended wing
> Deprest; and much they may, if all be mine,
> Not Hers who brings it nightly to my Ear.
>
> [IX.41–47]

"The skill of Artifice or Office mean" cannot contribute to the truly heroic poem (IX.39). All must be "Hers." This poet has achieved the divine vision and has been granted an attendant Spirit to translate that vision into poetry. But as he claims this authority, he expresses the fullest doubt. The ambitious suggestions of Book I account for the tremendous power of these lines, the final words of the final invocation. In a single conditional clause, the poet experiences a moment of absolute mistrust, beautifully controlled with the grim understatement of "and much they may." If Milton is the author of this poem, if he is the artist instead of the instrument, then he fails as poet and prophet. Since God particularly despises false prophets, failure in this context ranges from humiliation to something like damnation. The poet departs from his poem, leaving the conditional clause unanswered, uncompromised.

As the narrator invokes the many names of God, so he plays seriously with the many categories of prophetic inspiration. He invokes the Spirit that inspired Genesis and the Muse that inspired Du Bartas. He calls the roll of pagan prophets while requesting the plain vision of God. He pierces the cloud, sees the Father in the Son, and returns in Book VII to define his cooperative rapture. He compares the empty dreams of classical *furor poeticus* to the inspired dreams of Christian prophecy—and does so without discarding the classical names. Though the name "Son of God" must ever be his copious matter, still the names of Orpheus and Urania pass across his song. Because of Urania he is, though in "solitude," "not alone"—he knows her as a friend. He visits in dreams and is visited in dreams. Poems and visions come in his slumber. His inspiration is both visual and aural. When he awakens, still he is inspired with unpremeditated verse. What he chooses to sing appears to him unimplored. Provided that he add nothing of his own, the Muse allows him to fly, see, and speak. This prophet of many visions and many voices offers an example of almost every one of the traditional modes of prophetic inspiration. As copious as the matter of his song, he blends in one harmonious person the classical *vates,* the Christian poet, the biblical prophet. Once again, here is no mere frivolity. The narrator, like the Heavenly Muse, dares to "play / In presence of th' Almighty Father" (VII.10–11). He writes for a Celestial Patroness. She must approve his song, just as God was "pleas'd" with her "Celestial Song" (VII.11–12). When the narrator calls his verse "unpremeditated," he implicitly connects the inspired composition of the epic with the morning prayers of Adam and Eve. Our first parents also create "unmeditated" verse, seized by "holy rapture" (V.147–49). To sing he he does, the poet must repair the ruins of the Fall—the Heavenly Muse prefers "th' upright heart and pure." Should inspiration fail him, it would be a failure of purity.

The epic is a prophetic vision in dramatic form, dictated by a divine power. Milton had once planned to close his tragedy on the Fall with a prophetic masquerade of the evils of the world. Though all the allegorical characters are missing, this masque appears in the epic. History passes silently before Adam in Book XI, and the angel interprets the vision. As

Michael tells the story of mankind, Adam occasionally interposes a question. The epic itself has a similar form. At the beginning of *Paradise Lost,* the narrator formally gives up his voice to the attendant Spirit:

> Say first, for Heav'n hides nothing from thy view
> Nor the deep Tract of Hell, say first what cause
> Mov'd our Grand Parents in that happy State,
> Favor'd of Heav'n so highly, to fall off
> From thir Creator, and transgress his Will
> For one restraint, Lords of the World besides?
> Who first seduc't them to that foul revolt?
> Th' infernall Serpent; hee it was. . . .
>
> [I.27–34]

The question is answered and, presumably, the Heavenly Muse proceeds to "say" the epic. The personal "our Grand Parents" of this passage soon yields to the impersonal "Mother of Mankind" (l. 36), a general and distant name such as a divine agent might use when answering the questions of a mortal. Later in Book I, the poet interrupts with another question:

> Then they were known to men by various Names,
> And various Idols through the Heathen World.
> Say, Muse, thir Names then known, who first, who last,
> Rous'd from the slumber on that fiery Couch,
>
> . . . . .
>
> While the promiscuous crowd stood yet aloof?
>
> [I.374–80]

The impersonal, distant "known to men" again suggests that the Heavenly Muse is actually speaking the poem between the first question and this second question. As the divine authority speaks, the human auditor occasionally interrupts or interpolates a question. The first two books of the poem consistently maintain the tone of a divine educator addressing a privileged mortal—precisely the tone of Michael speaking to Adam:

> for neither do the Spirits damn'd
> Lose all thir virtue; lest bad men should boast
> Thir specious deeds on earth. . . .
>
> [II.482–84]

The voice says "Adversary of God and Man" (II.629), not "our Adversary." Removed from mortal perspective, the phrase "on earth" suggests that other dwellings are equally familiar.

Suddenly, this carefully established framework is broken and the identity of the speaking voice confused:

> Thus saying, from her side the fatal Key,
> Sad instrument of all our woe, she took. . . .
> [II.871–72]

Sin grasps the instrument of "all our woe." Calling attention to the shift in perspective, this first human possessive in the body of the epic repeats the first human possessive of the first invocation—the mortal fruit "Brought Death into the World, and all our woe." The human voice and the divine voice, initially separate, here mingle without difference. The shock of disorientation that should attend this moment has not been experienced, I believe, for several reasons. The homogenous syntax and diction of the verse disguise the initial dialogue, disguise the fact that *Paradise Lost* unquestionably begins with two speakers, one telling the story and one taking dictation. Also, readers are disposed to consider the invocations to the Muse as allegorical, fictional, or simply conventional. They do not attend seriously to a human speaker who asks a question and then transcribes the divine answer. Surely the man is being classical again. But surely the man is also being Christian again. The Muse "dictates to me slumb'ring." She is asked to "Say first," then does indeed say "The infernall Serpent," naming the essence of Satan with divine authority as later in the epic God Himself will literally transform Satan, who cannot understand "mysterious terms," into an "infernall Serpent," a snake in Hell. Readers have not allowed this change of voice to occur. "Of course he answers his own question," they observe in silence, repressing the language before them. But of course the Muse answers the question. The human request and the divine response give prophetic authority to the verse of the poem. Changing Satan into an "infernall Serpent," the inspired language acts with the power of God. In this prophetic theatre, we watch the divine spectacle unfold between the prophet and his source of inspiration. We watch the inspiring.

Milton continues to confuse the identity of the epic voice. The poem transcribed by the human narrator speaks of "our first parents" (IV.6), "our general Mother" (IV.492), and "our general Ancestor" (IV.659)—all epithets of a man speaking to mankind and for mankind, forming a bond between himself and his readers. Halfway through the poem, at the opening of Book VII, the mingled voice is separated once more:

> Say Goddess, what ensu'd when *Raphael,*
> The affable Arch-angel, had forewarn'd
> Adam by dire example to beware
> Apostasy, by what befell in Heaven
> To those Apostates. . . .
>
> . . . . .
>
> He with his consorted *Eve*
> The story heard attentive, and was fill'd
> With admiration, and deep muse. . . .
>
> [VII.40–52]

But this separation also returns to inseparable unity with the phrase "so spake our Sire" (VIII.39). An analogous shift in pronouns occurs during the Morning Hymn of Adam and Eve, which, like the epic, is unmeditated art:

> Witness If I be silent, Morn or Even,
> To Hill, or Valley, Fountain, or fresh shade
> Made vocal by my Song, and taught his praise.
> Hail universal Lord, be bounteous still
> To give us only good; and if the night
> Have gather'd aught of evil or conceal'd,
> Disperse it, as now light dispels the dark.
>
> [V.202–8]

The switch from "I" to "us" embodies not only the communal individuality of Adam and Eve but also the "Witness" of their prayer. "Us" includes the two speakers and includes as well the entire earth "Made vocal" by their song. All existence praises its Creator in a universal dance of motion. Our first parents give voice to a world; their song becomes all the mute songs of our pendant earth.[7] Similarly, the unpremeditated art of the epic narrator gives voice to his human audience; the plural possessive of a phrase like "sad instrument of all our woe" includes, not one man merely, but all the fallen progeny of Adam and Eve—quick, dead, and yet to live. The human possessive "our" signals the participation of fit audience. When the dialogue between prophet and Spirit collapses into a monologue, the new voice mingles heaven and earth in a single song. Secretary becomes speaker, spectator becomes spectacle, audience becomes actor. As the Muse replies to the human question, a divine voice speaks to men.

[7] As Adam and Eve ask God to "disperse" the darkness of the world, the narrator asks God to "Purge and disperse" his particular darkness.

But with the word "our" the prophetic theatre turns around so that men, like Adam and Eve in their daily orisons, may speak to God.

Though Adam "The story heard attentive," this attention left something to be desired. Identifying his unpremeditated epic art with the unmeditated art of Adam, the narrator also suggests that his "admiration, and deep muse" may be equally imperfect. The first invocation lists the powers necessary for the completion of the poem. The last invocation lists the ways in which the epic may fail in the absence of these powers. Should "all be mine," the whole endeavor is misguided. Yet the Heavenly Muse "brings it nightly to my Ear." The prophetic dream of *Paradise Lost* contains prophetic dreams, and these dreams within redefine both the possibility of success and the possibility of failure.

Eve spends an "irksome night" dreaming of "offense and trouble" (V.34–35). She awakens and, hand in hand with Adam, recounts a story which adumbrates not only the fall of man but also the possible failure of the epic narrator. The relationship between Eve and her devilish "Guide" (V.91) elaborately parodies the relationship between the slumbering narrator and his Celestial Patroness. As the Heavenly Muse brings the gift of heroic verse to the ear of the sleeping poet, so Satan squats obscenely at the ear of Eve: "Close at mine ear one call'd me forth to walk / With gentle voice" (V.36–37). Similarly, the Heavenly Muse calls the narrator forth to walk at night through Helicon and Sion. The poet, led by the Muse, flies "with bolder wing" until he is "rapt above the pole." The winged Satan seizes the dreaming Eve and carries her above the earthly pole:

> Forthwith up to the clouds
> With him I flew, and underneath beheld
> The Earth outstretcht immense, a prospect wide
> And various: wond'ring at my flight and change
> To this high exaltation; suddenly
> My guide was gone, and I, methought, sunk down
> And fell asleep. . . .
>
> [V.86–92]

In Book VII, the narrator is "up led" and "with like safety guided down" (ll. 12–15). But Eve is deserted at the height of her journey. She suffers the fate of Bellerophon that the narrator prays he may avoid in Book VII (ll. 17–20).

The Satanic dream is genuinely prophetic, but also genuinely ambiguous. Christian theologians often attributed imperfect or misleading prophecy to devils, citing the biblical examples of Baalim and the Witch of Endor, the classical example of Delphi.[8] Like the narrator, Eve dreams "Of Man's First Disobedience, and the Fruit"–yet her participation in this dream foreshadows her fatal sin. She becomes the woman she dreams. Eve literally "fell asleep." Her "high exaltation" foreshadows the coming exaltation of pride. The warning ambiguously hidden in the dream is of course the sinking down, the falling. Lying like truth, the dream conceals its true meaning. Moreover, her temptation in this dream seems calculated to appeal to the narrator as well:

> Taste this, and be henceforth among the Gods
> Thyself a Goddess, not to Earth confin'd,
> But sometimes in the Air, as wee, sometimes
> Ascend to Heav'n, by merit thine, and see
> What life the Gods live there, and such live thou.
> [V.77–81]

The narrator "with no middle flight intends to soar" and, in Book III, requests the heavenly vision denied to mortal eyes. Coming at the end of the line, the words "and see" receive special emphasis in the dialogue of Satan. To see "What life the Gods live there" could not but appeal to the blind prophet –it is precisely the vision he desires. Dreaming, Eve mistakes the voice of Satan for the voice of Adam. Perhaps the narrator has also confused fallen and unfallen voices. If "all be" his, the epic poet may himself be guided by a satanic spirit, may himself be sinfully participating in his narrative of the Fall, may himself be performing a "high exaltation," raised to a "bad eminence" of arrogant pride (II.6). Each night a satanic whisper dictates forbidden knowledge.[9]

[8] Milton's Christ voices this belief in *Paradise Regained* I.430–37. See also the sources cited in William B. Hunter, "Eve's Daemonic Dream," *ELH,* 13 (1946), 255–65. Thomas Fuller considers satanic prophecy in *The Holy State* (Cambridge, 1642), p. 370.

[9] Dreamers were thought to be exceptionally vulnerable to the suggestions of devils. See, for example, Thomas Nashe, *The Terrors of the Night or, A discoverie of Apparitions,* in *Works,* ed. Ronald McKerrow and F. P. Wilson (Oxford: Blackwell, 1958), I, 345–76. Nashe writes as if it were commonly understood that Satan appeared to dreamers in the likeness of relatives: "It will be demaunded why in the likeness of ones father, mother, or kinfolks, he oftentimes presents himselfe vnto vs? No other reason can bee given of it but this, that in those shapes which he supposeth most familiar vnto vs, and

The true model for divine prophecy is the vision of Adam in the last two books:

> but to nobler sights
> Michael from Adam's eyes the film remov'd
> Which that false Fruit that promis'd clearer sight
> Had bred; then purg'd with Euphrasy and Rue
> The visual Nerve, for he had much to see;
> And from the Well of Life three drops instill'd.
> So deep the power of these Ingredients pierc'd,
> Ev'n to the inmost seat of mental sight,
> That Adam now enforc't to close his eyes,
> Sunk down and all his Spirits became intranst:
> But him the gentle Angel by the hand
> Soon rais'd, and his attention thus recall'd.
> [XI.411–23]

The scene parallels exactly the daemonic dream of Eve. Michael assumes the role of comforter. Offering his gentle hand, the angel does for Adam what Adam did for Eve. Michael also replaces Satan. Whereas Eve had a devilish "Guide," Adam has a "Celestial Guide" (XI.785). The dreaming Eve was raised high only to be "sunk down," but here Adam is "sunk down" only to be "rais'd." From her height of rapture, Eve saw "a prospect wide." This vision occurs on the "top / Of Speculation" (XII.588–89) where "the amplest reach of prospect lay" (XI.380). Before receiving this vision, Adam feared that he would live in places "Nor knowing us nor known" (XI.307). But the gentle angel brings him to the Mount of Speculation and offers him a prophetic spectacle. Here is the true opening of the eyes, the inner sight that the narrator asks for in Book III. "Instill'd," "Ingredients," "inmost," "instranst"—the language of this passage expresses the dynamic cohesion of the "paradise within thee," for at this moment Adam discovers paradise a second time. Like the narrator, he is a fallen man given prophetic knowledge. He sees and knows.

After hearing the daemonic dream of Eve, Adam explains

---

that wee are inclined to with a naturall kind of love, we will sooner harken to him than otherwise" (p. 348).

Dreaming, Eve mistakes the voice of Satan for the voice of Adam. Since the devil was thought to be a wily shape-shifter and inspirer of devious prophecy, it seems possible to infer that the narrator implicitly questions the identity of his Muse in the invocation to Book IX. She may be a demon disguised in a shape most likely to tempt this ambitious man. The point is highly speculative.

that this dream could not have occurred without the complicity of her human faculties. During the sleeping hours, reason "retires / Into her private Cell" (V.108–9). Thus "Fancy wakes" and imitates the normal activity of the rational soul. In this sense, the entire dream was the creation of Eve herself —human nature is vulnerable to sinful slumber. If "all be" his, the narrator may be experiencing the irrational shapes of "mimic Fancy" (V.110). But Adam and Michael ascend "In the Visions of God" (II.376). The first prophet closes his eyes and awakens to a mime of history beyond the capacity of mortal sight. If "all be" hers, the relationship between Milton and his Muse will be that of Adam to Michael. Then the narrator would view time as space, hear prophetic speeches, understand both type and antitype, master the "mysterious terms" of divine allegory, and sing prophetically of the connections between time and eternity. His the singing, but the song is God.

Several Miltonic narrators claim degrees of prophetic inspiration, and in the next chapter I will discuss the nature and function of these figures. But the epic narrator, more than any other in the canon, insists that his poem appears without premeditation. The Muse dictates and the narrator transcribes. The epic dramatizes a familiar Christian paradox: submitting to the Heavenly Muse, the narrator loses his art to gain his art. He demonstrates the relationship between freedom and obedience. The choice of the secretarial prophet, then, binds together the poet with his poem. Adam fell because he misunderstood the relationship between freedom and obedience—the narrator manifests the themes of which he speaks. But perhaps the attribution of the poem to the Heavenly Muse is still more deeply involved in the nature of *Paradise Lost*. Perhaps this special kind of prophecy helps to define the moral and aesthetic difficulties of the whole endeavor. Milton chose to assume this role because the prophet as instrument and amanuensis gave his poem a special integrity. In fact, the epic would be disfigured if presented in any other way.

The central theological issue of *Paradise Lost* is freedom. The poem argues time after time that its major characters are free to stand or fall. Freedom is the primary concept that vindicates the goodness of the Creator and justifies His ways to man; freedom is the cornerstone of this great argument. I suggest that the problem of freedom became, for Milton, an aesthetic problem. God created Adam and Eve with free will. But as characters in a poem created by John Milton, they could hardly be free at all. If the human author formed them, imagined them, constructed them, their choices and actions would be predetermined, "premeditated." The calculated plans of the artist would direct his characters. Mere puppets, "Adam" and "Eve" would be fallen before the Fall and disobedient before their first disobedience. Characters in a fiction can never be free; no matter how much the author insists, he continues to manipulate his creations, doing all of their thinking, deciding, and acting for them. As God is to the world, so the author is to his book—an ancient metaphor, but also an imperfect one. In his *De Musica,* Augustine distinguished the artist from both the imitator and the genuine Creator. Imitation is simply mimicry and requires no rational understanding. The genuine artist comprehends, through divine illumination, the preexistent principles of harmonious creation. But he cannot, like God, create *ex nihilo.* Rather, he completes the divine Creation, realizing in matter what previously existed in essential forms; neither a creator nor an imitator, he participates with God in the perfecting of nature.[10] To create art without divine illumination would be impossible according to Augustine. In a poem like *Paradise Lost,* this effort would border on blasphemy. The epic hopes to justify the ways of God to men. If "this great Argument" appears to be contrived argument, mounted by a premeditating schemer, the epic might easily have the opposite effect. Attempting so much, the great argument might emerge as a great scandal, an impediment to faith. For if the characters remain obedient to the will of a human author, this contrivance would violate the delicate distinction between divine foreknowledge and predestination. God would appear as a human author, a puppet master. Instead of the artist being elevated, God would be humiliated. As Marvell feared, the epic would ruin the sacred truths.

Milton explores the aesthetic and moral dangers of his "advent'rous Song" by comparing himself to Satan.[11] In the

[10] See Emmanuel Chapman, *Saint Augustine's Theory of Beauty* (London: Sheed and Ward, 1939), 26–44.

[11] Some of the parallels between Satan and the narrator to be discussed here have also been noted by William Riggs in "The Poet and Satan in *Paradise Lost,*" in *Milton Studies II,* ed. James D. Simmonds (Pittsburgh: University of Pittsburgh Press, 1970), pp. 59–82. Working independently, both Riggs and I have connected these crucial parallels to the daring of the epic and to the

first four books especially, this mysterious relationship clarifies the difference between the poem we read and the poem we might have read. The narrator flies from Hell to Heaven:

> Thee I revisit now with bolder wing,
> Escap't the *Stygian* Pool, though long detain'd
> In that obscure sojourn, while in my flight
> Through utter and through middle darkness borne
> With other notes than to th' *Orphean* Lyre
> I sung of Chaos and Eternal Night. . . .
> [III.13–18]

Flying from Hell to Eden, Satan escapes "the Stygian Pool," journeys "Through utter and through middle darkness," and visits the court of "Chaos and Eternal Night." He offers, during this flight, two invocations. Disguised as a cherub "Alone thus wand'ring" (III.667), he requests directions from Uriel:

> and straight was known
> Th' Arch-Angel *Uriel,* one of the sev'n
> Who in God's presence, nearest to his Throne
> Stand ready at command, and are his Eyes
> That run through all the Heav'ns, or down to th' Earth
> Bear his swift errands over moist or dry,
> O'er Sea and Land: him *Satan* thus accosts.
> *Uriel,* for thou of those sev'n Spirits that stand
> In sight of God's high Throne, gloriously bright,
> The first art wont his great authentic will
> Interpreter through highest Heav'n to bring,
> Where all his Sons thy Embassy attend;
> And here art likeliest by supreme decree
> Like honor to obtain, and as his Eye
> To visit oft this new Creation round;
> Unspeakable desire to see, and know
> All these his wondrous works, but chiefly Man,
>
> . . . . .
>
> Hath brought me from the Choirs of Cherubim
> Alone thus wand'ring. Brightest Seraph, tell
> In which of all these shining Orbs hath Man
> His fixed seat, or fixed seat hath none,
> But all these shining Orbs his choice to dwell;

---

issue of freedom. I attempt to extend the argument by relating the blindness of the narrator, the "inverted" invocation of Book IV, and the aesthetics of inspired creation to this sustained contrast. See also, for general remarks about devilish creations in Milton, Dennis H. Burden, *The Logical Epic* (Cambridge: Harvard University Press, 1967), pp. 57–75.

> That I may find him, and with secret gaze,
> Or open admiration him behold
> . . . . .
> That both in him and all things, as is meet,
> The Universal Maker we may praise;
> Who justly hath driv'n out his Rebel Foes
> To deepest Hell, and to repair that loss
> Created this new happy Race of Men
> To serve him better: wise are all his ways.
> [III.647–80]

The poet introduces Uriel immediately before Satan, repeating the same information in similar phrasing, defines his audience. This repetition invites the reader to contrast the speech of Satan with the speech of *Paradise Lost.* Like the narrator, Satan expresses an "Unspeakable desire to see, and know" the works of God. The hortatory construction of "Brightest Seraph, tell" suggests the commanding question of Book I, "Say first, for Heav'n hides nothing from thy view . . . ?" As Milton will invoke Urania, classical muse of astronomy, so Satan addresses Uriel in search of astronomical guidance. At the beginning of Book III, the blind prophet asks for the *visio dei* and soon achieves the sight of God in Christ: "never shall my Harp thy praise / Forget, nor from thy Father's praise disjoin" (III.413–14). Here at the end of Book III, Satan asks that he may "behold" man in order to "praise" the "Universal Maker." The hypocrite adds that God banished the fallen angels "justly," for "wise are all his ways": to find his own way in this new world, Satan justifies the ways of God. When the devil finishes his speech, the narrator proceeds to explain why Uriel, the "Eye" of God, can be deceived:

> So spake the false dissembler unperceiv'd;
> For neither Man nor Angel can discern
> Hypocrisy, the only evil that walks
> Invisible, except to God alone. . . .
> [III.681–84]

Only God perceives the hypocrite, the nearly perfect liar. But the narrator, unmasking this "false dissembler," enjoys divine perception. "Invisible" Satan is one of the "things invisible to mortal sight" that the narrator, having been granted his vision, may now "see and tell." The vision of invisible hypocrisy is, for the author, a kind of inverted self-knowledge. Knowing Satan, the narrator knows what he is not and must not become. The devil speaks with malicious irony. Phrases such as "Unspeakable desire to see" and "secret gaze" mean one thing to the fiend who speaks them and another thing to the angel who hears them. Concealing his motives, Satan requires knowledge of Creation in order to destroy Creation. He desires to know so that he may, by corrupting man, engender ignorance. Successful thus far, Satan elicits the response from Uriel that the "advent'rous" poet hopes to receive from his Heavenly Muse:

> Fair Angel, thy desire which tends to know
> The works of God, thereby to glorify
> The great Work-Master, leads to no excess
> That reaches blame, but rather merits praise
> The more it seems excess. . . .
>
> [III.694–98]

The narrator asks, "May I express thee unblamed?" He recognizes, throughout the poem, the boldness of his intent: "Into the Heav'n of Heav'ns I have presum'd / An Earthly Guest" (VII.13–14). Here Uriel, for a moment the blind eye of God, praises the satanic desire to know as blameless excess. The narrator of the poem hopes to be worthy of the reply while offering the opposite of the request. On the visible surface, however, the parallel between Satan and Milton is alarmingly exact.

The narrator must attain an inner light to complete his poem. Before he discovers Uriel, Satan stands at a place where "the Air / Nowhere so clear, sharp'n'd his visual ray / To objects distant far" (III.619–21). From this advantageous position he "Saw within ken a glorious Angel stand, / The same whom John saw also in the sun" (III.623–24). The allusion to Revelation authenticates the angelology of *Paradise Lost;* the Uriel of this epic is found at his proper station, where the tradition of prophetic vision indicates he should be found. But the repetition of "saw" and "saw also" unavoidably connects the prophetic seeing of John with the seeing of the devil. As Satan lands in Eden, John Milton suggests his own relationship to St. John in the unanswered invocation of Book IV:

> O for that warning voice, which he who saw
> Th' *Apocalypse,* heard cry in Heav'n aloud,
> Then when the Dragon, put to second rout,
> Came furious down to be reveng'd on men,

Woe to the inhabitants on Earth! that now,
While time was, our first Parents had been warned
The coming of their secret foe, and scap'd
Haply so scap'd, his mortal snare; for now
Satan, now first inflam'd with rage, came down,
The Tempter ere th' Accuser of man-kind,
To wreck on innocent frail man his loss
Of that first Battle, and his flight to Hell:
Yet not rejoicing in his speed, though bold,
Far off and fearless, nor with cause to boast,
Begins his dire attempt, which nigh the birth
Now rolling, boils in his tumultuous breast. . . .

. . . . .

Now conscience wakes despair
That slumber'd, wakes the bitter memory
Of what he was, what is, and what must be
Worse; of worse deeds worse sufferings must ensue.
Sometimes towards *Eden* which now in his view
Lay pleasant, his griev'd look he fixes sad,
Sometimes towards Heav'n and the full-blazing Sun,
Which now sat high in his Meridian Tow'r:
Then much revolving, thus in sighs began.
[IV.1–31]

The syntax disguises the meaning of the first five lines until we arrive at "that now, / While time was, our first Parents had been warn'd." The narrator understands the futility of his invocation, for "had been warn'd" assumes that no warning appeared. The voice remained silent. What begins as a request for "that warning voice" finally reveals itself as an exclamation of regret. Desiring heavenly intervention and seeming to request it, the narrator indicates his prophetic equality with John. It would be as appropriate in *Paradise Lost* as in Revelation for God to provide a *vox de caelo*. Ranging easily through the expanse of time, the narrator compresses the entire spectacle of human destiny. Adam and Eve are unfallen and untempted in the narrative present; the "Dragon" is about to succeed; fallen history is about to begin. But this passage comprehends time from a visionary perspective. As Satan moves toward his success, the prophetic narrator speaks of the defeated Satan at the end of history in the past tense. He remembers the end of time: "Then when the Dragon, put to second rout, / Came furious down." Yet "now" Satan, "now first inflam'd with rage, came down." The devil of the Fall and the Dragon of the Apocalypse both "came down," as if their actions took place simultaneously. Manipulating temporal reference with astonishing complexity, the fragmentary invocation to Book IV defines the temporal paradoxes of prophetic vision. Arguably we can resolve these verb tenses within a realistic framework. The Apocalypse is presented in the past tense because John "saw" and "heard" the future before this narrator "saw" and "heard" the beginnings of man. "While time was" suggests that the Fall occurred before the writing of *Paradise Lost.* So Milton, writing in the seventeenth century, constructs his epic after the events of the Fall and after the vision of John. But the word "now" appears seven times between lines 5 and 31, confusing the temporal status of the narrator in relation to the events he describes. Satan "came" down, "Begins" to execute his plans, and finally "began" to speak. At the time designated by "now" Satan both "begins" and "began." The creation of the poem also takes place "now," in the present tense: "Thee I revisit now with bolder wing." The narrator is a man who, acting in the present, sees now and remembers now the same events—remembering St. John, he recalls even the future. His temporal position is that of a spectator enjoying the visionary illusions of divine art. A spectacle of the past unfolds before him in the present. Since the Fall is happening once again, the prophet reacts like an audience at a tragedy. "O for that warning voice," he cries, struck with woe, thinking of another man who looked on in this prophetic theatre. The irregular tenses of *Paradise Lost* represent the double perspective of the prophetic spectator. He sees now what has been before. The reader of the poem is liable to the same irregularity. Adam "falls" in Book IX, but "fell" long before. As the reader is to the art of the narrator, so the narrator is to the art of God.

In the mind of Satan "conscience wakes despair." His bitter memory concerns "what he was, what is, and what must be"—the surprising "Worse" of line 26 corrects the momentary suggestion that Satan, like the narrator, remembers his future. No prophet, Satan cannot know what is to be; yet we understand that "what must be" will indeed be "worse," for the narrator with his own memory of the Apocalypse has recently reminded us of the "second rout." Though Satan and the narrator differ in what they know of the future, the prophetic poet experiences a sequence of righteous emotions similar to the devilish sequence. As Satan ends his journey in the garden of delight, "conscience wakes despair" in the mind of the epic poet. He asks for a warning voice which he knows he cannot have; man must be disobedient, death and woe must enter the world. Both the history of mankind and the stated theme of the epic preclude a warning voice to announce the presence of Satan. But human conscience wakes the "bitter memory" of "what must be / Worse" as a result of this disobedience: our tragic history must proceed, ending on a wrathful day. If the poet were in fact to call down "that warning voice," John would never have heard *"Woe to the inhabitants on Earth!"* Satan would have been routed once and for all time; the narrator would not be writing an epic to justify the ways of God to men.

Deliberately lamenting a necessary absence, seemingly requesting an impossible event, the narrator expresses a kind of "bitter despair" in the unanswered invocation. His desire for a warning voice forces God to reply with silence. To offer a prayer knowing that God will refuse is, for the man of tragic conscience, a pious version of fighting against God knowing that He will win. As Milton looks forward to his "Sad task" (IX.13) of recounting the Fall, Satan weighs his "dire attempt" to cause the Fall. Two kinds of conscience wake two kinds of despair. Resembling each other, the prophet and the false prophet are exact opposites.

The Satan of *Paradise Lost* is Milton inverted. The devil arrives in Eden "not rejoicing in his speed, though bold" (IV.13). The narrator was "long detain'd" in Hell but, at the opening of Book III, rejoices in the speed of his "bolder wing" (III.13); emphasizing the negative parallel, Milton places these references to bold speed in the thirteenth lines of successive books. Satan, like a devilish engine, recoils upon himself to negate the success of his bold flight:

> horror and doubt distract
> His troubl'd thoughts, and from the bottom stir
> The hell within him, for within him Hell
> He brings, and round about him, nor from Hell
> One step no more than from himself can fly
> By change of place. . . .
>
> [IV.18–23]

Actually, Satan cannot journey at all. As he brings Hell to the universe of the sun, an angel forever at home, the narrator brings earthly blindness to the God of light:

> Thus with the year
> Seasons return, but not to me returns
> Day, or the sweet approach of Ev'n or Morn,
> Or sight of vernal bloom, or Summer's Rose,
> Or flocks, or herds, or human face divine;
> But cloud instead, and ever-during dark
> Surrounds me, from the cheerful ways of men
> Cut off. . . .
>
> [III.40–47]

Actually, Milton cannot see at all. Which way he looks is dark. Like Satan, the blind man may have good reason to approach his destination with "troubl'd thoughts" stirred to "horror and doubt." It cannot be easy for a blind man to worship light and pray to a God whose essence is perfect seeing. But the prayer of Book III does indeed exalt the God of light—and exalts this God without denying the pain and anguish of the blind. The great invocation transforms emotions close, very close to bitterness and self-pity into graceful pride and self-knowledge. What might understandably have emerged as an insuppressible indictment of God begins as a hymn to light and ends with a claim to divine favor. God will disperse the darkness visible. Because the narrator is blind, God will grant him extraordinary vision in the precincts of celestial light: "So much the rather thou Celestial Light / Shine inward." It is the faultless balance of moral tact and personal outrage that makes the invocation to Book III so unforgettable a moment in our literature. "So much the rather thou . . ."—the language is at once a request and an absolute command. Milton perfects himself as he prays to be perfected, heals himself as he examines his wound. When Satan invokes the light, his malicious self-pity expresses itself without restraint:

> O thou that with surpassing Glory crown'd,
> Look'st from thy sole Dominion like the God
> Of this new World; at whose sight all the Stars
> Hide thir diminisht heads; to thee I call,
> But with no friendly voice, and add thy name
> O Sun, to tell thee how I hate thy beams. . . .
>
> [IV.32–37]

He calls the name in order to insult the meaning. For the devil, the important point about the sun is that it diminishes the stars. Though he understands the kingly nature of this particular "sovran vital Lamp" (III.22), Satan offers his dark hymn to light "with no friendly voice." He hates the world he is excluded from. Whereas the narrator, "from the cheerful ways of men / Cut off," continues to love the "holy light," Satan blasphemes the light that is not his. When he concludes "Evil be thou my good," the devil ironically defines his own exclusion from the divine rhythms of the universe. Evil does end in surpassing good for mankind; Satan alone is exempt from the *felix culpa.* The implicit formula of the blind prophet—Blindness be thou my sight!—joins with the harmonies of a redemptive order. Hell is uniquely unregenerate. Like the narrator, Satan accepts what he is and makes the best of it. The difference is that, for the devil, all is his and his alone.

Alien, despairing, and envious, Satan offers the invocation to light which the blind poet, trusting in his better guide, would never have spoken:

> Thus while he spake, each passion dimm'd his face,
> Thrice chang'd with pale, ire, envy and despair,
> Which marr'd his borrow'd visage, and betray'd
> Him counterfeit, if any eye beheld.
> For heav'nly minds from such distempers foul
> Are ever clear. Whereof he soon aware,
> Each perturbation smooth'd with outward calm,
> Artificer of fraud; and was the first
> That practis'd falsehood under saintly show,
> Deep malice to conceal, couch't with revenge. . . .
> [IV.114–23]

Satan inadvertently reveals his nature. Here is all the unconscious spite and disdain that never disfigures the invocation to Book III. The narrator himself seems to recognize the contrast: "For heav'nly minds from such distempers foul / Are ever clear." The treachery of this false angel can be seen "if any eye beheld." We immediately learn that the "eye" of Uriel "pursu'd him down" and "Saw him disfigur'd" (IV. 125–28). But the eye of the blind prophet also "saw" the marred visage. Viewing "things invisible to mortal sight," the blind poet understands his invisible counterpart—understands what he has not, by the grace of God, become. "Counterfeit" Satan, invoking the power he hates, is the inverse poet of this epic song. His thoughts involuntarily move inharmonious numbers. He is the "Artificer of fraud; and was the first / That practis'd falsehood under saintly show." As we follow the parallel journeys of Milton and Satan, both culminating in an address to light, the creation of *Paradise Lost* answers the negative creation of Satan. Both the devil and the narrator perform their actions "now": line by line the epic verse fills in the vacuum of decreation, perfecting human obedience even as Satan corrupts it. The plot of *Paradise Lost* contains and redefines the plot of Satan. The inspired poem contains an inverted poet who, inspired by himself alone, parodies the ways of the prophet as surely as he parodies the ways of God. A fruitless Fall is the theme of his antiepic. Reading this invisible poem, we discover a definition by negation of *Paradise Lost*. As Satan tells the angels of God, "Not to know mee argues yourselves unknown" (IV.830). But only fallen men know the world by contraries. To illuminate what he was Milton created, in the figure of Satan, what he was not.[12]

The negative creator of *Paradise Lost* is Satan. Parodying the birth of Eve and the birth of Athena, Sin springs full-blown from the left side of his head:

> All on a sudden miserable pain
> Surpris'd thee, dim thine eyes, and dizzy swum
> In darkness, while thy head flames thick and fast
> Threw forth, till on the left side op'ning wide,
> Likest to thee in shape and count'nance bright,
> Then shining heav'nly fair, a Goddess arm'd
> Out of thy head I sprung. . . .
>
> . . . . .
>
> Thyself in me thy perfect image viewing
> Becam'st enamor'd, and such joy thou took'st
> With me in secret, that my womb conceiv'd
> A growing burden.
>
> [II.752–67]

From the Hell of the mind she comes, "thy perfect image." God creates "Divine Similitude" in the Son and imposes his harmonies on the universe. The difference is a matter of freedom. Copulating with his perfect image, Satan can only

[12] The possibility of defining oneself by negation appealed to many seventeenth-century poets, supremely to John Donne in his "Nocturnall upon S. Lucies Day." Herbert made use of negative definition in "The Answer." Marvell's "Upon Appleton House" burgeons with contrasting opposites and balanced antitheses. Perhaps a more relevant example is the use of Archimago in Book I of the *Faerie Queene*.

In *Areopagitica* Milton wrote that "*Adam* fell into . . . knowing good and evill, that is to say of knowing good by evill" (CE IV, 311). See my discussion of logical negatives on pp. 180–83.

create himself. All is truly his. "Sin" and "Death" are other names for Satan—his created world is an allegory of his own psychological divisions. Sin turns to him and says:

> Thou art my Father, thou my Author, thou
> My being gav'st me; whom should I obey
> But thee, whom follow?
>
> [III.864–66]

But she has no being, no freedom to obey or disobey. God is "Author of all being" (III.374), and the devil merely pays homage to himself. Eve echoes the words of Sin when she turns to Adam and says:

> My Author and Disposer, what thou bidd'st
> Unargu'd I obey; so God ordains,
> God is thy Law, thou mine. . . .
>
> [IV.635–37]

"Daughter of God and Man" (IX.291), Eve freely decides to be obedient. Her free will allows her independence from both God and man—that is why her obedience is to be cherished and her disobedience to be mourned. If all be his, "Adam" and "Eve" would have the same relationship to the narrator that Sin has to Satan, her sole "Author." The epic would have no being, its characters enacting a psychological allegory of the divisions within a human mind. The poem is usually read in precisely this way: when Milton addresses the "Heavenly Muse" he simply names that part of himself which has the power to write poetry; when he surrenders his voice to this Muse he simply begins to speak out of the other side of his mouth. But the narrator insists that the relationship between himself and the epic is closer to that between Adam and Eve. The poem emerges through his person, but its true Creator is divine.

The question of freedom in the fictional world often appears in the work of modern novelists such as Nabokov, Mailer, and Robbe-Grillet. Recently John Fowles has offered a solution to this difficulty which, though impressive, is typical of modern fiction. Aware of the problems in calling his creations "free," Fowles eventually lights on a way to solve the dilemma of a character named Charles, who is on a train to London:

> I preached earlier of the freedom characters must be given. My problem is simple—what Charles wants is clear? It is indeed. But what

the protagonist wants is not so clear; and I am not at all sure where she is at the moment. Of course if these two were two fragments of real life, instead of two figments of my imagination, the issue to the dilemma is obvious: the one want combats the other want, and fails or succeeds, as the actuality may be. Fiction usually pretends to conform to the reality: the writer puts the conflicting wants in the ring and then describes the fight—but in fact fixes the fight, letting that want he himself favors win. And we judge writers of fiction both by the skill they show in fixing the fights (in other words, in persuading us that they were not fixed) and by the kind of fighter they fix in favor of: the good one, the tragic one, the evil one, the funny one, and so on.

. . . So I continue to stare at Charles and see no reason this time for fixing the fight upon which he is about to engage. That leaves me with two alternatives. I let the fight proceed and take no more than a recording part in it; or I take both sides in it. I stare at that vaguely effete but not completely futile face. And as we near London, I think I see a solution; that is, I see the dilemma is false. The only way I can take no part in the fight is to show two versions of it. That leaves me with only one problem: I cannot give both versions at once, yet whichever is the second will seem, so strong is the tyranny of the last chapter, the final, the "real" version.

I take my purse from the pocket of my frock coat, I extract a florin, I rest it on my right thumbnail, I flick it, spinning, two feet into the air and catch it in my left hand.

So be it. And I am suddenly aware that Charles has opened his eyes and is looking at me. There is something more than disapproval in his eyes now; he perceives I am either a gambler or mentally deranged. I return his disapproval, and my florin to my purse. He picks up his hat, brushes some invisible speck of dirt (a surrogate for myself) from its nap and places it on his head.[13]

Writers fix their fights. If they try to fight clean and fair, readers impose "the tyranny of the last chapter." So up goes the coin—a peculiarly modern form of unpremeditated art.

Milton would not have flipped a coin because he would not have equated the blind resolve of probability with freedom. Instead, this prophetic poet invites the God who created Adam and Eve free also to create "Adam" and "Eve" free. Milton prays for inspiration so that his epic characters will not spring full-blown from his seventeenth-century mind. The invocations ask God to repeat in verse the miracle of the first inspiration, giving *anima* to "Adam" as He breathed into the

[13] *The French Lieutenant's Woman* (Boston: Little, Brown and Company, 1969), pp. 405–7, copyright © 1969 by John Fowles, quoted by permission of the publisher.

dust of historical Adam; there must be no essential difference between "Adam" and Adam. Throughout "this great Argument" about human freedom, the inspired poem "may assert Eternal Providence"—the word "assert" retains as a crucial overtone its Latin root *ad-serere,* "to join to." The argument of the narrator, joined to Eternal Providence, is indistinguishable from "this great Argument." Creating the fiction that he is no creator, the poet forfeits his plan and even at times his voice. But the prophet as amanuensis allows the poet and his poem to mirror more perfectly the relationship of God to the world; writing unpremeditated verse, the narrator has foreknowledge about the outcome of his epic but does not actually manipulate the plot and characterization. With his obedient transcription, he promises himself and his fit readers that the characters of *Paradise Lost* have a will of their own. This much assured, the poem may undertake its great labor of justification. The question of aesthetic freedom disappears into the question of prophetic authority.

Traditionally, critics have recognized *Paradise Lost* as the poem of an inspired man or, at least, as the poem of a man who thought himself inspired. Masson observed, "The author is, in a real sense, an inspired man." [14] Hanford stated this position elaborately in 1939, contending that Milton believed himself an English Moses who apprehended unveiled truth and accommodated this truth to the understanding of his fallen readers.[15] William Madsen, using Hanford as convenient *locus classicus,* has recently attacked this view:

> It is therefore difficult to understand what it means to say that Milton uses the *method* of accommodation in *Paradise Lost,* since he would hardly arrogate to himself a mode of understanding and expression that he denies to the human authors of the Bible and reserves to God alone. He of course uses the Biblical *language* by which God has accommodated Himself to our understandings, but this does not make him a Moses who has "looked on the face of truth unveiled." Nor does the fact that Raphael, as a fictional character, tells Adam that he must use the method of accommodation in describing the War in Heaven mean that Milton thought that he himself was in possession of truths so ineffable that he had to "accommodate" them to ordinary human understanding by veiling them in myth and allegory. As a fictional character the narrator does indeed lay claim to such knowledge, but

[14] Masson, ed., *The Poetical Works of John Milton* (London, 1882), III, 333.
[15] "That Shepherd Who First Taught the Chosen Seed," pp. 403–19.

unless we are willing to grant that John Milton was literally inspired, there seems to be no meaningful way to relate this fictional claim to the language of *Paradise Lost*.[16]

I can find no place in the poem where the narrator "does indeed lay claim" to knowledge that he cannot communicate to the reader. There is only one accommodation in the epic: the Muse accommodates divine truth for the narrator, who transcribes this accommodation for the reader. Both poet and reader are spectators at the heavenly court. Aside from this defect, Madsen seems to emerge victorious.

He is reacting against a Platonic conception of the poem. Readers of *Paradise Lost* should discard the notion of the natural world as an imitation or "shadow" of a world of essential ideas. No Platonic or Neoplatonic allegorist, Milton speaks as a Christian typologist, imitating the modes of figurative discourse he found in the Bible. But having reduced the author to an imaginative exegete, Madsen finds his typological conception of the epic inconsistent with the inspired narrator. There is "no meaningful way" to relate this "fictional character" with his grandiose claims to the language of the poem—and thus, it would seem, no way to relate him meaningfully to anything in the poem. The narrator is surely "fictional," but "fictional," as Madsen uses the term, conceals real problems. Who is the "John Milton" to whom, Madsen implies, we cannot easily grant literal inspiration? To arrive at these statements, Madsen examines a long tradition of biblical exegesis in relation to Milton's prose. Byt why is "John Milton" the speaker of the prose works any less "fictional" than the narrator of *Paradise Lost?* I am not quibbling. Later on Madsen concludes that Milton is more a preacher than a prophet: "Milton is a Christian poet who lives in the full light of the Gospel day, not a prophet under the old dispensation of types and shadows, and his function is to create 'lively images' of the truths that are available to every faithful Christian. Like the preachers who defended the 'putting of lively colours upon common truths' by appealing to the example of the Bible, Milton turned to the Bible not only as the source of Christian truth but also as a model of expression" (p. 81). The narrator of *Paradise Lost* repeats

[16] *From Shadowy Types to Truth* (New Haven: Yale University Press, 1968), pp. 74–75. Since he argues overtly what other critics have argued implicitly, Madsen is a somewhat arbitrary choice here.

the visionary experience of Moses, and when he dreams, a divine power accommodates itself to his ear. He is anything but a purveyor of common truth. Madsen requires suspiciously Platonic means to reach this rejection of prophetic inspiration. He appears to assume that prose is more real than poetry, that philosophy is more real than fiction, and that theologians speak more truly than artists. He sees no alarming difference between Milton and any other exegetical typologist. The epic he describes is ungodly safe—no disturbing ambition, no horror, no misdoubting of the attempt. The burning voice becomes a genteel candle; his Milton speaks no more ambitiously than any preacher who tricked out vulgar doctrine in the colors of biblical allegory. I have chosen Madsen as my own convenient *locus classicus* because his is typical of a scholarly approach to Milton ever more prevalent these days. Almost unconsciously, he marshals his impressive historical knowledge to level the untoward ambitions of his subject, emerging with a Milton of temperate and unassuming ego—a man of only modest pretensions, easy to come to terms with. The submerged argument of *From Shadowy Types to Truth* is that Milton attempted nothing very startling to a seventeenth-century reader, and certainly nothing very startling to a critic who has done his homework in the appropriate traditions. But Andrew Marvell was seized by horror and delight at the easy gravity of this epic song. Such confident fluidity to contain such tremendous intentions! To Marvell, the epic was sublime.

The inspired narrator is not inconsistent with a typological approach to the epic language. Rather, the inspired creation of the poem invests the shadowy types with substance, for typology is a divine art, not a human one. The prophet who narrates this poem attempts to become a major instrument in the continuing revelation of the Word of God. He sings with the upright rectitude of prelapsarian Adam and sees with the authority of Moses. He endeavors, as far as possible, to minimize the difference between the world of his poem and the world itself. In his prophetic theatre, we learn what God would say to man and what man should say to God. The dreams within the epic represent both the possible success and possible failure of an effort which is paradoxically not an effort at all. Marvell recognized that only the gift of prophecy could explain an enterprise so ambitious as *Paradise Lost:*

Where couldst thou words of such a compass find?
Whence furnish such a vast expence of mind?
Just Heav'n thee like Tiresias to requite
Rewards with Prophesie thy loss of sight.

If Milton did indeed receive new sight, it was the culmination of that extraordinary sense of preparation evident in "At a Vacation Exercise," the Latin elegies, and the autobiographical sections of the political prose. He must have realized some signs of success as early as 1629, when he finished the Nativity Ode and announced his dedication to sacred song in Elegy VI. In 1645 Milton believed that "Lycidas," first published in 1638, "by occasion foretels the ruine of our corrupted Clergy then in their height." This famous subtitle is probably best understood as a remark about the triviality of the "occasion" in relation to the grand speech elicited. Donne's *An Anatomie of the World* was a poem "Wherein, By occasion of the untimely death of Mistress ELIZABETH DRVRY, the frailty and the decay of this whole World is represented." [17] Milton granted prophetic power to the pastorals of Spenser as well, observing in his characteristic negative construction that the May Eclogue is "not without some presage of these reforming times" (CE III, 166). The Renaissance understood that Virgil's fourth or "messianic" eclogue had foretold the birth of Christ. By 1645 Milton understood that his own pastoral had foretold a new age of spiritual perfection. Certainly it was no small matter for Milton to have prophesied the "ruine of our corrupted Clergy," for he thought this "ruine" the beginning of the most important historical change since apostolic times:

Every one can say that now certainly thou hast visited this land, and hast not forgotten the utmost corners of the earth, in a time when men had thought that thou wast gone up from us to the farthest end of the Heavens, and hadst left to doe marvellously among the sons of these last Ages. O perfect, and accomplish thy glorious acts; for men may leave their works unfinisht, but thou art a God, thy nature is perfection. . . . And he that now for haste snatches up a plain ungarnish't present as a thanke-offering to thee, which could not be deferr'd in regard of thy so many late deliverances wrought for us one upon another, may then perhaps take up a Harp, and sing thee an elaborate Song to Generations. In that day it shall no more bee said as in scorne, this or

[17] I am grateful to Professor Jeffrey Ford for calling my attention to the similarity between the two subtitles. See also the contrast between "direct or by occasion" in *Paradise Lost* IX.974.

that was never held so till this present Age, when men have better learnt that the times and seasons passe along under thy feet, to goe and come at thy bidding, and as thou didst dignifie our fathers dayes with many revelations above all the foregoing ages, since thou tookst the flesh. . . . [CE III, 147–48]

When God has completed His great acts, then the poet may seize his harp and complete his own great acts of praise. But "Lycidas" had already prophesied these revelations. Milton had spoken the word and God had begun to perfect the deed. Like the Old Testament prophets, the poet was a singer of power. His words could be read as adumbrations, however incidental, of the providential scheme; his words took the flesh of historical fact. God and Milton collaborated on allegories in the two overlapping worlds of art and life.

The phamphleteer who wrote this "ungarnish't present" in "haste" displayed the lowest of the traditional grades of prophetic inspiration. He was a man prompted (in the terms of John Smith) by the *Filia Vocis* or *Spiritus Sanctus,* a man moved to passionate activity. The narrator of *Paradise Lost,* however, seems to experience almost every prophetic mode but this one. He appears to bear no burden of political denunciation and no mandate for righteous action in contemporary affairs. But the visionary narrator does in fact indicate his relationship to the fervent activist. This relationship cannot be appreciated apart from the evolution of Milton's sense of prophetic authority.

The young poet did not slumber over that place in Revelation where the company of the Lamb apprehends the celestial harmonies. A position before this choir, the ultimate consolation, justifies the early deaths of Diodati in the *Epitaphium Damonis* and Edward King in "Lycidas." [18] But Milton desired to hear the unexpressive nuptial song not, like Lycidas and Damon, as a saint in the afterlife, but rather as a prophet in this life. Prophetic inspiration is one of the gifts demanded of "divinest Melancholy" in "Il Penseroso":

There let the pealing Organ blow,
To the full voic'd Quire below,
In Service high, and Anthems cleer,
As may with sweetness, through mine ear,

[18] Barker (pp. 7–12) discusses Milton's early interest in the choir of the Lamb.

> Dissolve me into extasies,
> And bring all Heav'n before mine eyes.
> [Ll. 161–66]

As often in Milton, an essentially classical notion is, in context, inseparable from the Christian notion that replaced it. The "extasies" are simultaneously the frenzies of the pagan oracle and the raptures of the Christian prophet. The two prophets of different religions unite again in the closing lines of "Il Penseroso" to define the utmost reward of melancholic rigor:

> And may at last my weary age
> Find out the peaceful hermitage,
> The Hairy Gown and Mossy Cell,
> Where I may sit and rightly spell
> Of every Star that Heav'n doth shew,
> And every Herb that sips the dew;
> Till old experience do attain
> To something like Prophetic strain.
> These pleasures *Melancholy* give,
> And I with thee will choose to live.
> [Ll. 167–76]

These lines recall stanaz XIX of the Nativity Ode, "the pale-ey'd Priest from his prophetic cell." But whereas the Christ of that poem divides the pagan *vates* from the true prophet, silencing the oracles, Milton here conflates the classical astrologer and diviner with the Christian ascetic. The "Mossy Cell" and the "Hairy Gown" appear in the same heritage, as if Christ had not distinguished them absolutely. Prophetic vision rewards, in this life, the "old experience" of the scholarly exile. Announcing his birthday poem for Christ, the incipient poet of Elegy VI contrasted his chaste Muse with the dissipate Muse of Diodati; he who would sing of the gods must live a "chaste youth" with "stainless hands" (ll. 63–64). The young Milton was not so concerned with chastity and rigorous purity because he simply wished to color old truths with rhetorical allegories.[19] He associated retirement from the world with heavenly vision, with "something like Prophetic strain."

But the pressure of history, equally the creation of God,

[19] Parker treats the anxious concern with virginity somewhat coyly in *Milton: A Biography,* I, 56, 67, 74–75, 226–29. It is evident from the autobiographical digression in *An Apology* (CE III, 303–6) that Milton at one time vowed absolute chastity and associated this vow with poetic power.

moved him away from the private life of solitary study. Milton accepted a different kind of prophetic melancholy in *The Reason of Church Government* (1641). Though prophets are "selected heralds of peace"—that is, forerunners of the Prince of Peace—still they are required to bring "a very sword and fire both in house and city over the whole earth":

This is that which the sad Prophet Jeremiah laments, *Wo is me my mother, that thou hast born me a man of strife, and contention.* And although divine inspiration must certainly have been sweet to those ancient profets, yet the irksomenesse of that truth which they brought was so unpleasant to them, that every where they call it a burden. Yea that mysterious book of Revelation which the great Evangelist was bid to eat, as it had been some eye-brightening electuary of knowledge, and foresight, though it were sweet in his mouth, it was bitter in his belly; bitter in the denouncing. Nor was this hid from the wise Poet Sophocles, who in that place of his Tragedy where *Tiresias* is call'd to resolve K. *Edipus* in a matter which he knew would be grievous, brings him in bemoaning his lot, that he knew more then other men. . . . But when God commands to take the trumpet and blow a dolorous or a jarring blast, it lies not in mans will what he shall say or what he shall conceal. [CE III, 230–31]

In his pamphlets Milton returned over and over to the question behind this passage. How can the Christian controversialist justify his hatred for his enemy, his derision and his bitter denouncing? Here as elsewhere, Milton referred to the precedent of Hebraic prophecy; the controversialist was a man of strife, at one with Jeremiah. This defense of bitterness and denunciation resembles the self-righteous zeal of John Knox. But to Milton, the zeal of the controversialist was a burden and the self-righteous tone is balanced by a sense of regret. Knox took delight and Milton apologized. Milton found that, though the same God offered both the trumpet and the harp, the zeal of the pamphleteer contradicted the aims of divine poetry; topical rebuke was in fact the opposite of divine poetry. The sacred singer endeavored to join and imitate the celestial harmony; he celebrated, praised, and immortalized. In *Of Reformation* the pamphletter imagined the time when "one may perhaps bee heard offering at high *strains* in new and lofty *Measures* to sing and celebrate thy *divine Mercies,* and *marvelous Judgments* in this Land throughout all AGES" (CE III, 78). But the controversialist helped to deliver and not to celebrate these judgments; he denounced, rebuked, and damned to oblivion. He was more often concerned that trivial books be forgotten than great deeds be remembered.

The identification with Jeremiah and John immediately precedes the famous autobiographical account in which Milton made a "covnant" with the "knowing reader" to deliver his immortal song (CE III, 233–42). The poet was, like the pamphleteer commanded by God to blow the trumpet, moved with an inner prompting. He vowed to accomplish his great poetic works by praying to the same Spirit that touched the lips of Isaiah—a prayer which the speaker of the Nativity Ode had already offered. In context with the entire pamphlet, the covenant with the reader does not itself explain Milton's decision to recount in such detail his evolving spiritual and literary dedication. Nor is this autobiographical section merely, as it has been described, an example of "self-justification," one of the formal divisions of Aristotelian rhetoric.[20] Milton never used classical conventions unless they could be defended with a Christian precedent as well. So here the denouncer presented his credentials. In *Paradise Regained* Christ contrasts the pagan orators with the Hebrew prophets, concluding that the prophets were greater teachers of the rules of civil government (IV.353–64). Introducing a discussion of church government, the autobiographical passage is at once an Aristotelian self-justification and a claim of prophetic authority. It was to provide this authority, theologians argued, that the lives of every one of the prophets appear in the Bible.[21] So the ambitions of the prophetic poet justified the tirades of the prophetic pamphleteer. By recounting the growth and issue of his inward prompting, Milton authorized himself to attack the Prelates, to take upon himself the bitter burden of John, Isaiah, Jeremiah, and all the prophets who chastised the wicked priests and kings of ancient Israel. The art of the poet, associated with private study, mental calm, and immortal praise, strengthened the pamphleteer against his burden of public display, mental turbulence, and bitter dispraise. His covenant with the knowing reader issued from his covenant with the all-knowing God.

Yet Madsen states correctly that Milton was a Christian poet, living in the shadowless light of the new dispensation. Like other reforming theologians, Milton conceived of a

[20] Wilbur Gilman, *Milton's Rhetoric: Studies in Defense of Liberty* (Columbia: University of Missouri Press, 1939), pp. 55–65.

[21] See chapter I, p. 29.

Christ who recapitulated, summarized, and absorbed the Old Testament prophets. "Christ alone," he wrote in *De Doctrina Christiana,* "is, properly speaking, and in a primary sense, the Word of God, and the Prophet of the Church" (CE XIV, 369). Christ spoke through all the prophets, and when the word "Spirit" applies to prophetic inspiration in the Bible, this word "must be understood of the Spirit which supplied the place of Christ the Word and the Chief Prophet" (CE XIV, 369). Calvin maintained that the prophets received dictation, but Milton carried the argument one step further into heresy. "Though he was ministering on earth in the body, his whole spirit and mind, as befitted a great prophet, were in the Father" (CE XIV, 315). The subordinationalist Christ of *De Doctrina Christiana* is himself a Calvinist prophet, deriving his authority, power, and intellect from the Father.

If Christ is properly speaking the only prophet and the last prophet–the only mediator and agent of divine accommodation–still the *triplex munus* scheme allows His followers some recourse to the prophetic gift. Milton interpreted the prophetic office as the instruction of the church in heavenly truth and the declaration of the "whole will (*plenam voluntatem*)" of the Father. This formulation broadens slightly the Calvinist position, for Christ's prophetic office begins with the first revelation of the divine will–the Creation (CE XV, 287–89). But the conception is primarily that of Calvin, and the emphasis falls on teaching. Christ, or the Holy Spirit acting in his place, illuminates His audience so they may understand the truth He speaks:

> His prophetical function consists of two parts; one external, namely, the promulgation of divine truth; the other internal, to wit, the illumination of the understanding. [CE XV, 289]

> For although all real believers have not the gift of prophecy, the Holy Spirit is to them an equivalent and substitute for prophecy, dreams, and vision. [CE XVI, 119]

> Nor is the name of prophet applied exclusively to such as foretell future events, but to any one endowed with extraordinary piety and wisdom for the purposes of teaching. [CE XVI, 245]

> Hence under the gospel likewise, the simple gift of teaching, especially of gospel teaching, is called 'prophecy.' [CE XVI, 245]

It is unfair to say that Milton was inspired as a preacher and not as a prophet, for he himself saw no difference in kind between the two offices. All believers have the gift of prophecy or its equivalent. The words of Scripture must be interpreted "by means of that Holy Spirit promised to all believers" (CE XVI, 259–60). As Milton wrote in *Paradise Regained,*

> God hath now sent his living Oracle
> Into the World to teach his final will,
> And sends his Spirit of Truth henceforth to dwell
> In pious Hearts, an inward Oracle
> To all truth requisite for men to know.
> [I.460–64]

The passage summarizes the prophetic office—we become oracles in understanding the Oracle.

Milton held the ancient theory of necessary correspondence between the knower and the known. But to "know" is to understand the Bible. Thus the relationship between knowing subject and known object fades into the relationship between inspired Word and inspired interpreter:

> The *wisdome* of *God* created *understanding,* fit and proportionable to Truth the object, and end of it, as the eye to the thing visible. If our *understanding* have a film of ignorance over it, or be blear with gazing on other false glisterings, what is that to Truth? If we will but purge with sovrain eyesalve that intellectual ray which *God* hath planted in us, then we would beleeve the Scriptures protesting their own plainnes, and perspicuity, calling to them to be instructed, not only the *wise,* and *learned,* but the *simple,* the *poor,* the *babes,* foretelling an extraordinary effusion of *Gods* Spirit upon every age. [CE III, 33]

Understanding is to the truth understood "as the eye to the thing visible," and the knower is "fit and proportionable" to what he knows. But knowledge requires the illumination of God's Spirit. The brotherly relationship between divine illumination and divine prophecy may be suggested by comparing this passage to the prophetic inspiration of Adam in *Paradise Lost.* The "film of ignorance" reappears as "the film . . . / Which that false Fruit that promis'd clearer sight / Had bred" (XI.412–14). The admonition to "purge with sovrain eyesalve that intellectual ray" reappears as the "visual Nerve" of Adam "purg'd with Euphrasy and Rue" (XI.414–15). This parallel indicates that Milton perceived no difference in kind between prophetic understanding and any other sort of understanding. He wished his own words to be measured against the inward oracle of the Spirit, the only source of knowledge; in the preface to *De Doctrina Christiana* he wrote, "Judge of my present undertaking according to the admonishing of the Spirit of God, and neither adopt my sentiments, nor reject them, unless every doubt has been removed from your belief by the clear testimony of revelation" (CE XIV, 15). The word "revelation" refers to both the Bible and the internal "ray which God hath planted in us," for both are equally the "Spirit of God." Teachers and pupils, preachers and congregations, books and readers must correspond in inspiration before education can take place.

Milton, of course, believed that the function of poetry is to teach. Great poems were "doctrinal and exemplary," Spenser was a greater teacher than Aquinas. In *The Reason of Church Government* he contrasted the patriotic benefits of truly didactic art with the dispiriting effects of those contemporary poets who sweetened the vicious and vitiated the sweet:

> Lastly, whatsoever in religion is holy and sublime, in vertu amiable, or grave, whatsoever hath passion or admiration in all the changes of that which is call'd fortune from without, or the wily suttleties and refluxes of mans thoughts from within, all these things with a solid and treatable smoothnesse to paint out and describe. Teaching over the whole book of sanctity and vertu through all the instances of example with such delight to those especially of soft and delicious temper who will not so much as look upon Truth herselfe, unlesse they see her elegantly drest, that whereas the paths of honesty and good life appear now rugged and difficult, though they be easy and pleasant, they would then appeare to all men both easy and pleasant though they were rugged and difficult indeed. And what a benefit this would be to our youth and gentry, may be soon guest by what we know of the corruption and bane which they suck in dayly from the writings and interludes of libidinous and ignorant Poetasters, who . . . doe for the most part lap up vitious principles in sweet pils to be swallow'd down, and make the taste of virtuous documents harsh and sour. [CE III, 238–39]

Though Milton seems to endorse the Horatian formula of "Teaching" with "such delight," his understanding of this ancient encapsulation is not, finally, Horatian. Teaching was, for Milton, the work of the inspired disseminating their inspiration. Because the activity of the divine teacher embodied and continued the prophetic office of Christ, any poet who wished to teach "the whole book of sanctity and vertu" would naturally aspire to become a prophetic poet. But a page later in *The Reason of Church Government* Milton, once again disparaging the vinous inspiration of modern poets, asserts without compromise the need for "devout prayer to that eternall spirit who can enrich with all utterance and knowledge": his conception of the Christian *vates* absorbs, stands precedent to, the classical conception of poetry as delightful teaching.

Milton discussed the capacity of a patriotic literature to inculcate moral lessons "beside the office of a pulpit" (CE III, 238). Aquinas, comparing the prophet with the teacher, stressed the limitations of human educators: "Now the gift of prophecy confers on the human mind something which surpasses the natural faculty in both these respects, namely as to the judgment which depends on the inflow of intellectual light, and as to the acceptance or representation of things, which is effected by means of certain species. Human teaching may be likened to prophetic revelation in the second of these respects, but not in the first. For a man represents certain things to his disciple by signs of speech, but he cannot enlighten him inwardly as God does" (II–I.clxxiii.2). But Milton attributed great honor and heavenly favor to the preachers of the Word, granting them exactly the power denied them by Aquinas:

> for certainely there is no imployment more honourable, more worthy to take up a great spirit, more requiring a generous and free nurture, then to be the messenger, and Herald of heavenly truth from God to man, and by the faithfull worke of holy doctrine, to procreate a number of faithfull men, making a kind of creation like to Gods, by infusing his spirit and likenesse into them, to their salvation, as God did into him; arising to what climat so ever he turne him, like that Sun of Righteousness that sent him, with healing in his wings, and new light to break in upon the chill and gloomy hearts of his hearers, raising out of darksome barrennesse a delicious, and fragrant Spring of saving knowledge, and good workes. [CE III, 164]

God infuses His "spirit and likenesse" into the preacher who, "making a kind of creation like to Gods," infuses this same spirit and likeness into his listeners. As in the narration of *Paradise Lost,* there is only one accommodation: the preacher receives the gift of "heavenly truth" and transmits the gift intact. The word "infusing" links the teachers of this passage with commentaries about prophetic knowledge. Donne said of

John the Baptist: "He knew *per scientiam infusam,* by infused knowledge; as he was a Prophet."[22] The word appeared regularly in discussions of the subject, and was enough of a cliché to elicit some Latin wit from Hobbes:

> So likewise where God sayes (Joel 2.28) *I will powre out my Spirit upon all flesh, and your Sons and your Daughters shall prophecy, your Old men shall dream Dreams, and your Young men shall see Visions,* wee are not to understand it in the proper sense, as if his Spirit were like water, subject to effusion or infusion; but as if God had promised to give them Propheticall Dreams, and Visions. For the proper use of the word *infused,* in speaking of the graces of God, is an abuse of it; for those graces are Vertues, not Bodies to be carryed hither and thither, and to be powred into men, as into barrels. [p. 441]

The narrator of *Paradise Lost* is the vessel for infused knowledge, the model of which is the first inspiration and first gift of human "being"–the breath of God giving *anima* to the dust of Adam. God repeats this miracle when Michael gives the prophetic Adam his "fill / Of knowledge, what this Vessel can contain" (XII.558–59). Milton believed that God repeats this miracle yet again when educating his ministers, that they repeat it when educating their congregations. In *An Apology* Milton said that the "chaste and holy mysteries" came to him "with timeliest care infus'd" (CE III, 306). Whether through God or his minister, Milton awakened to the inward oracle. As the inspired poet of *Paradise Lost,* inseparably Protestant teacher and visionary prophet, he attempted to recreate the miracle of knowledge within his fit reader.

Of all the servants of God and vessels of inspiration defined in *De Doctrina Christiana,* those most nearly in accord with Milton's conception of himself as a controversialist are the extraordinary ministers: "EXTRAORDINARY MINISTERS are persons inspired and sent on a special mission by God, for the purpose of planting the church where it did not before exist, or of reforming its corruptions, either through the medium of preaching or of writing. To this class belong the prophets, apostles, evangelists, and the like" (CE XVI, 239). This conviction of special destiny hardens the tone of the political pamphlets, for the definition of extraordinary ministers corresponds with the definitions of the *Filia Vocis* in the traditional ranking of prophetic inspiration. "Inspired and sent on

[22] *Sermons,* IV, 147.

a special mission by God," these men are prompted to act in the theatre of history. The category is uncomfortably broad, perhaps, but it would be misleading to define the pamphleteer with any greater precision. Because Milton allowed no essential difference between teaching and prophecy, we should not expect to find him constructing a detailed scale of prophetic experience. What we find instead is an emotional and psychological distinction between prophetic prose and prophetic verse, the prophet as active denouncer and the prophet as visionary praiser. This division is more a matter of the individual than of his beliefs. In *An Apology* Milton presented a magnificent description of the kinds of ministry, a description which closely resembles the myth of divided Truth in *Areopagitica.* Christ possessed all the gifts of prophetic speech. In each of his speeches, he perfectly adjusted his tone to the occasion. When Christ departed, these verbal gifts were divided among the various ministers, some receiving the tone of gentle wisdom and others the tone of harsh denunciation (CE III, 312–13). The finest servants of God will gather together, as occasion requires, the dismembered portions of the perfect ministry. These men will be evangelists, prophets, and teachers, true friends of Truth who hew the rock only to build the temple.

When Milton spoke of those extraordinary ministers bearing the burden of zealous contempt, he for a moment abandoned the cooler element and held the pen unmistakably in the right hand:

> Some also were indu'd with a staid moderation, and soundnesse of argument to teach and convince the rationall and sober-minded; yet not therefore that to be thought the only expedient course of teaching, for in times of opposition when either against new heresies arising, or old corruption to be reform'd this coole unpassionate mildnesse of positive wisdome is not anough to damp and astonish the proud resistance of carnall, and false Doctors, then (that I may have leave to soare a while as the Poets use) then Zeale whose substance is ethereal, arming in compleat diamond ascends his fiery Chariot drawn with two blazing Meteors figur'd like beasts, but of a higher breed then any the Zodiack yields, resembling two of those four which Ezechiel and S. John saw, the one visag'd like a Lion to expresse power, high authority and indignation, the other of count'nance like a man to cast derision and scorne upon perverse and fraudulent seducers; with these the invincible warriour Zeale shaking loosely the slack reins drives over the heads of Scarlet Prelats, and such as are insolent to maintain traditions, brusing their stiff necks under his flaming wheels. Thus did the true Prophets of old combat with the false; thus Christ himselfe the fountaine of meeknesse

found acrimony anough to be still galling and vexing the Prelaticall Pharisees. [CE III, 313–14]

Once again, the "true Prophets" justify the militant pamphleteer. Their words crush the heads of the unregenerate as Christ shall bruise the head of the serpent. The single standard for the appearance of these special ministers is the character of the time. In 1641 God commanded the poet to leave his private studies and work toward the perfecting of history. Milton believed that the entire nation was under a similar obligation: "The doore of grace turnes upon smooth hinges wide opening to send out, but soon shutting to recall the precious offers of mercy to a nation: which unlesse Watchfulnesse and Zeale two quick-sighted and ready-handed Virgins be there in our behalfe to receave, we loose: and still the ofter we loose, the straiter the doore opens, and the lesse is offer'd" (CE III, 225). All actions best performed in season, the conjunction of human corruption, the intolerance of God, and divine inspiration creates the zealous denouncer. So long as institutions are evil, God will require prophets to rouse His people.

The seasons of history, the patterns of corruption and reform, are represented by the biblical history of Israel. These temporal patterns can never be superceded because they reflect an eternal pattern—or so Milton came to believe. The personified "Zeale" of *An Apology* evolves into the military Christ of *Paradise Lost.* An invincible warrior, ten thousand thunders in his hand, wheels turning like a whirlwind, his flaming jeweled chariot breaking the heads of devilish foes—the triumphant Son appears at the war in heaven to epitomize the zeal of human prophets in all ages. Christ is both the goal of the visionary and the example for the denouncer. He harmonizes all forms of prophecy in his perfect office. Soaring "as the Poets use," Milton elaborated the visions "which Ezechiel and S. John saw." Yet what he saw inspired "combat with the false," divine "acrimony." The prophet as spectator envisioned the prophet as public spectacle and active warrior. Even the visionary knew that the time was ripe for extraordinary zeal.

Like other Puritan apologists, Milton presented England as a new Israel seeking for deliverance. In *Of Reformation* he attacked the prelate with biblical equations: "Have they not been as the *Canaanites,* and *Philistins* to this Kingdom?" (CE III, 45) The prayer of *Animadversions* implores God not "to bring us thus far onward from *Egypt* to destroy us in this Wildernesse" and imagines the time when England will be "standing on the shoare of that red Sea into which our enemies had almost driven us" (CE III, 147–48). Later, in *Areopagitica,* Milton looked forward to the fulfillment of the words of Joel, when the Spirit of God would pour out on all men and "all the Lords people are become Prophets" (CE IV, 342–43). The time was near when England would become "a Nation of Prophets" surpassing the seventy elders of Israel. Truth, now scattered, was once a "lovely form," and Englishmen were to reform its reformers. The patterns of Old Testament history, when God favored a nation with his Word, had revived once more in Puritan England: "Now once again by all concurrence of signs, and by the generall instinct of holy and devout men, as they daily and solemnly expresse their thoughts, God is decreeing to begin some new and great period in his Church, ev'n to the reforming of Reformation it self: what does he then but reveal Himself to his servants, and as his manner is, first to his English-men; I say as his manner is, first to us, though we mark not the method of his counsels, and are unworthy" (CE IV, 340). Despite the qualification, England bore the standard of a new covenant. As a prophet of this new *promissio,* Milton received a vision of the English nation roused from sleep in the image of the Nazarite Samson. Throughout the pamphlet, with its constant references to building the temple, Milton identified implicitly with Haggai and Zechariah, the post-exilic prophets who exhorted the people to rebuild the Temple of Solomon. At this point in his life, Milton's sense of himself and of history resembled that of Oliver Cromwell: "I am one of those whose heart God hath drawn out to wait for some extraordinary dispensations, according to those promises that he hath held forth of things to be accomplished in the later times, and I cannot but think that God is beginning of them."[23] Really, *Areopagitica* offered the hope that the extraordinary might soon become the ordinary, that a time might soon appear in which there would be no need for zealous contempt because all schisms would be benign. With brotherly zeal, patience, and tolerance, Englishmen might reassemble the broken body of Truth. But the pamphlet was midwife to a nation never born.

[23] A. S. P. Woodhouse, *Puritanism and Liberty* (London: J. M. Dent, 1938), pp. 103–4.

Like the Israelites before them, Englishmen lusted after strange gods. The *Second Defence* (1654) noted signs of irrevocable decline. England was no longer a nation of potential prophets, but a nation whose great accomplishments resided in the past. The qualification of *Areopagitica* replaced the rule. Whereas the speaker of the earlier pamphlet looked forward to the end of his extraordinary mission, the author of the *Second Defence* dwelled obsessively on his own particularity, his special power as a zealous warrior. The tone of regret in *The Reason of Church Government* turned proud and disdainful. The blind prophet was, like Elijah, "too sacred to attack" (CE VIII, 73). Insofar as the two can be separated, he seems to have taken comfort from the divine favor shown himself, rather than from the divine favor shown his nation. His words were as powerful as a sword. Armed only with the language and the truth, he had vanquished his adversaries; Salmasius fell to an immortal pamphlet in the wars of truth. An inward prompting equated duty with blindness:

> Hence, when that office against the royal defence was publicly assigned me, and at a time when not only my health was unfavorable, but when I had nearly lost the sight of my other eye; and my physicians expressly foretold, that if I undertook the task, I should in a short time lose both —in no wise dismayed at this warning, methought it was no physician's voice I heard—not the voice even of Aesculapius from the shrine of Epidaurus—but of some diviner monitor within; methought, that, by a certain fatality in my birth, two destinies were set before me, on the one hand, blindness, on the other, duty—that I must necessarily incur the loss of my eyes, or desert a sovereign duty. [CE VIII, 67–69]

The shrine of Epidaurus contained a spring thought to be particularly efficacious in the cure of ocular diseases.[24] The voice Milton heard was "diviner"; the Latin *divinioris* puns on the relationship between pagan diviners and diviner Christian prophets. But the conjunction of duty and blindness was not without some relationship to the healing streams of Epidaurus. "There is a way through weakness, as the Apostle teaches, to the greatest strength." Through his ever-during shadows, "the light of the divine countenance may shine

[24] W. R. Halliday, *Greek Divination* (London: Macmillan, 1913), pp. 109, 129, 135.

forth all the more clearly." Remarkably, Milton emerged from this major crisis with his sense of divine guidance unimpaired. The decision to defend the revolution in zealous prose—a decision in which gain and loss coincided—became the sanction of prophetic power. The inward prompting grew into "a voice I heard." Having chosen to blind himself, Milton discovered "an inward and far surpassing light" (CE VIII, 73). An angel folded its wings across his eyes in order that he might see the Lord alone. As the defender of liberty went blind to see, so the narrator of *Paradise Lost* will give up his voice in order to speak. If the lame and the mighty are one, the strong man will choose to be blind and mute.

At the end of the *Second Defence,* Milton warned the people against flagging zeal in the search for truth. No matter how completely the English might fail, however, God had once again kept His promise to Moses that Israel would never be without at least a single prophet. This sightless pamphleteer no longer distinguished between the praise of poetry and the rebuke of prose. The author of the *Defence of the English People* now looked back on his labor of blinding duty and found in that acerbic diatribe an epic of just praise:

> I have celebrated, as a testimony to them, I had almost said, a monument, which will not speedily perish, actions which were glorious, lofty, which were almost above all praise; and if I have done nothing else, I have assuredly discharged my trust. But as the poet, who is styled epic, if he adhere strictly to established rules, undertakes to embellish not the whole life of the hero whom he proposes to celebrate in song, but, usually, one particular action of his life . . . so likewise will it suffice for my duty and excuse, that I have at least embellished one of the heroic actions of my countrymen. The rest I pass by: for who could do justice to all the great actions of an entire people? If, after achievement so magnanimous, ye basely fall off from your duty, if ye are guilty of any thing unworthy of you, be assured, posterity will speak, and thus pronounce its judgment: The foundation was strongly laid, the beginning, nay more than the beginning, was excellent; but it will be inquired, not without a disturbed emotion, who raised the superstructure, who completed the fabric! To undertakings so grand, to virtues so noble, it will be a subject of grief that perseverance was wanting. It will be seen that the harvest of glory was abundant; that there were materials for the greatest operations, but that men were not to be found for the work; yet, that there was not wanting one, who could give good counsel; who could exhort, encourage; who could adorn, and celebrate, in praises destined to endure forever, the transcendent deeds, and those who performed them. [CE VIII, 253–55]

The temple of *Areopagitica* may never be built, unfinished through the ages to come. But in the ruins of its foundation Milton has harmonized the two conceptions of prophecy. The pamphleteer is like the poet "who is styled epic" and writes "praises destined to endure forever." He assumes a double mission. He is both a zealous defender celebrating virtues and a zealous denouncer bearing divine warning. His words, like the words of Hebrew prophets, will be vindicated in the future. The present "will be seen" in the future, but the speaker sees the future in the present. The daughter of God is also the daughter of Time—there wants not one to see her. Solitary, powerful, he stands the watch in history.

By the time Milton finished *Paradise Lost,* the solitary watchman became for him the principle of divine truth in human societies. Within the epic, the eternal type of the extraordinary minister is Abdiel. This solitary servant of God, surrounded by satanic dangers and satanic tongues, rises to speak the Word of God in zealous tones. For his great defense, he receives that fame which does not grow on mortal soil:

> Servant of God, well done, well hast thou fought
> The better fight, who single hast maintain'd
> Against revolted multitudes the Cause
> Of Truth, in word mightier than they in Arms. . . .
> [VI.29–32]

Of course he immediately begins to fight the lesser fight, joining with the "Powers Militant" to strike Satan physically. But the unshaken, unseduced, and unterrified speech to the devils remains his most important action and one of the most significant actions of the epic. The example of Abdiel (that Protestant angel) reverberates in human history. Enoch dared "single to be just," "The only righteous in a world perverse" (XI.701–3). Noah, too, opposed the entire world. Michael sings his praises in one of the finest passages of the poem:

> One Man except, the only Son of light
> In a dark Age, against example good,
> Against allurement, custom, and a World
> Offended; fearless of reproach and scorn,
> Or violence, hee of thir wicked ways
> Shall them admonish, and before them set

> The paths of righteousness, how much more safe,
> And full of peace, denouncing wrath to come
> On thir impenitence; and shall return
> Of them derided, but of God observ'd
> The one just Man alive. . . .
>
> [XI.808–81]

Working in secret ways, God places His judgment on the tongues of solitary outcasts.

The narrator explicitly connects the zealous speech of Abdiel with the creation of his poem:

> I sing with mortal voice, unchang'd
> To hoarse or mute, though fall'n on evil dayes,
> On evil dayes though fall'n, and evil tongues;
> In darkness, and with dangers compast round,
> And solitude;
>
> [VII.24–28]

A good man in an evil time, "compast round" with satanic tongues, the narrator repeats the solitary heroism of Abdiel, Enoch, and Noah. He has no praise for his time or for his nation. It is "an age too late."

At the beginning of his public career, Milton believed that God prompted his extraordinary ministers to perfect and complete history. God made promises to nations and inspired unique men to explicate those promises. Though such men denounced corruption with zealous rebuke, their primary concern was the reformation of institutions and the conversion of the misguided. The door was open, the *promissio* to be seen—prophets roused the people to Watchfulness and Zeal, those ready-handed virgins. Tearing down the corrupt church, prophets delivered the plans for a new temple. In the *Second Defence,* the extraordinary minister deplored the failure of his audience but held in trust the design of the temple. Like an epic poet, he had praised the great deeds of the past. Now he could offer good advice and needed exhortation, even if no one listened. In the future better men would understand why the foundation never became a building. But the extraordinary ministers of *Paradise Lost* appear in evil times, alone and without immediate audience. They denounce their nations, and they bring down the promise of judgment. Noah and Enoch have no one to praise. The historical situation that produces these two fearless speakers recurs after the coming of Christ. *Paradise Lost* offers no possibility for a new nation of prophets, no possibility for a true church in the time of the narrator. Only the evil man thinks his days benign:

> What will they then
> But force the Spirit of Grace itself, and bind
> His consort Liberty; what, but unbuild
> His living Temples, built by Faith to stand,
> Thir own Faith not another's: for on Earth
> Who against Faith and Conscience can be heard
> Infallible? Yet many will presume:
> Whence heavy persecution shall arise
> On all who in the worship persevere
> Of Spirit and Truth; the rest, far greater part,
> Will deem in outward Rites and specious forms
> Religion satisfi'd; Truth shall retire
> Bestruck with sland'rous darts, and works of Faith
> Rarely be found: so shall the World go on,
> To good malignant, to bad men benign,
> Under her own weight groaning, till the day
> Appear of respiration to the just. . . .
> [XII.524–40]

I find this passage unequivocal. Truth shall retire, the temple be dismantled. After the apostolic times, history returns to its condition before the Covenant. Since there can be no public temple to represent a community of the just, the Spirit will be found, if found at all, in the hearts of solitary men:

> And chiefly Thou O Spirit, that dost prefer
> Before all Temples th' upright heart and pure,
> Instruct me, for Thou know'st. . . .

In this situation, the ordinary ministers defined in the *De Doctrina Christiana* lose their function, which is predicated on a true church externally established in a just society. When corrupt human institutions refuse to embody the prophetic office of Christ, God acts through men extraordinarily raised to admonish and denounce. The one just man of the *Second Defence* reappears in *Paradise Lost* as an inspired singer who finds his precedent in pre-Covenant biblical history, in the lonely heroism of Enoch and Noah. For what remains of time there can be no return of Israel. A poem which was once to be doctrinal and exemplary to a nation ultimately emerges as a poem for fit audience though few.[25] Until that day of just wrath, God will continue to inspire a succession of just men—fearless, mighty, alone. For his part, the just man will live in a manner discontinuous with normal life. He will be scorned, ridiculed, he will face dangers all around. He will enter the paradise within and compare it with the corruption without. Surrounded by evil tongues, his tongue is free—and free because he speaks nothing of his own.

It is extraordinarily difficult to speak of Milton's "development," his movement from one position to another. He returns again and again to the same metaphors, same biblical texts, same themes, same words. The zealous Presbyterian attacking the prelates becomes, with no change in tone, the zealous defender of regicide attacking the Presbyterians. Above all, Milton writes the most fully equivocal English one is likely to find outside of Melville. He glories in the negative construction, especially when speaking about himself. In *The Reason of Church Government* Milton offers the following vow: "at mine own peril and cost I refuse not to

[25] My differences with that most influential of recent books about Milton, Stanley E. Fish's brilliant *Surprized by Sin: The Reader in Paradise Lost* (New York: St. Martin's, 1967), should be evident by now. The hypothetical "reader" assumed throughout this study is, apart from his remarkable appetite for being duped, an ordinary Christian sharing broad doctrinal sympathies with the author of *Paradise Lost.* But the poem, written by a fugitive "On evil days . . . fall'n, and evil tongues," adopts a more defensive and protective posture than Fish suggests. In the pamphlets Milton certainly does address large audiences—the English nation, the European community. However, it should be noted that whenever he speaks of his poetic ambitions, he endeavors to purge his audience: "let rude ears be absent," he says, and makes his covenant with "the knowing reader." In his epic Milton never addresses the reader directly, and those passages which acknowledge his presence, such as the invocation to Book VII and the progress toward the innermost bower in Book IV, seem designed to exclude rather than invite. Given Milton's assessment of Restoration England and Michael's account of the worldly successes of falsehood in the time between the apostolic missions and the Apocalypse, his "fit audience" is by implication a group of solitary outcasts judged "perverse" by their contemporaries. The relationship of Milton to the large body of Christian readers is not, as Fish assumes, that of a didactic preacher to his congregation, but rather that of a prophet to his evil nation. The "affective stylistics" of Milton cannot be appreciated in terms appropriate to Bunyan, who provided a compendium of pious attitudes, hoping to cure by wise anticipation all kinds of Christian discouragement. He is more likely to be understood in terms appropriate to Michelangelo, who painted figures on the Sistine Ceiling that cannot be seen from any angle on the floor. The fit audience, knowing beforehand, will require no education within the work itself. In *Paradise Regained* Christ remarks that a good reader will bring "A spirit and judgment equal or superior" to his text, "(And what he brings, what needs he elsewhere seek)" (IV.324–25). An audience of such readers could hardly be surprised by sin.

sustain this expectation from as many as are not loath to hazard so much credulity upon the best pledges that I can give them" (CE III, 241). The phrase "I refuse not to sustain" functions as a kind of logical double negative. I am not speaking of the grammatical double negative, for the history of that complex construction is an altogether different matter. In this context, to "refuse" means "not to sustain"—the man promises, then, "not not to sustain" his expectation for poetic success. The digression on poetry in *An Apology* contains many similar phrases. As a young man, Milton "was not unstudied in those authors" (CE III, 302). That is, he was "not not studied" in those authors. He now hopes that he may one day be "the object of not unlike praises" and "he who would not be frustrate of his hope to write well hereafter in laudable things, ought him selfe to bee a true Poem" (CE III, 303). Logically, the word "frustrate" already negates the possibility of "hope," and the phrase "frustrate of his hope" functions as "not achieve his hope." The poet of the delicate and equivocal phrase would "not not achieve his hope" by becoming himself a true poem. His constant reliance on the doubly negative phrase may represent more than a Latinate mannerism or, in autobiographical contexts, a modest finesse of forthright vanity. This point is worth pursuing briefly, and anyone in search of why Milton writes as he writes will eventually come to *Areopagitica*.

Milton appears to reason about how to discover truth. What he does in fact is reason about how to read John Milton. The metaphysical assertions of *Areopagitica* comprise the nearest thing we have to a Miltonic aesthetic. The metaphors and myths of this pamphlet often concern the activities of separation and unification: Psyche separates "confused seeds," good and evil leap from the rind of one apple tasted, and the sad friends of Truth recollect her shattered form. A major theme of the oration is how to regard division and disagreement when Christian truth is by definition absolute. The solution to this difficulty can be understood, I think, as a metaphysic of the logical double negative. Here Milton shows that one cannot build a temple without both pulling apart and pulling together:

Yet these are the men cry'd out against for schismaticks and sectaries; as if, while the Temple of the Lord was building, some cutting, some squaring the marble, others hewing the cedars, there should be a sort of irrationall men who could not consider there must be many schisms and many dissections made in the quarry and in the timber, ere the house of God can be built. And when every stone is laid artfully together, it cannot be united into a continuity, it can be contiguous in this world; neither can every piece of the building be of one form; nay rather the perfection consists in this, that out of many moderat varieties and brotherly dissimilitudes that are not vastly disproportionall arises the goodly and the gracefull symmetry that commends the whole pile and structure. [CE IV, 342]

The reader must unbuild and build a temple to understand this passage. Are the "not vastly disproportionall" stones in fact proportional? Yes and no. Logically, the phrase means "not vastly not proportional" and this double negative, like all logical double negatives, cannot be reduced to either a positive assertion or a negative assertion: "not not proportional" occupies some middle ground between "proportional" and "not proportional." The double negative makes "yes" and "no," positive and negative, contiguous in this verbal world. When we negate any quality, we immediately divide all things into those which possess this attribute and those which do not. The word "disproportionall" hews the world in two—negation is the way of the dualist. If, however, we hew again and negate the negation, the second negative reunifies our initial division without destroying that division. Because Milton writes "not vastly disproportionall," the qualities of proportion and disproportion touch each other: the world is at once two halves and one whole. The "brotherly dissimilitudes" of this passage recall good and evil, those fundamental twins who "cleave together" since the fall of man (CE VIII, 310). As the primal pun on "cleave" suggests, the two actions of hewing apart and fitting together are almost inseparable. To discover truth we must perform them simultaneously, as we do in either constructing or understanding a logical double negative. Trying to categorize the stones of the temple as "proportional" or "disproportional," we pull apart the phrase "not vastly disproportionall." But ultimately we realize that both the positive and the negative have been pulled together in the double negative. Schism twice applied will make the temple whole. Milton writes in *The Doctrine and Discipline of Divorce* that "Gods doing ever is to bring the due likenesses and harmonies of his workes together, except when out of two contraries met to their own destruction, he moulds a third existence" (CE III,

418). In God's eternity, the temple of *Areopagitica* is "united into a continuity." But man imitates the methods of God as best he can, writing "not vastly disproportionall" to unite in a third and contiguous existence the two contraries met to their own destruction. "The end then of Learning is to repair the ruines of our first Parents by regaining to know God aright, and out of that knowledge to love him, to imitate him, to be like him" (CE IV, 277). The double negative is one of the ways in which Milton endeavors to "re-pair" the ruins of the Fall. His discourse continually offers alternatives that are not merely alternatives.[26]

Translating his discourse, the critic cannot help but do violence to this poise of contraries. But I offer a not unstudied summation. Milton tends to associate the zealous warrior, the bearer of prophetic burden, with his pamphleteering. The precedent of Old Testament prophecy, strengthened by the prophetic office of Christ, both informs and justifies his derisive tone. Until the end of the *Second Defence*, he conceives of this burden as a conditional one. Often he interrupts the pamphlets, imagining a time when he can cease to act as a public spectacle and turn to another prophetic function. This second form of prophecy, associated with praise and poetry and musical harmony, allows the prophet to act as a visionary spectator. When England fulfills her covenant and rebuilds the temple of God, the prophet may become more of a comforter, bringing all heaven before the eyes of his audience. The language of the warrior commands a nearly physical force; Harapha in *Samson Agonistes*, like Salmasius a victim of righteous taunting, slinks from the stage "somewhat crestfall'n" (l. 1244). Similarly, the song of the visionary prophet bears the power of arranging the physical world into benign and orderly combinations, like the first harmonies of the Nativity Ode which "the well-balanc't world on hinges hung" (l. 122). At the end of the *Second Defense*, the blind

[26] Professor Edward Tayler suggested to me that the passage about temple-building in *Areopagitica* might be central to an understanding of Milton's peculiar way with dualisms. He is not responsible, though, for the small theory that I have erected.

The biblical metaphors of the passage were often evoked in the various controversies between Puritans and Conformists during the reign of Elizabeth. See the second chapter, "Christian Liberty and Edification," of John S. Coolidge's *The Pauline Renaissance in England: Puritanism and the Bible* (Oxford: Clarendon Press, 1970), pp. 23–54. The passages Coolidge quotes on pp. 74 and 95 may serve to illustrate the tradition of political temple-building within which Milton speaks.

prophet defines himself as both a singer of praise and a deliverer of judgment. But now he is alone, his audience is posterity. In *Paradise Lost* the world goes on from bad to worse. The need for denunciation and zealous warfare is historically permanent, no longer a condition of the provisional present. Except for solitary men, there can be no audience in posterity. Michael's own prophetic burden makes obsolete those sections of the *De Doctrina Christiana* about the ordinary ministers who inherit the prophetic office of Christ. In the theological treatise, the definition of the visible church is simply "those who are called" (CE XVI, 219). But in *Paradise Lost* the number of those who abhor idols, live by pure doctrine, and build the temple dwindles as low as one. Successfully completed in an age too late, this epic is the inspiration of a Calvinist prophet with no faith in the public institution of the church.

The ultimate consolation of the early poems, the nuptial song of the Lamb, appears in Book III of the epic. After a lifetime of preparation, the visionary poet finally comes to the court of heaven, sees without cloud, and joins his voice to the angelic choir. He celebrates the immortal vision in immortal verse. When he returns to "mortal voice" in Book VII, he immediately identifies himself with Abdiel:

> Standing on Earth, not rapt above the Pole,
> More safe I Sing with mortal voice, unchang'd
> To hoarse or mute, though fall'n on evil days. . . .
> [VII.23–25]

So the consolation of heavenly song appears alongside the eternal praise for Abdiel, Enoch, and Noah. The prophetic narrator seeks the divine commendation, "Servant of God, well done"—he speaks when other tongues are mute. He has sung in heaven and he hopes to be sung of in heaven. Writing *Paradise Lost,* Milton did not slumber over that place where it says that prophets are not without honor, save in their own country.

The solitary just man, in the figure of the narrator, unites the two functions of the prophet. He receives an inspired vision and speaks inspired words with the fearlessness of Abdiel. His vision is inseparable from his burden: "And long it was not after, when I was confirm'd in this opinion, that he who would not be frustrate of his hope to write well hereafter in laudable things, ought him selfe to bee a true

Poem, that is, a composition, and patterne of the best and honorablest things; not presuming to sing high praises of heroick men, of famous Cities, unlesse he have in himselfe the experience and the practice of all that which is praise-worthy" (CE III, 304). *Paradise Lost* reconfirms this opinion. The connection between the narrator and Abdiel, essentially an autobiographical one, lends authority to the heroic art of the epic. As theologians argued, God does not choose His instruments arbitrarily. This dictated, inspired, and unpremeditated poem is also the work of a solitary individual. How are we to know whether the narrator is a prophet? How are we to establish the authority of a text purporting to have been inspired? Issues that for centuries had clustered about the authentication of Holy Word also inform the presentation of *Paradise Lost*. We recognize the divine origins of the epic if Urania "finds" us, inspiring its readers as she inspired its author—but the poem invites another traditional test.

Only a free man can speak with authority of freedom. *Paradise Lost* exactly reverses the self-justifications of the political pamphlets. The controversialist appeals to his visionary promptings as authority for his zealous rebukes; the poet alludes to his fearless zeal as authority for his prophetic visions. Having lived a life heroic, Milton wrote his inspired epic knowing that he contained within himself the heroism he celebrated and was therefore, in this very special sense, the hero of his own poem. He included his life within Urania's epic because, through the accomplishments of his prophetic office, fit readers might come to God. His life was his authority.

The dangerous inference that *Paradise Lost* intends to transcend a portion of the Bible matches the equally presumptuous suggestion that its narrator believes himself, if not the one just man alive, then a man prominent in the line of great and solitary servants extending from Abdiel to Enoch and Noah. Milton was certainly aware of his abiding self-righteousness. Having crushed the hapless Remonstrant of *Animadversions* with one verbal brutality after another, the author finally permitted him a single insight in his final speech: "In the mean time I beseech the God of Heaven to humble you" (CE III, 178). Perhaps God tried. But Milton understood that he was, in his time of weakness, a prophet almost too sacred to attack. Since God wounded so that he might heal, dismembered so that He might make whole again, the seal of blindness led Milton to attempt what no other Christian poet had ever attempted. He elaborated the Bible with new inventions, claiming an authority at least as emphatic as the Old Testament itself. He made Abdiel as much a divine creation as Adam. Moses, in writing the Pentateuch, had represented the course of his own inspiration. Milton followed this model. In his epic the blind prophet dramatized his inspiration and therefore, inseparably, his regeneration. Fallen Adam lost the privilege of speaking to God and angel as a friend, "Venial discourse unblam'd" (IX.5). The narrator himself asked in Book III, "May I express thee unblam'd?" He requested a sign of approval, a relaxation of ancient prohibitions, inviting God to perfect his healing. The answer was affirmative. The God who made Milton blind, his "ever-during dark" not dissimilar from the "darkness visible" of Hell, gave him the compensatory sight of "Divine Similitude." As the "brightness invisible" of Heaven canceled, linguistically and physically and spiritually, that "darkness visible" at the dregs of the universe, so the perception of that imperceptible light counteracted the blindness of the prophet. Speaking his epic with fearless conviction, Milton asked God to repeat this miracle. As he lost his eyes to see the divine vision, he would surrender his voice to speak the divine poem. Then he could not be mute: if all was Hers, all was his.

But the poem dramatized the attaining as well as the attainment. *Paradise Lost,* representing the process of its inspiring, allowed for its own failure. Henry More wrote in his attack on enthusiasm that an inspired "melancholist" must "be very highly puffed up, and not onely fancy himself *inspired,* but believe himself such a special piece of *Light* and *Holiness* that God has sent into the world, that he will take upon him to *reform,* or rather *annull,* the very *Law* and *Religion* he is born under, and make himself not at all inferiour to either *Moses* or *Christ*" (p. 11). Defying the conservative revolt against enthusiasm, Milton persisted with his inspired epic knowing that its aesthetics would render the achievement of the poem inseparable from the spiritual achievement of the man. His bets were absolute. He risked humiliation before man and God, his poem left incomplete by failure of spirit or by death. He risked proving by conspicuous example the skepticism of a Henry More, for submerged in the full dream of his epic was an empty dream; behind the inspired poet was a destructive poet of pride, malice, and revenge. Lacking the miracle of divine afflatus, his inventions would have no true being and the unpremeditated verse of the inspired prophet would be revealed as the scandalous, premeditated scheme of a vain man. Satan created Sin and Death in his own image—an uninspired author could do no better. If Milton wrote without heavenly inspiration, if he alone created *Paradise Lost,* his "Satan" would be a self-portrait drawn in perfect likeness to the hidden image of himself. Milton unassisted would be the invisible hypocrite, pretending not to be exactly what he was. It is abundant testimony to the integrity of fallen man that the last words of the last invocation refuse to disallow this possibility.

CHAPTER IV

Prophetic Actors

MILTON often encircled a "double frame" around his poetic creations. "On the Morning of Christ's Nativity," "The Passion," "Lycidas," *Paradise Lost,* and *Paradise Regained* all begin with a narrator who establishes his authority to sing the ensuing poem, to preside over the forthcoming creation. The narrators, then, are simultaneously outside of one frame and inside the larger frame of the entire fiction. Each of them explores the nature of his inspiration and defines the limit of his knowledge, the agent of his prompting, and the extent to which he is a composer or merely an instrument. When the song itself begins, framed within the larger frame, the narrator usually retreats from our sight. Like the Attendant Spirit of Comus—his obvious relative—the narrator "must be viewless now." The Attendant Spirit, however, reappears in a disguise to join the masquerade he introduces. Similarly, the narrator of *Paradise Lost* displays his metaphorical, perhaps typological, identification with figures in the epic. The events and characters and themes within the smaller frame often reflect back upon the inspired narrator of the larger frame. Disguised, veiled, these narrators participate in the creations over which they preside.

In *Paradise Regained*, for example, Satan and Christ debate at length the proper relationship between an action and the time of its performance. Christ obediently withholds his action, refusing to attack his Adversary until the appointed time and proper season. He resists all satanic exhortations for the immediate establishment of His Kingdom or the immediate revelation of His power. Imitating this example, the narrator of the poem places his own action, the creation of *Paradise Regained,* in context with the necessary development of a divine poet. *Paradise Regained* is itself an action performed in the proper season, after the proper preparation: "I who erewhile the happy Garden sung, / By one man's disobedience lost, now sing. . . ." The rhetorical (but not the metrical) emphasis is on "now," a present made necessary and decorous by his singing "erewhile." Imitating the opening lines of the renaissance *Aeneid,* the narrator suggests a chiasmic relationship between the seasons of Christian and classical poetry.[1] The classical *vates* established the correct relationship between time and poetic action by writing pastoral or bucolics before epic, but the Christian *vates* must write epic before pastoral or bucolics. As classical pastoral is to classical epic, so Old Testament epic is to New Testament "pastoral." The brief epic is a pastoral in that it defines the perfect ministry of Christ. As Christ fulfills Adam and obedience fulfills disobedience, so the smaller epic fulfills the large. The Christian poet advances his career by reversing the career of the classical poet. He moves forward by moving backward.

This chiasmic proportion, like the sage words of Christ, defines the proper relationship between classical and Christian. The similes of the poem, comparing "Small things with greatest" (IV.564), reenact the proportion, for Milton's small things were Virgil's great things. Milton treats the world of classical epic as Virgil treated the world of classical pastoral. God defines the action of the narrator and the action of the Son when He remarks, "His weakness shall o'ercome Satanic strength" (I.160). The narrator merges with the themes of his own creation. In his similes, Christian weakness triumphs over classical strength—his seasonal song duplicates the example of Christ. Singing of victory over all temptation, he represents the divine type of his singing within the song itself:

> and as he fed, Angelic Choirs
> Sung Heavenly Anthems of his victory
> Over temptation and the Tempter proud.
> [IV.593–95]

The narrator accepts his prompting from the same Spirit that leads Christ into the wilderness, a dovelike Spirit "With prosperous wing full summ'd" (I.14). In the song thus prompted, Christ remembers His baptism:

> And last the sum of all, my Father's voice,
> Audibly heard from Heav'n, pronounc'd me his,
> Mee his beloved Son, in whom alone

[1] Lewalski, *Milton's Brief Epic,* pp. 5–6.

> He was well pleas'd; by which I knew the time
> Was full. . . .
>
> [I.283–87]

The sum of all announces that the time is full. Both Christ and the narrator begin their great actions "now," in the fullness of time. "Full summ'd," the poet and his subject correspond.

Only "Lycidas," of the poems with two frames, varies the usual pattern significantly, for in this poem the narrator is part of the smaller, not the larger, frame. His continuing search for inspiration appears, as we read the poem in sequence, to frame his song. He invokes the "Sisters of the sacred well" (l. 15) and twice returns to the rivers and fountains of classical pastoral. He is spectator at a pageant of mourners, passively recording their reactions to the death of Lycidas. His words are also part of this pageant:

> But the fair guerdon when we hope to find,
> And think to burst out into sudden blaze,
> Comes the blind Fury with th' abhorred shears,
> And slits the thin-spun life. "But not the praise,"
> Phoebus replied, and touched my trembling ears. . . .
>
> [Ll. 73–77]

The characters in this pastoral masque can hear the narrator as well as he can hear them; this "uncouth swain" is both a passive secretary and an active participant. But the whole pageant is itself contained by the surprising narrative turn of line 186:

> Thus sang the uncouth swain to th' oaks and rills,
> While the still morn went out with sandals gray. . . .
>
> [Ll. 186–87]

An unseen spectator has been hidden throughout the poem. Suddenly he appears, turning "the uncouth swain" into a character, an actor, a spectacle. He reveals the dramatic pageantry of the poem as imaginary convention. The only real audience to this song was "th' oaks and rills."

"Lycidas" also differs from the other poems, particularly from *Paradise Regained,* because its "uncouth" narrator acts out of season, at the improper time. He alone, of all Milton's narrators, disturbs the "season due." Yet still he corresponds with his subject. As Lycidas is "dead ere his prime," so the uncouth swain sings of Lycidas "before the mellowing year."

Framing the framer, the closing passage comments on the disturbance of poetic seasons:

> And now the Sun had stretch't out all the hills,
> And now was dropt into the Western bay;
> At last he rose, and twitch't his Mantle blue:
> Tomorrow to fresh Woods, and Pastures new.

Consolation has been achieved within the smaller frame. The opening statement, "For Lycidas is dead, dead ere his prime," has been redefined. "For Lycidas, your sorrow, is not dead"—the dead shepherd, like the sun, "sunk low, but mounted high." This final passage redefines the disturbance of poetic seasons to accord with the redefinition of "dead ere his prime." As the uncouth swain resolves the unseasonable death of Lycidas, so the second narrator resolves the unseasonable poetry of the uncouth swain.

The uncouth swain discovers the meaning of death in comparing Lycidas to the sun. Both sink "in the ocean bed" and both rise "in . . . the morning sky." But as a metaphor for death and rebirth, the sun can only adumbrate the divine rhythm; the sun measures time, and Lycidas has been translated to "other groves and other streams" in "the blest kingdoms meek of joy and love." The second narrator also accomplishes his redefinition with a passage about the sun. His repeated "And now" has the effect of suspending sequential time. The sun "had stretch't out all the hills," as if the entire afternoon were visible "now" in a single glance at the shadows across the land—but "now" the sun has dropped beneath the horizon. The ambiguous antecedent of "he" establishes an imaginative connection between the suspended sun and the uncouth swain. For this shepherd, like a sun everywhere and nowhere in the sky at once, has contracted the sequential movement of time into a single action. Disturbing the season due, he has sung today what he will be ready to sing tomorrow. He has pursued consolation and understood the death, cried and wiped his "melodious tear." Touched by Apollo, addressed by "the Pilot of the *Galilean* lake," he has matured in the extraordinary moments between the going out of the "still morn" and the coming down of the evening sun. The future has been revealed in the present. Lycidas is not dead and the poet who sung for Lycidas has not acted out of season. During one suspended day, the shepherd has been exempt from the normal rhythm of his sequential career.

The last two lines seem to destroy this arrested motion, reasserting temporal development and poetic seasons. With the words "At last" and "Tomorrow," balancing the double "And now," time seems to reorder itself as a sequence. But "At last he rose and twitch't his Mantle blue" may refer to the sun as well as to the uncouth swain. For a moment, the reader imagines that "he" does in fact stand for the sun. Even the "Mantle blue" does not dispel this illusion entirely, since the phrase might well describe the clear morning sky; it is not until the next line that our meaningful confusion can be resolved with certainty. The words "Tomorrow to fresh Woods" must refer to the wanderings of the uncouth swain in a future yet to appear, a "Tomorrow" yet to dawn. If "he rose" referred to the sun, then this "Tomorrow" would already exist in the past; the dawn yet to appear would have risen in the previous line. We therefore discard the illusion that "he" stands for the sun. But it is precisely this illusion which redefines the poetic action of the uncouth swain—he has sung his future. "At last he rose" while "the Sun had stretch't out all the hills." In the last line, time does indeed become a normal sequence. The second narrator indicates the success of unseasonable song, but he also reminds us of the imperfections of all human elegies and human elegists. Living in the sweep of time, we forget those whom we mourn. True fame cannot reside in a world ever fresh, ever new. "Now" that Lycidas has been mourned "at last," Lycidas can be forgotten in the new concerns of "Tomorrow." Similarly, the elegist cannot sustain his violation of poetic seasons any more than he can sustain his grief. As the uncouth swain contracts time, performing the future in the present, he must also serve time, meeting the fresh and new "Tomorrow" in harmony with temporal measures. Sometime, in time, he will sing at the season due.

Milton provided "Lycidas" with a stunning conclusion by placing his major narrator inside the smaller frame, hiding the true structure of the poem until its final seven lines. But elsewhere the inspired narrator inhabits the larger frame, and the act of writing the poem is redefined within the relatively impersonal narration of the smaller frame. This pattern emerges clearly in the Nativity Ode. Here the double frame is typographically explicit, the four stanzas naming the occasion, motive, and inspiration of the hymn standing separate from the hymn proper. As in *Paradise Lost,* the narrator disavows authorship of the forthcoming poem. The "Heav'nly Muse" is the true creator. The voice of this divine author issues "From out his secret altar toucht with hallow'd fire" (l. 28), like the prophetic voices of Isaiah and Jeremiah.

Critics have noticed that the verb tenses of this poem vary in a way grammatically inconsistent but thematically coherent.[2] The poem opens, "This is the Month, and this the happy morn," with the present tense denoting Christmas Day 1629. Yet in stanzas 2 and 3 of the introduction, the narrator moves into an imaginary present tense denoting the first Christmas Day. He sees "The Star-led Wizards haste" toward the stable and implores the Heavenly Muse to "prevent them with thy humble ode." Thereafter, the hymn alternates between a past tense referring to biblical Christmas ("It was the winter wild") and a present tense referring to biblical Christmas ("All meanly wrapt in the rude manger lies"). In stanza 14, the ode begins to consider a typological relationship between the Incarnation and the Last Judgment; the future tense refers to the Apocalypse. But in the climactic summary of this theme, the present tense opens up to absorb the future:

And then at last our bliss
Full and perfect is
  But now begins. . . .
[Ll. 165–67]

The temporal difference is retained in the metrical and grammatical antithesis of "then" and "now." But both events are designated with the present tense. The poem establishes one tense to signify Christmas 1629, biblical Christmas, and "Full and perfect" bliss outside of time. This new present tense unfolds—and enfolds—the meaning of the Incarnation as an moment simultaneously inside and outside of history.

Perhaps the model for these temporal "confusions" is the prophetic books of the Bible, especially the Psalms. Many commentators, notably Augustine, remarked that David often used the past tense and the present tense when speaking of events yet to happen.[3] In *A Preparation for the Psalter,* George Wither summarized the traditional explanations for this grammatical irregularity. David spoke in irregular tenses

[2] See for example Lowry Nelson, *Baroque Lyric Poetry* (New Haven: Yale University Press, 1961), pp. 32–34, 41–52.

[3] For Augustine on this subject, see *NPNF,* VIII, 142, 651.

to convey the certainty of his predictions. Also, his true audience was not contemporaneous with him; he knew that men in the Christian era would sing these songs "rather Historically than Prophetically," and therefore chose the appropriate tense. Finally, the language of the Psalms was divine as well as human: "the Prophet spake as in the person of the Holy Spirit. For, although the mysteries of the Gospell, of which the Psalms treat, were not then fulfilled in act, in respect of vs to whom they were to be manifested in *Time:* yet in regard of God, with whom all Times are present, they might be properly anough mentioned as things alreadie effected."[4] Old Testament prophecy was the work of two authors. Though the prophet and the Spirit acted in accord, their language conflicted—as did their audience. "In regard of God," but not in regard of Israelites, the future already existed at the time it was foretold. Human language bent to accommodate this divine perspective. As men are to the past, so God is to the future; this imperfect analogy is still instructive for the student of biblical tenses. Prophecy, viewed from the vantage point of eternity, was historical from the beginning. Prophets were divine historians of the gospel and, at the Incarnation, the historicity of their foretelling was revealed to men. The irregular tenses of the Bible revolve about this moment of revelation—a moment which was in time, because it happened, and outside time, because it had already "happened." After the Incarnation, the irregular tenses of Hebrew prophecy are no longer irregular to Christian readers. Christians were the true temporal audience of Old Testament prophecy, as their analysis of biblical grammar proved to them without question. The Incarnation narrowed the difference between divine and human perspective. After Christ "appeared," the past tense was proper both "in respect of vs" and "in regard of God."

The narrator of the Nativity Ode begins by distinguishing himself from the Old Testament prophets. Temporally, they are on one side of the Incarnation and he on the other. "For so the holy sages once did sing" of redemption and peace (l. 5). But the narrator, like the prophets before him, refuses to accept the "proper" tense. Having placed the "holy sages" in the past tense, the narrator then creates his imaginative present, locating Christmas 1629 and biblical Christmas on

[4] P. 106. I summarize Wither's argument on pp. 103–7.

the same temporal plane. The Muse must "join [her] voice unto the Angel Choir" and sing with the "hallow'd fire" of Isaiah. In the Ode that follows, the Heavenly Muse joins with the angel choir at just the moment when Hebraic prophecy is judged by the Incarnation, at just the moment when predictions are revealed as Christian history and pagan oracles are struck dumb. The past tense of "once did sing" proves incomplete. As the prophets could not contain their vision of the future in the future tense, so the Christian cannot contain his vision of the past in the past tense. They meet in the eternal present. At the Incarnation, the songs of all the holy sages, prophets and historians, join together in the angel choir. The great song, like the great subject, is at once within and without time.

Yet who is the singer here? The narrator of the Nativity Ode, like the narrator of *Paradise Lost,* forfeits his voice to the Heavenly Muse. He asks "thy voice" to sing the poem, but the hymn itself seems to contradict this humble abdication. This voice, like the epic voice of *Paradise Lost,* expresses human sentiments:

> Ring out ye Crystal Spheres,
> Once bless our human ears,
> (If ye have power to touch our senses so). . . .
> [Ll. 125–27]

The double voice does not threaten orthodox conceptions of artistic creation—everyone attributes this poem to John Milton, and anthologies of renaissance literature do not include poems by the Heavenly Muse (1608–1674). Rather, the dual identity of this inspired voice offends the modern notion of "speaker" or "persona." Twentieth-century readers educated in the manipulation of point of view have been taught to expect some minimal consistency in these matters, a single speaker who, as his words proceed, reveals a coherent "personality" in confronting a "dramatic situation." But how can such a vocabulary accommodate a narrator who promises not to speak and reappears in the speech of another? From what point of view does one man come to represent the collective voice of humanity? Even allegory cannot resolve the fundamental mystery of a divine voice which is also a human voice. If the Heavenly Muse were purely an allegorical character, embodying the poetic powers of the speaker in the introduction, why does this speaker divide his voice from "thy voice" so absolutely? Critics have yet to accuse Milton of schizophrenia.

Milton comments on the narration of the Nativity Ode in the opening stanza of "The Passion":

> Erewhile of Music and Ethereal mirth,
> Wherewith the stage of Air and Earth did ring,
> And joyous news of heav'nly Infant's birth,
> My muse with Angels did divide to sing. . . .

The second stanza begins with the word "Now," and the conjunction of "Erewhile" and "Now" looks forward to the beginning of *Paradise Regained.* In both cases, this conjunction informs the reader that the writing of an earlier poem makes possible and necessary the writing of the present poem. "The Passion" was clearly meant to be a companion poem for the Nativity Ode. The "mirth" of the Incarnation changes to the "sorrow" (l. 8) of the Passion—a holy version of the antithetical moods of "L'Allegro" and "Il Penseroso." In this first stanza, the poet characterizes the Nativity Ode as an action performed on a stage. Later he writes of the Incarnation:

> He sovereign Priest, stooping his regal head
> That dropt with odorous oil down his fair eyes,
> Poor fleshly Tabernacle entered,
> His starry front low-rooft beneath the skies;
> O What a Mask was there, what a disguise!
> [Ll. 15–18]

The Nativity was a masquerade. The art of the Nativity Ode joins the art of God in transforming nature into the setting for this divine entertainment. Nature becomes "the stage of Air and Earth." The Heavenly Muse and the angels "divide" the singing of the gospel news. Though the song has two parts, the two parts create a single artful harmony. Framing a divine entertainment, the Nativity Ode participates in the prophetic theatre. Allegorical Peace, commanded by her "Maker," comes "softly sliding" through the "turning sphere" like the personification of a Jonsonian masque. The prophetic vision of Psalm 85 appears "as at some festival":

> Yea, Truth and Justice then
> Will down return to men,
> Th'anamel'd *Arras* of the rainbow wearing,
> And Mercy set between,

> Thron'd in Celestial sheen,
> With radiant feet the tissued clouds down steering,
> And Heav'n as at some festival,
> Will open wide the Gates of her high Palace Hall.
> [Ll. 141–48]

The Last Judgment, the definitive Christian spectacle, is here a palace masquerade in which the righteous, having performed in the theatre of history, are allowed to view the festival within the "high Palace Hall." Like the Apocalypse, the Nativity is a theological event especially well-suited to the epistemological implications of the masque, for the *theatrum mundi,* normally a spectacle in which God judges the acts of men, turns around at the Incarnation so that men may know the acts of God.

The imaginative genre of prophetic masque clarifies somewhat the ambiguous role of the human speaker. He promises to listen to the song of the Heavenly Muse, yet he reappears as the author of phrases such as "our human ears." These reversals of audience and participant are, of course, normal in the court masque, a form which collapses the spectators with the spectacle.[5] The Attendant Spirit of *Comus* introduces a work of art to his spectators, but at the end of the entertainment, the actors turn and address "Noble Lord, and Lady bright" (l. 966). The masked dancers greet their spectators; actors and audience mingle without difference as art reaches out a hand to life and life reaches in to clasp that hand. Like the biblical prophets, the narrator of the Nativity Ode receives a vision in which he himself is an actor, hears a song of which he himself is the singer. The entire poem takes place on the stage of a prophetic and inspired imagination. The narrator is analogous to both the Attendant Spirit and the audience at Ludlow.

The ambiguous role of the narrator echoes throughout the poem. Nature, doffing her gaudy trim, acts in the divine pageant—"And let the Bass of Heav'n's deep Organ blow" (l. 130). Yet Nature, "that heard such sound / Beneath the hollow ground" (ll. 101–2), is also an audience. This second role is a dangerous temptation for the natural world. Hearing the celestial harmonies, Nature almost comes "To think her

[5] The major work on this defunct genre is still Enid Welsford's *The Court Masque* (Cambridge: Cambridge University Press, 1927). But there are many helpful observations in *Ben Jonson,* II, and in Stephen Orgel's *The Jonsonian Masque* (Cambridge: Harvard University Press, 1965).

part was done" (l. 105). At the Incarnation, however, time does not receive "its last fulfilling" (l. 106). The initial truncated foot of line 153, "Must redeem our loss," emphatically returns our joyful world to the sober necessities of history. Until the last fulfilling, Nature must remain primarily a spectacle for heaven. It is the function of the narrator to direct the decorous performance of humanity at this moment of partial, not "perpetual peace." Joining the choir with a collective "our," he teaches by example how best to order our individual celebrations and act with propriety in this great masque. We must cover our "naked shame" in imitation of the guilty earth (l. 40). We must be ashamed of our wars in the presence of the Prince of Peace (ll. 53–60). Modesty is our harmonious response to the season; like Nature, the human voice of this poem has "doff't her gaudy trim" in order "With her great Master so to sympathize" (ll. 33–34). Hearing the prophet speak in our name, we learn what will be lost and how to regard that loss. No more will innocent shepherds sit "simply chatting in a rustic row" (l. 87), for "mighty *Pan*" has "kindly come to live with them below" (ll. 89–90). In his tone the collective narrator imitates the gentle kindness, the sweet restraint of "mighty *Pan,*" yet also imitates His refutation of pastoral simplicity–the shepherds with their "silly thoughts" are ignorant as well as innocent (l. 92). The prophet directs our pride to its appropriate end. We may ask to hear celestial music provided we add the modest qualification, "(If ye have power to touch our senses so)" (l. 127). Our human part, like the part of Nature, is not done; these ravishing songs must not "Enwrap our fancy long" (l. 134). Comparing "full and perfect" bliss to "this happy day" (l. 167), the narrator tempers human joy to fit the occasion, enhance the spectacle. He comprehends the happiness we have by defining what we have lost and what we have yet to gain. He perfects humanity in acting for us all. With moderate joy and impeccable taste, he joins the divine celebration. His inspired voice divides the singing with angels and does us proud: the collective speech of humanity enters the angelic choir without disgrace, with only self-imposed humiliation.

The double role of the angelic host mirrors the double role of Nature. In the introduction, "all the spangled host keep watch in squadrons bright" (l. 21), a divine audience at the spectacle of the Incarnation. But in stanza XI, the angels "Are seen in glittering ranks with wings display'd." The watchers become the watched, displaying their glory, a spectacle for an indeterminate audience including all of Nature. At the end of the poem, the command "But see!" directs the vision of both audiences, human and divine. Earlier, the narrator beseeched his Heavenly Muse to "See how far upon the Eastern road / The Star-led Wizards haste" (ll. 22–23). But the final injunction to "see" commands all eyes. "Bright-harness'd Angels sit in order serviceable." They are eternally seated as an audience and eternally arranged as a spectacle. In this "Courtly Stable" the watchers act and the actors watch. The star is in place. The poem ends with our universe gazing in rapt attention.

The Nativity Ode represents an experiment with the form of poetry which a prophet would be expected to create. Its poet-prophet acts in a divine theatre as both seer and seen, transcriber and voice transcribed. "The Passion" is a failed experiment with the same genre. The "Mask" and "disguise" of the Nativity yield to a sorrowful vision of "These latter scenes" (l. 22). Milton proceeds to ring changes on the reversal of spectacle and spectator so pervasive in the Nativity Ode:

> See, see the Chariot and those rushing wheels
> That whirl'd the Prophet up at *Chebar* flood;
> My spirit some transporting *Cherub* feels,
> To bear me where the Towers of Salem stood,
> Once glorious Towers, now sunk in guiltless blood;
>   There doth my soul in holy vision sit,
> In pensive trance, and anguish, and ecstatic fit.
> [Ll. 36–42]

This passage defines a narrative structure far more complicated than anything in the companion poem. Here the speaker is a spectator of himself as a spectator; he watches himself watching a holy vision. Then, in the following stanza, he immediately switches to the point of view of the watched watcher. He is the soul in visionary rapture:

> Mine eye hath found that sad Sepulchral rock
> That was the Casket of Heav'n's richest store,
> And here though grief my feeble hands up-lock,
> Yet on the soft'ned Quarry would I score
> My plaining verse as lively as before. . . .
> [Ll. 43–47]

Finding himself in the role of prophetic spectator, the narrator becomes what he sees. All at once his eye finds both himself and the setting of the poem. The two spectators collapse into one. In the next stanza, the last of this unfinished poem, the narrator considers another change of perspective:

> Or should I thence hurried on viewless wing,
> Take up a weeping on the Mountains wild. . . .
> [Ll. 50–51]

The vision of Ezekiel now yields to the weeping of Jeremiah. In this poem, the Muse is reduced to a "viewless wing" capable of moving the narrator from biblical landscape to biblical landscape, from one prophetic identification to another.

The structure is excessively complex. What suited Marvell in "Upon Appleton House"—also a poem concerned with ocular oddities—frustrated the more theological art of Milton. It is interesting that the visionary narrator does not attribute his song to an agent of divine prompting. He never gives up his voice. Here the poem is "my song," "my roving verse"; because the narrator does not forfeit his voice to a heavenly creator, the poem lacks the initially divisive double frame of its companion piece. Without a double frame, "The Passion" winds through a series of mirrorlike visions within visions. The visionary prophet moves from place to place. He does not, like the singing prophet of the Nativity Ode, move gracefully from time to time; the art of the poem never intertwines with the art of a Heavenly Muse. Certainly Milton came to realize the structural advantages of the Nativity Ode. When the "I" of the introduction surrenders his voice, he can reemerge as the composite voice of humanity. Shedding his individuality, he can direct the sympathies of his human audience without acknowledging this audience, teaching the decorous apportionment of praise through the activity of praising. Poetry, Milton wrote in *The Reason of Church Government,* has the power "to allay the perturbations of the mind, and set the affections in right tune, to celebrate in glorious and lofty Hymns the throne and equipage of Gods Almightinesse" (CE III, 238). The composite voice of the Nativity Ode, celebrating the great birth, does in fact "set the affections in right tune." A reader participates in the celebrating by including himself within the collective "our." The method of the Ode became the method of *Paradise Lost.* Once again, the individual "I" of the invocations reappears in a composite voice dignified with prophetic authority. Defining what is praiseworthy, the various "Hail" passages invite the reader to participate in wise celebration. The role of the Calvinist prophet, adding nothing of his own, allows both narrators to find their lost art in the prophetic masquerade of a divine creator. "My roving verse" of "The Passion" turns in upon itself without conclusion, whereas "thy humble ode" arrives through the exposition of divine mysteries at the order serviceable. In "The Passion" Milton was his own spectator; in "An Ode on the Morning of Christ's Nativity" he was a masker watched by heaven. The double frame, dividing human from heavenly and narrator from poem, permitted Milton to complicate and repair these initial distinctions by dramatizing the paradoxes of prophetic art.

The prophetic poems are held within the larger context of the Word of God. Their various narrators join a community of inspired visionaries. The speaker of Nativity Ode is touched with a sacred coal like Isaiah, the roving versifier of "The Passion" sees himself receiving the vision of Ezekiel, the blind prophet of *Paradise Lost* must have the inspiration of Moses to complete his adventuresome song, and the seasoned poet of *Paradise Regained* must be led by the same Spirit that prompted Christ. The continuing revelation of the Word through history is a single masquerade of divine complexity in which all the prophets, all the types, participate. The art of God, by accommodating the Word to prophets, by adumbrating the providential scheme in historical types, and by disguising the Son as a man, makes history into a spectacle for heaven. Prophets, however, are seers. They witness the divine masque while they are absorbed into its spectacle. They imitate Christ the mediator and, within and without the spectacle of history, give other godly men some sense of the divine prospects.

Most readers believe that *Samson Agonistes* is Milton's final work.[6] If so, this "dramatic poem" represents a radical departure in form. There is no inspired narrator, no narrator at all. The Chorus might have served as an inspired inter-

[6] W. R. Parker, the original dissenter, reviews the whole issue in *Milton: A Biography,* II, 903–17. See also Allan H. Gilbert, "Is *Samson Agonistes* Unfinished?" *PQ,* 28 (1949), 176–94, and John T. Shawcross, "The Chronology of Milton's Major Poems," *PMLA,* 76 (1961), 45–58.

preter of the dramatic action, but Milton chose Israelites to people his Chorus and gave them ironic myopia. "Or do my eyes misrepresent?" the friends of Samson say upon encountering him for the first time (l. 124). They are no more perceptive—or rather, consciously perceptive—in announcing the arrival of Dalila (l. 710): "But who is this, what thing of sea or land?" In *Paradise Lost,* God, Christ, the angels, the narrator, and ultimately Adam all understand to varying degrees the actions of the epic. They understand these actions as well or better than the reader. But no character within the dramatic frame of *Samson Agonistes* ever comes to understand the events in which he participates. No character fully possesses the gift of prophecy.

Samson Agonistes offers many dramatic ironies lost to its Old Testament characters but available to its Christian readers. The characters seem to make associations half-consciously—as it turns out, for example, Dalila is a thing of both sea and land. The Chorus first compares her to "a stately Ship" (l. 714) and later, when she has departed, to "a manifest Serpent" (l. 997). Samson thinks of his temptress as an adept in sorcery:

> Thy fair enchanted cup, and warbling charms
> No more on me have power, thir force is null'd,
> So much of Adder's wisdom I have learn't
> To fence my ear against thy sorceries.
>
> [Ll. 934–37]

The hero will close his ears to these "warbling charms," like the deaf snake that cannot hear the charmer. The Chorus also connects the temptress with sorcery. When Harapha appears, they warn Samson to "Look now for no enchanting voice" (1065). This "enchanting" female of sea and land, both serpent and snakecharmer, is the very image of the god Dagon. Abraham Cowley explained his characterization of Dagon in *Davideis* as follows: "Some make *Dagon* to be the same with Jupiter Aratrius, deriving it from *Dagon,* Corn; but this is generally exploded, and as generally believed, that it comes from *Dag, a Fish;* and was an Idol, the upper part *Man,* and the lower Fish. . . . I make it rather *Female* then *Male,* because I take it to be the *Syrian Atergatis* (*Adder dagan,* the mighty *Fish*) and *Derecto,* whose *Image* was such" (p. 80). Cowley cited John Selden's *De Dis Syris* (1617) as the source of this female *"Adder Dagon."* He concluded, following Selden, that "Their Goddess Dagon" was "a kind of Mermaid-Deity" (p. 108). Milton once called Selden "the chief of learned men reputed in this land" (CE IV, 309), and it seems obvious that he adapted this *"Mermaid-Deity"* to enrich his presentation of Dalila. The metaphors of the drama characterize her as serpent, sorceress, and enchanting siren—Samson twice says that he is a shipwrecked pilot (ll. 198, 1044). This hero of romance has been trapped by the sorceress of Dagon because, unlike Odysseus, he lacked foresight when passing by the sirens. But the comparative mythology of the author and his understanding reader is superior to the knowledge of the Hebrew characters. The ideal reader seems to know more Syrian mythology than the captives of the Syrians. He alone understands that the idolatry of Samson for Dalila is precisely analogous to the idolatry of the Philistines for Dagon.

This kind of dramatic irony makes the tone of the drama exceedingly difficult to apprehend. There is no narrator authorized by God to guide our human response. When Samson claims to have learned "Adder's wisdom," his remark is ironic, elaborately ironic. Protecting himself from "warbling charms," Samson has learned the wisdom of the wicked in Ps. 58:3–6: "The wicked are estranged from the womb: they go astray as soon as they be born, speaking lies. Their poison is like the poison of a serpent: they are like the deaf adder that stoppeth her ear; which will not hearken to the voice of charmers, charming never so wisely. Break their teeth, O God, in their mouth." But learned it with a difference—he closes his ears to the wicked charms and threatens to tear his charmer limb from limb. The ironic parallel is striking. A Nazarite, one separate to God, Samson is in a holy sense "estranged from the womb." He has been poisoned by the serpent, as his constant references to mental disease suggest. Perhaps Samson speaks these lines with contempt: to deal with his enemy he has been forced to adopt the base means of an adder. Perhaps the reader is meant to apprehend connections between wicked wisdom and divine wisdom unrecognized by the fallen champion. Is the speech about "Adder's wisdom" an occasion to notice the bitterness of Samson or to appreciate the irony of Milton? The inspired narrators of *Paradise Lost, Paradise Regained,* and the Nativity Ode assume the voice of humanity in order to direct our understanding of history; the narrator of *Paradise Lost,* for example, introduces speakers and comments on their dialogue, guiding our apprehension of tone. In the absence of his prophetic guide, the reader of *Samson Agonistes* must often mediate between what he knows and what the characters may know.

Yet even in this shadow world the inspired narrator of the epics is not entirely absent. The blind hero evokes him constantly. Learned though we be in the complex interactions of art and life, it would be perversely sophisticated to deny the autobiographical resonance of this work. They are not naive literalists who insist that Harapha is a lot like Salmasius, Dalila a lot like Mary Powell, and Samson himself an awful lot like Milton and his narrators. These connections are unavoidable and unavoidably significant, for the poet must perform the heroic actions of which he writes. Unless the poet and his subject correspond, true creation cannot take place: the triumphs of the blind hero are not dissimilar from the triumphs of John Milton. But in *Samson Agonistes* half of the zealous visionary who narrated *Paradise Lost* seems to have fallen away. The prophet as divine visionary seemingly disappears, replaced by the prophet as zealous warrior. The types of Abdiel move to the center of the stage. Samson judged Israel for twenty years, for twenty years the one just man alive.

Lacking a prophetic narrator, *Samson Agonistes* still deals with a prophesied or destined action. The hero, led by a guiding hand, begins the drama in open air:

> The breath of Heav'n fresh-blowing, pure and sweet,
> With day-spring born; here leave me to respire.
> [Ll. 10–11]

Samson wishes to quietly "respire" even when the breath of heaven suggests "inspire." He has lost the sense of destiny that informed his previous career. "Restless thoughts" present him with "Times past, what once I was, and what am now" (l. 22), but not with times future. Foretelling his birth, an angel turned to flame. Samson cannot reconcile this prophetic emblem with his present state:

> O wherefore was my birth from Heaven foretold
> Twice by an Angel, who at last in sight
> Of both my Parents all in flames ascended
> From off the Altar, where an Off'ring burn'd,
> As in a fiery column charioting
> His Godlike presence, and from some great act
> Or benefit reveal'd to Abraham's race?
> [Ll. 23–29]

Samson cannot understand what this "benefit" might be. According to tradition, he exemplifies the lowest category of prophetic experience. Though he is "motioned" toward future actions by the *Fila Vocis,* his relationship with God includes no elaborate visions and little knowledge of the meaning of his prompted acts. Throughout this play, Samson utters prophecies correct in letter but false in spirit. His thoughts "portend" the "double darkness" of death and blindness (ll. 590–91). "And I shall shortly be with them that rest," he says to his father (l. 598). As Samson leaves with the Philistine messenger, the Chorus recalls in detail the divine emblem of the angel ascending in flames (ll. 1431–35). By this time Samson has regained his faith in "some great act" of his future and learned not to doubt "Divine Prediction" (l. 44). Yet even as he takes the guiding hand of the Philistine, obeying two masters at once, he remains uncertain of divine purposes. "The last of me or no I cannot warrant" (l. 1426). He obeys the motion ignorant of its ends. There is, when he leaves the stage, merely "aught of presage in the mind" (l. 1387)—a sense, and not a command, of the future. Pulling down the temple, the great metaphor of the Phoenix represents him as the "Holocaust" (l. 1702) adumbrated by the fiery angel of his nativity. Only then does Samson see.

Despite the absence of the visionary narrator, this drama concerns inspiration, prophecy, the relationship between conscious actor and passive instrument—nor did Milton abandon entirely the device of double framing. There is a drama within this drama, and the central character is doubly an actor. One of the many meanings of "agon" is "actor."[7] Samson endorses this description of himself:

> I was to do my part from Heav'n assign'd,
> And had perform'd it if my known offense
> Had not disabl'd me, not all your force:
> [Ll. 1217–19]

"By some great act" Samson will complete his destiny (ll. 28, 1389). Despairing, he often compares his former role of hero with his current role of fool.[8] Like the other Hebrew characters, Samson separates his past "race of glory" from his present "race of shame" (l. 597)—a metaphor seemingly derived from the athletic games of Greece and Rome. The

[7] Krouse, p. 111.

[8] See Arnold Stein, *Heroic Knowledge* (Minneapolis: University of Minnesota Press, 1957), pp. 111–30.

drama moves toward the games of Dagon, the "Sacrifices, Triumph, Pomp, and Games" of the festival day (l. 1312). At first, Samson reacts to these festivities with all the scorn of Tertullian for the remarkably similar spectacles of Rome:

> Have they not Sword-Players, and ev'ry sort
> of Gymnic Artists, Wrestlers, Riders, Runners,
> Jugglers and Dancers, Antics, Mummers, Mimics,
> But they must pick mee out with shackles tir'd,
> And over-labor'd at thir public Mill,
> To make them sport with blind activity?
> [Ll. 1323–28]

He will not be "thir fool or jester" (l. 1338). But roused by the motions of God, the champion submits. Before an audience of Philistines in "a spacious Theater" (l. 1605), Samson plays fool to the Philistines and hero to God. Surviving this "so horrid spectacle" (l. 1542), the Israelite Chorus define their cathartic experience in the final octosyllabic sonnet. The characters have the "true experience" of purging "all passion"; a catharsis exists apart from whatever may occur in the mind of the reader. So, in simplest terms, the dramatic poem contains a drama with a hero and two human audiences. The evil audience dies in the "horrid spectacle." The better audience of countrymen survive to define their tragic experience.

Blind and chained, Samson is a spectacle to all men. He is "expos'd" (l. 75), "obnoxious" (l. 106), and agonizes over his public execration.[9] He can only "see" by virtue of the Chorus, who tell him the name, nature, and aspect of each visitor. But he is seen by all, "to visitants a gaze" (l. 567). The two evil visitors claim this privilege triumphantly. Dalila, the Chorus says, "eyes thee fixed" (l. 726) and Harapha comes "each limb to survey" (l. 1089). Even gentle Manoa hopes to "view" Samson in his own house (l. 1491). The blind hero painfully recalls the time when he was a spectacle to God, not men: "Under his special eye / Abstemious I grew up and thriv'd amain" (ll. 636–37). While exercising righteous hatred toward Harapha, Samson begins to regain the sense of God's watch. He assures the giant that "his eye" is always "Gracious to re-admit the suppliant" (ll. 1172–73).

[9] Northrop Frye also notes the primitive horror of public shame in this drama (*Anatomy of Criticism: Four Essays* [Princeton: Princeton University Press, 1957], pp. 220–21).

Inevitably, the drama converges on the "spacious Theater" where Samson is seen by an entire city. The messenger, who would not be absent "at that spectacle" (l. 1604), enters fleeing "The sight of this so horrid spectacle" (l. 1542).

At the temple of Dagon, the roles of the drama within the drama are suddenly reversed. The Philistines are "with internal blindness struck":

> But he though blind of sight,
> Despis'd and thought extinguish't quite,
> With inward eyes illuminated
> His fiery virtue rous'd. . . .
> [Ll. 1687–90]

The true relationship between spectacle and spectator is just the reverse of what it appears to be. Samson is the genuine spectator, "With inward eyes illuminated." Now both audience and actor, he watches the spectacle of his own victory, "eyes fast fixed" (l. 1637). For a moment eye to eye with providence, Samson puns knowingly and prophetically in his final words:

> Hitherto, Lords, what your commands impos'd
> I have perform'd, as reason was, obeying,
> Not without wonder or delight beheld.
> Now of my own accord such other trial
> I mean to show you of my strength, yet greater;
> As with amaze shall strike all who behold.
> [Ll. 1640–45]

Following the Philistine messenger, Samson simultaneously obeys two masters. Here he addresses two audiences, playing for them both. He begins speaking to Philistine "Lords" but finishes speaking ambiguously to "Lords" and "the Lord"—the "you" of line 1644 can refer to both. Of course the God of "rousing motions" knows what his actor is about to do. But the man who came to "play before their god" (l. 1340) is now playing before his own God. Only the divine audience, knowing the end of the drama, can appreciate the final irony here. The hero is displaying his "own accord" with God—that is, his "agreement" with God. He means "to show" his Lord that he is no passive instrument. Rather, he is an actor who knows what he is about, a free man, and he knows that God enjoys the free obedience of His creations. So he constructs an elaborate irony for God to understand in delight and the Philistines to misunderstand in sorrow. Like any good actor, he is proud to bring his Philistine audience "wonder and delight"; soon he will bring them woe, the unmentioned but imminent other half of tragic experience.[10] He accepts the role of spectacle, one "beheld," and promises to "show" even greater strength. Since the Philistines are metaphorically blind, Samson and heaven truly constitute "all who behold." All those who think themselves beholding will be struck indeed. In the theatre of Dagon, Samson is a spectacle for Philistine Lords, but these lines create an imaginative theatre of God. In this second theatre, Samson watches "With inward eyes" while the Philistines unknowingly act "with internal blindness struck." Here the true spectator displays this "internal blindness" by speaking to the Philistines in such a way that they cannot hear.

An intricate comparison between Samson and David further elucidates the two theatres at the climax of *Samson Agonistes.* When the Chorus says that Harapha is the father of Goliath (l. 1249), Milton establishes a similarity with a difference.[11] As Samson slays Harapha in verbal combat, so David will slay Goliath in actual combat. Ironically, the biblical Samson possesses literal strength whereas David is better known for his verbal cunning. Samson is as much like Goliath as he is like David. While Samson is weak in his strength, David is strong in his weakness. Soon after the reference to Goliath, the hero refuses the command of the Philistines, saying that he will not "show them feats, and play before thir God" (l. 1340). But ultimately Samson does play before Dagon, and the description of this "act" both evokes and parodies the play of David before the Ark:

> before him Pipes
> And Timbrels, on each side went armed guards,
> Both horse and foot before him and behind,
> Archers, and Slingers, Cataphracts and Spears.
> At sight of him the people with a shout
> Rifted the Air clamoring thir god with praise,
> Who had made thir dreadful enemy thir thrall.
> [Ll. 1616–22]

[10] J. V. Cunningham discusses "woe," "wonder," and renaissance theories of tragic catharsis in *Tradition and Poetic Structure* (Denver: Swallow, 1960), pp. 142–231.

[11] John M. Steadman discusses this parallel in "Milton's Harapha and Goliath," *JEGP,* 60 (1961), 786–95. He concludes that Milton intended to represent the superiority of words to physical battles by having his strong hero defeat Harapha in a parody of David defeating Goliath.

"And David and all the house of Israel played before the Lord on all manner of instruments made of fir and wood, even on harps, and on psalteries, and on timbrels, and on cornets, and on cymbals" (2 Sam. 6.5). Armed soldiers preceded the Ark. When the disapproving Michael rebuked him, David replied that he danced because the Lord had chosen him king, vanquishing his enemies (2 Sam. 6.21–22). The head of his chief enemy, Saul, was fastened in the temple of Dagon (1 Chron. 10.10). Here the Philistines become the joyful celebrants and Dagon the god praised. Samson is the vanquished foe, as much Goliath and Saul as David, celebrating his own defeat. But then again, he is also approaching his triumph. The playing of Samson and David represents a "brotherly dissimilitude."

As this parallel suggests, *Samson Agonistes* is concerned with the relationship between blasphemous and godly play. The hero, obeying the dictates of his religion, first refuses to take part in the pagan feast. But the inner motions of God exempt him from external obedience. It is not unlikely that Milton himself was playing with the arguments of the early Fathers, particularly Tertullian, against the pagan spectacles. When the temple falls, it sounds "As if the whole inhabitation perish'd" with a "universal groan" (ll. 1511–12). These lines direct the Christian reader to the Christian fulfillment of Samson's heroic action. The Philistine audience has become a group of actors at a typological foreshadowing of what Tertullian called the only true Christian spectacle—the Last Judgment. Like David, Samson plays before his Lord. Though he acts in a blasphemous pagan festival, he ends an inward audience to a divine spectacle. Samson, disobeying the injunctions of Tertullian, follows him to the letter. The spectacle he "acts" and "sees" is the only one Tertullian allowed the Christian to imagine himself acting and seeing; the ironic reversal of audience and actor makes the theatre of Dagon into the sacred theatre of God. *Samson Agonistes* both accepts and rejects the arguments of *De Spectaculis*.

Since the hero joins the audience in the reversed theatre of God, his final action can be understood as a kind of catharsis.[12]

[12] The catharsis of Samson has been noted by Martin Mueller, "*Pathos* and *Katharsis* in *Samson Agonistes*," *ELH*, 31 (1964), 156–74, and Sherman Hawkins, "Samson's Catharsis," in *Milton Studies II*, ed. Simmonds, pp. 211–28. Both commentators interpret the episodes with the three visitors as representing a precise scheme for the progress of Samson's purgation.

The surviving Israelites define their own "true experience" as divine consolation:

> Oft he seems to hide his face,
> But unexpectedly returns
> And to his faithful Champion hath in place
> Bore witness gloriously; whence Gaza mourns
> And all that band them to resist
> His uncontrollable intent;
> His servants he with new acquist
> Of true experience from this great event
> With peace and consolation hath dismist,
> And calm of mind, all passion spent.

In context, "His servants" may include the "faithful Champion" along with Manoa, the Chorus, and the nation of Israel. God "re-turns" his hidden "face" to bear glorious "witness" for Samson and replaces those myopic choral eyes, seeing Samson and seeing for Samson. Earlier in the play, the Chorus explains that it can hardly be a "fair dismission" (l. 688) when the appointed champion "Unseemly falls in human eye" (l. 690). At the end of the drama, the champion has been once more under the eye of God and is among those servants "dismist" without a murmur of dissatisfaction, "all passion spent."

Throughout this tragedy the notions given final emphasis—"peace," "consolation," and "calm of mind"—represent by their very absence some future state of just fulfillment or "fair dismission" for the hero. Samson and the visitors often allude to his mental turbulence, his restless "disease." The Chorus prays that he may achieve a "peaceful end" (l. 709). They offer him "consolation" (l. 183), yet later assert that the genuinely reviving consolation must come from God. Comparing "Consolatories writ" with inner consolation, the Israelites foreshadow the end of the drama:

> But with th'afflicted in his pangs thir sound
> Little prevails, or rather seems a tune,
> Harsh, and of dissonant mood from his complaint,
> Unless he feel within
> Some source of consolation from above;
> Secret refreshings, that repair his strength,
> And fainting spirits uphold.
>
> [Ll. 661–66]

"The breath of Heav'n fresh-blowing" in which Samson wished to "respire" does in fact return as "Secret refreshings"

—he pulls down the temple with the terrible "force of winds" (l. 1647). A "source of consolation from above" does in fact "fainting spirits uphold." At the beginning of the festival day Samson cannot "once look up, or heave the head" (l. 195). Yet between the pillars he stands "At last with head erect" (l. 1639), receiving the consolation which upholds. The Samson who appears before the Philistines is calm before his storm. He walks in "patient but undaunted" (l. 1623). He stands "a while" leaning against the columns "as one who pray'd" (ll. 1636–37). He delivers his ironic speech to the audience. Samson is unhurried, at ease in time. In the catharsis of this tragic actor, "calm of mind" precedes "all passion spent."

Introducing his dramatic poem, Milton compared the purgations of art with those of homeopathic medicine:

> Tragedy, as it was anciently compos'd, hath been ever held the gravest, moralest, and most profitable of all other Poems: therefore said by *Aristotle* to be of power by raising pity and fear, or terror, to purge the mind of those and such like passions, that is to temper and reduce them to just measure with a kind of delight, stirr'd up by reading or seeing those passions well imitated. Nor is Nature wanting in her own effects to make good his assertion: for so in Physic things of melancholic hue and quality are us'd against melancholy, sour against sour, salt to remove salt humors.

Catharsis is not only for readers and audiences. The same effect can be found in "Nature." *Samson Agonistes* suggests that the same effect can be found in the order of grace as well. The hero is a constant victim of restlessness and interior motion. Thoughts rush upon him like insects. His anguish "suffers not / Mine eye to harbor sleep, or thoughts to rest" (ll. 458–59). "Wounds immedicable" torment him (l. 620). The only rest he can imagine at the beginning of the play is "death's benumbing Opium" (l. 630). Indeed, the only rest he seems to find is in the monument that Manoa, whose name means "rest," promises for his corpse. His ceaseless "ferment and rage" cause his thoughts to raise

> Dire inflammation which no cooling herb
> Or med'cinal liquor can assuage,
> Nor breath of Vernal Air from snowy *Alp*.
> Sleep hath forsook and giv'n me o'er
> To death's benumbing Opium as my only cure.
> [Ll. 626–30]

The "cooling herb" and "Vernal Air" cannot cure this "inflammation" because, in spiritual disease as in physical disease, only like cures like. God knows the way to heal.

Like the tragic poet and the homeopathic physician, God treats disease in kind. To heal this victim of internal motion He applies another internal motion:

> Be of good courage, I begin to feel
> Some rousing motions in me which dispose
> To something extraordinary my thoughts.
> [Ll. 1381–83]

Afflicted with a "Dire inflammation," the roused Samson proceeds to fulfill the emblem of the "fiery angel" with his act of "fiery virtue" (l. 1690). God moves the restless, turning one inflammation into another. Unable to sleep, the champion must be "rous'd" (l. 1690) by "rousing motions"—he is metaphorically asleep throughout most of the drama. The divine physician awakens the sleepless, fires the inflamed. He applies a motion directed toward a destined end as cure for the endless turmoil of guilt and self-reproach. Where Samson saw sleepless activity, God saw slumbering inaction—that is one of the differences between divine and human spectators. Rousing his champion, God motions the hero toward his ultimate purgation.

No one would be surprised to hear that Samson ends his life in a symbolic rebirth. He is, like the Phoenix, reborn from an "ashy womb" (l. 1703). The fiery virtue of his new birth recreates the emblem "Of thy conception" (l. 1434). However, this metaphor receives a more detailed presentation than is usually recognized. There are indications that the "rousing motions" of God signal the beginning of a symbolic labor to precede the symbolic emergence from the ashy womb. Just before the Philistine arrives, the Chorus remarks, "This Idol's day hath been to thee no day of rest, / Laboring thy mind" (ll. 1297–98). These are the false motions of inner restlessness. Refusing to leave, Samson will not serve his God "but by labor / Honest and lawful to deserve my food" (ll. 1365–66). One might argue with some force that the "rousing motions" prod Samson to accept a new kind of "labor," thus submitting to his divine rebirth. We confront a problem of discernment. Associations that the modern reader is predisposed to consider "unconscious" in earlier literature are, in this renaissance drama, the conscious patterns of a rational artist. There are unnumbered ways to brutalize a text. We may become crudely psychoanalytic: ignorant of Freud, Milton was not innocent of the ashy womb—he lost two wives in childbirth. Licensed by the metaphors in the drama, we may complete the patterns with a psychological art of our own invention: that reader is subtle indeed who decides to push "deserve my food" into the symbiosis of Samson and God. Should we relinquish our sense of history for even a moment, the drama will reveal configurations undreamt of in its philosophy. Imagine these lines in relation to a foetal Samson who refuses, like the "Brave Infant" of Jonson's Cary-Morison Ode, to emerge from his womb:

> *Chorus.* Consider, *Samson;* matters now are strain'd
> Up to the height, whether to hold or break;
>
> [Ll. 1348–49]

> *Samson.* . . . Besides, how vile, contemptible, ridiculous,
> What act more execrably unclean, profane?
>
> [Ll. 1361–62]

> *Samson.* Where outward force constrains, the sentence holds;
> But who constrains me to the Temple of *Dagon,*
> Not dragging?
>
> [Ll. 1369–71]

> *Samson.* Be of good courage, I begin to feel
> Some rousing motions in me which dispose
> To something extraordinary my thoughts.
>
> [Ll. 1381–83]

> *Officer.* I praise thy resolution; doff these links:
> By this compliance thou wilt win the Lords
> To favor, and perhaps to see thee free.
> *Samson.* Brethren farewell, your company along
> I will not wish. . . .
>
> [Ll. 1410–14]

On such grounds a huckster might pitch the guady tents of a psychoanalytic carnival. The Chorus says that the waters are "strain'd," about "to hold or break." Samson refuses to follow this urge because he sees no difference between defecation and birth "execrably unclean." The umbilical cord, he loyally replies, does not constrain him to leave, "Not dragging." Then the great rhythms of the mother assert themselves—the "rousing motions" are upon him irresistibly. Pleased with his complicity, the attendant Officer has him "doff these links," severing the new hero from the womb "perhaps to set thee free." Samson bids farewell to his "Brethren," he the adventuresome first-born. Hideously enough, *Samson Agonistes* has collapsed into a textbook illustration of the birth trauma.

We must collect our wits. In *Samson Agonistes* the historical critic faces a challenge to his discrimination, taste, and good sense at least as acute as the reading of *Hamlet*. It is curious that the criticism of this work has not centered about the issue of psychological as well as theological interpretation, since the connection between defecation and birth is undeniably present in the drama, and upon this association depends the significance of the climactic moment between the pillars.

Samson often defines his moral weakness as a failure of manhood: "O impotence of mind, in body strong!" (l. 52) Body and mind have failed to mate; the marriage of "strength" and "virtue" has been severed:

> But thee whose strength, while virtue was her mate,
> Might have subdu'd the Earth. . . .
>
> [Ll. 173–74]

> Immeasurable strength they might behold
> In me, of wisdom more than mean;
> This with the other should, at least, have pair'd. . . .
>
> [Ll. 206–8]

The man for whom cords were as threads in fire surrendered to "foul effeminacy" that held him "yok't" long before the Philistine mill (l. 410). He calls himself a "tame wether" (l. 538). At the end of the drama virtue is restored, mated with strength, and the result "From out her ashy womb now teem'd" (l. 1703).

There are two false "conceptions" in *Samson Agonistes*. Undone by a sniff of gold, Dalila "conceiv'd / Her spurious first-born; Treason against me" (ll. 390–91). Manoa, hearing that "*Samson* is dead," delivers a "windy joy":

> What windy joy this day had I conceiv'd
> Hopeful of his Delivery, which now proves
> Abortive as the first-born bloom of spring
> Nipt with the lagging rear of winter's frost.
>
> [Ll. 1574–78]

What he "conceiv'd" for the "Delivery" of his son has proved "Abortive." The "lagging rear" of winter has "nipt" this "first-born bloom." Instead of giving birth, his conception broke wind. Ironically, he has in fact a "windy joy this day." The heavenly Father also conceived rebirth through windy purgation:

> This utter'd, straining all his nerves he bow'd;
> As with the force of winds and waters pent
> When Mountains tremble, those two massy Pillars
> With horrible convulsion to and fro
> He tugg'd, he shook, till down they came, and drew
> The whole roof after them with burst of thunder
> Upon the heads of all who sat beneath,
> Lords, Ladies, Captains, Counsellors, or Priests,
> Thir choice nobility and flower. . . .
> [Ll. 1646–54]

These are no vernal airs, no fresh breezes from the Alpine slope. Samson purges all the bile, rancor, fester, gangrene, rage, and mortification of the mind. He does so in the posture of relieved constipation, "straining" and "bow'd," the release coming "With horrible convulsion" and at last "with burst of thunder." The "first-born" of Dalila and Manoa parody this genuine birth: the ironic association between the "windy joy" of Manoa and this triumph "As with the force of winds and waters pent" is there in the poem—both are births that emerge as anal discharges. The Philistines also parody the eruption of Samson: "And fat regorg'd of Bulls and Goats" (l. 1671).[13] The several associations which inform this climactic passage were far more natural to Milton than to ourselves, even to our Freudian selves. Milton understood that an earthquake took place in the "bowels" of the earth, an ancient metaphor still pervasive in the seventeenth century.[14] In the note prefixed to

[13] Compare Raphael's definition of knowledge and appetite in *Paradise Lost* VII.126–30:

> But knowledge is as food, and needs no less
> Her Temperance over Appetite, to know,
> In measure what the mind may well contain,
> Oppresses else with Surfeit, and soon turns
> Wisdom to Folly, as Nourishment to Wind.

The base gluttony of the Philistines is the outward form of mental intemperance. Samson exchanges "Wisdom" for "Folly" and "Nourishment" for "Wind"—yet that wind, measure of his folly, becomes the means of his triumph.

[14] On earthquakes in the "bowels" of the earth, see Kester Svendsen, *Milton and Science* (Cambridge: Harvard University Press, 1956), pp. 103–6. The devils of *Paradise Lost* "Rifl'd the bowels of thir mother Earth" (I.687), an anal and therefore fruitless rape.

the drama, Milton wrote that tragic poetry was "of power . . . to purge the mind" and proceeded to speak of "Physic." The physicians and patients of the seventeenth century understood by "purgative" what our gentler age understands by "laxative." [15] The God of this play is no delicate sentimentalist. He would not resent scatological metaphors, especially when applied to the destruction of Philistines, for in the near future (1 Sam. 5.6) the Lord of Israel will smite the Philistine followers of Dagon with "emerods"—that is, with hemorrhoids.

The ways of inspiration are both "unsearchable" and "uncontrollable." In *An Apology* Milton considered whether or not violent derision befit a Christian speaker. Arguing the affirmative, he cited the precedent of Luther, who wrote with such "tart" fervor "that his own friends and favourers were many times offended with the fierceness of his spirit" (CE III, 314). Moreover, "the Spirit of God who is purity it selfe, when he would reprove any fault severely . . . abstains not from some words not civill at other times to be spoken" (CE III, 315). There follows a catalogue of immodest language in the Bible and a denunciation of those "Fools who would teach men to read more decently than God thought good to write" (CE III, 316). What tart rhetoric is to the wars of truth, the catharsis of *Samson Agonistes* is to the wars of history. With prophetic irony, the "breath of Heav'n fresh-blowing, pure and sweet" eventually blows again "with the force of winds and waters pent" to scourge the "choice nobility and flower" of the Philistines. One critic of *Samson Agonistes* believes that the use of "flower" in this passage is among the weakest of Miltonic metaphors, showing the master in his dotage.[16] In fact, the use of "flower" in this passage is one of the most magnificently scornful touches in all of English literature. This purgative catharsis forever soils the choicest flowers of Philistia. Metaphorically, they suffer the ultimate indignity.

God, wrote Basil in his tract *Against Anger,* "does not forbid that anger be directed against its proper objects, as a medicinal device, so to speak." [17] The divine physician of *Samson Agonistes* cures like with like and motions his hero

[15] Milton writes of purgatives in Prolusion VII, *Complete Prose Works,* I, 305.

[16] Christopher Ricks, *Milton's Grand Style* (Oxford: Clarendon Press, 1963), pp. 55–56: "The word 'flower' is dead."

[17] *Saint Basil: Ascetical Works,* trans. Sister M. Monica Wagner, Fathers of the Church (New York, 1950), p. 458.

toward an act of scornful release. His "rousing motions" result in a symbolic rebirth which is also a symbolic defecation. As Samson revives from the "ashy womb," he purges from the other end of divine inspiration. He lives and dies at once. This double triumph creates a probable pun in the closing lines of the play. God "bore witness gloriously": He gave birth to a "spectator" and also to a "martyr," for the Greek root of "martyr" means "witness." The final sonnet, then, defines the "true experience" of both Samson and those who remain after his death. As an actor Samson releases his restlessness in physical violence. But as spectator of his own action, "With inward eyes illuminated," he achieves a kind of peacefulness. Unhurried, he waits with patience, prays in peace, and decimates the theatre. Both for the man who performs and the man who sees, the purgation of inward motion in the form of outward deed is the "true experience" of "all passion spent."

The sleepless Samson awakens fit to play before his God in a masquerade of prophetic action. As the inspired narrators of the Nativity Ode and *Paradise Lost* are to speech, so Samson is to deed. As they preside over the masque of prophetic song, both obedient and free, so Samson performs in the masque of typological history, a free man moving in "accord" with the divine motions. As they lose their voice in order to speak, so Samson is chained in order to act. But words and actions are not perfectly separable. Heroic singers must correspond to their heroic subjects, performing the deeds they celebrate. If heroic singers are strong, then perhaps strong heroes are not without all recourse to the power of the word. Samson defeats Harapha with zealous words and speaks with great cunning to the Philistines. There are many ways to serve Israel. The life of Samson moves away from words and toward a prophetic action. The life of David, his mysterious counterpart, moves away from physical battle and toward the prophetic Psalms. But granted all differences, Samson the strong man and David the visionary singer are heroic brothers.

The life of John Milton echoed them both. He moved away from sweet visions to the rancorous disputes of public politics and back again to inspired praise. Raising his harp once more, he displayed outright contempt for the martial pageants of literary tradition:

> Not sedulous by Nature to indite
> Wars, hitherto the only Argument

Heroic deem'd, chief maistry to dissect
With long and tedious havoc fabl'd Knights
In Battles feign'd; the better fortitude
Of Patience and Heroic Martyrdom
Unsung; or to describe Races and Games,
Or tilting Furniture, emblazon'd Shields,
Impresses quaint, Caparisons and Steeds. . . .
[IX.27–35]

He parodied these conventions in the heavenly battles of Book VI and the races, jousts, and games held by the fallen angels in Book II. With his ironic art he, like the heroic martyr of *Samson Agonistes,* could attend the godless spectacle to perform a divine action. But for twenty years of public controversy there was no distance comparable to the ironies of art. His Samson speaks of obeying two masters, the Philistine and the Lord:

Masters' commands come with a power resistless
To such as owe them absolute subjection;
And for a life who will not change his purpose?
[Ll. 1404–6]

They came with power resistless to the author of *The Reason of Church Government,* commanded by God to blow a jarring blast. Sweet to the tongue, the Word of God was "bitter in the belly" and "bitter in the denouncing." In the closing lines of his drama, Milton wrote about the hidden face of God and the dismissal of calm servants. The passage might well have been conceived as a happy resolution to the anguish of David in Ps. 27.9: "Hide not thy face from me; put not thy servant away in anger: thou hast been my help; leave me not, neither forsake me, O God of my salvation." In *Samson Agonistes* the presumed desertion of God mystifies and embitters His servants until the tragic catharsis averts their threatened quarrel. But the passions involved are not so much disowned as they are relocated. The wrathful discontent of man and the wrathful disapproval of heaven both find, in the Philistines, object fit—this is a play about the good purgation of hatred. The author of *Samson Agonistes* praised the restless prophet who, inspired by God, delivered himself of all that vile rebuke.

CHAPTER V

Prophetic Time

Time,
the sine-pondere, most
imperturbable of elements
assumes its own proportions
silently, of its own properties—
an excellence at which one
sighs.
Yvor Winters,
"Quod Tegit Omnia"

PROPHETS speak about history. In some cases their knowledge of distant events may be duplicated without inspiration. The scientist may predict the future by inferring effect from cause; the historian may recreate the past by deducing cause from effect. But the mode of prophetic knowing is unique. A prophet does not reason within the sequential movement of history, deriving effect from cause, conclusion from premise. As Augustine remarked, a holy prophet beholds "the immovable causes of things future in that very highest pinnacle of the universe itself." From the privileged vantage point of eternity, he apprehends the shape of time in a way unavailable to those scientists and historians reasoning within the temporal flux. Prophets neither deduce nor conclude—in essence they merely know. Locked inside the succession of moments, men understand events with the logic of action and reaction. The prophet, standing outside of history, understands connections between discrete events that cannot be expressed in the mortal formulas of scientific and historical causation. A prophetic artist, Milton was ever intent on unveiling the eternal shapes of time—time the most elusive of human necessities.

Time, said Aristotle, is the measure of motion. Though Augustine confessed his inability to define time, and Christians disagreed with Aristotle about the eternity of the world, the Greek concept became a Christian commonplace. Time might be compared with eternity, its nervous flux deprived of noble permanence. It might be personified as a winged flyer, a toothed devourer, and a fleet runner, father of Truth and History. But in nonfigurative contexts, the Aristotelian conception often appeared essentially unchanged.[1] Time measured sublunary motion, and in the end motion was decay. Men strove to enact their destinies, pursued their compelling motives until at last the force of motion itself drove them back into the dust:

> Tell time it meets but motion,
> tell flesh it is but dust.[2]

Time, which "meets but motion," provided the fundamental premise from which Renaissance authors developed their ethical logic. The argument went in two directions. For the *carpe diem* poet, the incessant motion of time indicated the necessity for action and pleasure in the immediate world—time revealed the tragic immorality of coyness. For the religious poet, the same view of time demanded retirement from the immediate and merely momentary—time revealed the virtue of eternity. In either case, time as the measure of motion taught human beings how to act.[3]

With the gradual repudiation of this notion by the physicists and philosophers of the last three centuries, our western

[1] Aristotle's major treatment of time is in *Physics* IV. Augustine, in *The City of God* XII.xxvi, found the classical definition perfectly compatible with his faith. Jehovah was Lord of Time: "For what other creator could there be of time, than He who created those things whose movements make time?"

For "Time" in medieval and renaissance iconography, see Erwin Panofsky, *Studies in Iconology* (New York: Harper and Row, 1962), pp. 69–94; Jean Seznec, *The Survival of the Pagan Gods,* trans. Barbara Sessions (New York: Pantheon, 1953), pp. 137, 248, 420; Klibansky *et al.,* pp. 133–36, 153–70, 207–14.

Richard Gale has edited an anthology, *The Philosophy of Time* (Garden City: Doubleday, 1967), with interesting selections, brilliant introductions, and adequate bibliographies.

[2] "The Lie," ll. 33–34, in *Poems of Ralegh,* p. 46.

[3] For the relationship between time, action, and ethics in renaissance literature, particularly in Shakespearean tragedy, see Cunningham, pp. 135–41; Frank Kermode, *The Sense of an Ending* (New York: Oxford University Press, 1967), pp. 67–89.

The *carpe diem* conventions—the withering rose, the fleeting day, the momentary dew—prove the imperfections of this world in religious poems like George Herbert's "Virtue" and Henry Vaughan's "The World." The *carpe diem* tradition itself is virtually an inverse religion. Eternity becomes a vast desert, and the place of eternity in devotional verse is usurped by sensual time, the immediate instant, the "now." Coyness is sin, orgasm is resurrecting death. Cf. Ralegh's "Serena bee not coy," Donne's "The Canonization," Lord Herbert's "An Ode upon a Question Moved," Carew's "The Golden Age," Lovelace's "Love Made in the First Age," and of course Marvell's "To His Coy Mistress."

culture would seem to be, for the first time in some time, without a communal definition of time. The various attempts to provide such a definition—the popularized relativity of Einstein, the serialism of J. W. Dunne, the eternal recurrences of P. D. Ouspensky, the synchronicity of Jung and Pauli—have succeeded only in dividing parapsychological adventurers from rationalist scoffers.[4] We live in, with, through, or high above time. We save and spend it, give and are given it, take and are taken by it, glance at it on our tables and check it on our wrists. Yet we know not what "it" is. Nor do we, as a society, think very deeply about what "it" means. In the renaissance, death moved the lover to embrace his immediate love and prompted the divine to contemplate his eternal God. Death was the universal antidote to inordinate pride. When Queen Elizabeth toured the streets of London, the common people staged allegorical pageants to remind her of the common doom.[5] Though one might draw an oblique analogy with contemporary demonstrations, the parallel is weak indeed. Our culture—where the aged go away to die in hospitals and special communities, a failure too shameful to be seen—dwells on violence and not temporal decay. Violence is death as an unexpected surprise. What once was inevitable has now become sudden, a lifetime of process concentrated in an instant. I expect that we fear violence less because of its own terrors than because it reminds us with a shock of what our

[4] Dunne's most popular book is *An Experiment with Time* (New York: Macmillan, 1927). One can taste sufficient Ouspensky from *Tertium Organum* (New York: Knopf, 1922) and *A New Model of the Universe* (New York: Knopf, 1931). For the bizarre tale of the Jung-Pauli collaboration, see Arthur Koestler, *The Roots of Coincidence* (New York: Random House, 1972), pp. 88–104, and for the bizarre results, see *The Collected Works of C. G. Jung*, ed. Gerhard Adler *et al.*, *trans.* R. F. C. Hull, Bollingen Series 20 (Princeton: Princeton University Press, 1968), VIII. The effect of modern physics on the philosophy of time is treated by J. J. C. Smart, *Philosophy and Scientific Realism* (London: Routledge, 1963) and Milic Capek, *The Philosophical Impact of Contemporary Physics* (Princeton: D. Van Nostrand, 1961). With recent discoveries about the DNA molecule, we will doubtless have a spate of books about how the biological present contains the biological future in its cellular wrappings—time, once circles and lines, will reemerge on the wings of a double helix.

In *Man and Time* (London: Aldus, 1964), J. B. Priestley considers the dilemma of "time-haunted" modern man in a sometimes entertaining, sometimes tedious, always amateurish fashion. Try instead Priestley's amusing gothic novel about the haunting of time, *The Old Dark House* (New York: Grosset and Dunlap, 1928). The best time-travel stories are Robert Heinlein's "By His Bootstraps" and Anthony Burgess's "The Muse."

[5] J. E. Neale, *Queen Elizabeth I* (Garden City: Doubleday, 1957), pp. 61–62.

mass culture would have us forget. Though time measures man at least as precisely as man measures time, we find ourselves impossibly tongue-tied whenever we venture a formal definition of time or ponder for a while its implications.

One would suppose that the absence of a concept of time would threaten the sense of history and historical continuity in our culture. If the very instant eludes us, then the generation, the decade, the period, the era would also seem in danger of disintegration. Marxists, of course, know when they are—and Christians used to know. But it might be argued that the irreligious noncommunists of our culture are in precisely this situation. Even the firmest patriot no longer speaks of the "manifest destiny" of his society. The "idea of progress," once our most important product, remains in the official rhetoric of politicians, advertisers, developers, road builders, city planners, con men, and Timothy Leary. But for many of us, the fine old words no longer move. For better or for worse, we have no prophet to dispose our present toward a common future.

Prophecy invites men to join their various motives with the divine motions of history. The future, known in the present, attracts and focuses many disparate commitments. Prophecies tend to fulfill themselves because prophets, exempt from causal reasoning, inspire other men to animate the processes of cause and effect. We accede to the vision, organizing our time to flow gracefully into the destined hour. Plato attributed extraordinary virtue to normal eyesight: "Vision, in my view, is the cause of the greatest benefit to us, inasmuch as none of the accounts now given concerning the Universe would ever have been given if men had not seen the stars or the sun or the heaven. But as it is, the vision of day and night and of months and circling years has created the art of number and has given us not only the notion of Time but also the means of research into the nature of the Universe." [6] If normal vision comprehends motion and therefore time, prophetic vision comprehends temporal motion from the standpoint of eternal rest. The prophet sees all time at once, the past, present, and future indivisible. His function is to offer an understanding of history to his community. Without a prophet, unsure of where and when we are in history, we act in time like blind men. At the

[6] *Timaeus* 47AC, trans. R. G. Bury, in *Plato,* VII, 63. A. B. Chambers relates this passage to the invocation to Book III.

beginning of the English Revolution, the Puritans grasped a plan of history which, giving form to past and future time, showed them how to act in the present time. For a time they were, as Milton said, "a nation of prophets." They attempted to realize a communal vision of time.[7] Insofar as we can see ourselves, we appear to lack such a vision.

Actually we do, in a sense, possess in common a definition of time and history. Time, as Winters says, "assumes its own proportions" wholly oblivious to our philosophical, scientific, and cultural confusions.[8] He is speaking of the excellence of poetry. Time disposes itself in the language we live in, with, through, and sometimes beyond. The language which cannot accommodate a definition of time also provides that definition; our elaborate systems of verb tenses, temporal conjunctions, and adverbs force us to sort out time in order that we may think and speak. As Plutarch realized, the understanding of time implicit in language makes possible logical thought. We assume time in order to think about thinking. A syllogism, like other logical operations, is really a temporal sequence: knowing from previous investigation that *X* is *Y*, *when* we know that *Z* is *Y*, *then* we know that *X* is *Z*. Conclusions *follow* from premises. Many of the organizational words that appear in logical discourse, such as "now," "then," "subsequently," and "consequently," are also temporal words. Logic is a highly sophisticated way of organizing time into repeatable sequences, a kind of "tick-tock" for understanding the processes of cognition.[9]

Words provide a communal sense of history because we use them to tell stories. History, like fiction, is time given shape and form. Accepting the conventions of narrative technique, audiences grant storytellers the freedom to escape from the mundane clock and manipulate temporal phenomena. A rough but useful way to measure the shape of time in fiction is to consider the proportion between the "real time" or clock-time of the reading experience and the "dramatic" or narrative time of the fiction thus experienced. It is permissible, in this heuristic framework, to convert the reader's clock-time into

[7] I am, once again, much indebted to Cohn's *The Pursuit of the Millenium.*

[8] *Collected Poems,* rev. ed. (Denver: Swallow Press 1960), p. 37. "Quod Tegit Omnia," copyright 1960 Yvor Winters, is quoted by permission of the publisher.

[9] On the assumption that, if art is an imitation of life, then plot is an imitation of history, Kermode examines the literary resonance of our sequential apprehension in *Sense of an Ending.*

linguistic space. So, one sentence or three lines of verse may indicate the passing of years of narrative time in a work which also expands an instant of narrative time into pages of paragraphs or lines. In *Paradise Lost,* the epic similes usually occur while an action is being performed. They arrest the action and interrupt the sequence of fictional time. Of course we understand that Satan does not stop arranging himself so that Milton may compare him to an orator. The effect, however, is exactly that—a moment suspended, prolonged, a gap created in dramatic time. But the real time of the reading experience can never be arrested. So the reader experiences, within the continual flow of clock-time, the illusion of time speeding, slowing, stopping. Once again, the reader is to the narrator as Adam is to Michael; the prophetic vision of the last two books also moves in various tempos. Time is the little world of narrators, and they spin it for their recreation.

One important difference between drama and narrative concerns the necessary redefinition of these effects. In drama, the fictional time of the characters tends toward an identity with the real time of the audience. Although the breaks between scenes and acts may indicate the passing of no time or much time, any given scene abides (sooner or later) by the clock that audience and actors hold in common. As characters in a dramatic representation, actors may measure their time by any standard their creator wishes to impose; but spectators are particularly conscious of this manipulation, and throughout history many audiences have preferred to keep their clock-time in perfect synchronization with the time of the dramatis personae. Fiction approaches such unity only when characters speak—otherwise, the narrator winds a very special clock of his own creation. One way for a dramatist to escape from rigorous clock-time without violating the expectations of a fastidious audience is to have his characters create fiction, tell stories. In classical Greek drama, the chorus performed this function:

From another point of view the Chorus releases us from the captivity of time. The interval covered by a choral ode is one whose value is just what the poet chooses to make it. While the time occupied by the dialogue has a relation more or less exact to real time, the choral lyrics suspend the outward action of the play, and carry us still farther away from the world of reality. What happens in the interval cannot be measured by any ordinary reckoning; it is much or little as the needs of the piece demand. A change of place directly obtrudes itself on the senses, but time is only what it appears to the mind. The imagination travels easily over many hours; and in the Greek drama the time that elapses during the songs of the Chorus is entirely idealised.[10]

Milton creates this effect in *Samson Agonistes*. Indeed, he emphasizes the triumphant escape from dramatic necessity by having the same story told more than once, each version disposing the narrative time in a different manner. At its climax, this most undramatic drama approaches narrative verse. The catastrophe occurs off-stage, and we learn of the event from characters turned storytellers. Our first narrator, the Messenger, tells his story in 63 lines, compressing into this real and dramatic time all the narrative time from "Sunrise" (l. 1597) to noon. *Samson Agonistes* itself begins at "dayspring" (l. 11). The Messenger, then, creates a fictional or narrative time in 63 lines which precisely equals the dramatic time passed in 1,508 lines. This equation calls attention to the temporal possibilities of literary artifice, as if Milton desired his readers to examine the difference between drama and narrative, between two kinds of temporal illusion. Within his story, the Messenger (as we might expect) extends the moments between the pillars with simile. The physical action alone takes up 13 lines (ll. 1647–59). When the Messenger finishes, the Chorus returns to dramatic time. They define the death of the hero with reference to the dramatic present, for just "now," just after noon, Samson "li'st victorious" (l. 1663). Then the first Semichorus returns from dramatic to narrative time and enters, as it were, the gap in clock-time opened by the Messenger. They retell the story, ending with Samson again between the pillars. Continuing the narrative, the second Semichorus redescribes the moment of physical labor, arresting this moment for the prolonged space of 21 lines (ll. 1687–1707). Immediately, Manoa breaks the spell of this enchanted instant and says, "Come, come, no time for lamentation now" (l. 1708). His emphatic "now" calls the drama and its characters back to clock-time.

But during this suspension, the climactic moment has twice escaped the special conditions of dramatic representation. The noontime event has been twice told, extended in time for 34 lines. As we will see, the hero of this drama is a man impelled by "motions" that cannot be measured in Aristotelian clock-

[10] S. H. Butcher, *Aristotle's Theory of Poetry and Fine Art* (New York: Dover, 1951), pp. 292–93.

time. These divine motions lead him out of sequential time and into a moment of great temporal mystery. Since drama naturally transpires in clock-time, Milton had to break down the conditions of drama in order to represent this mysterious instant, measure these transcendant motions; the linear time of Aristotle must bend to accommodate an eternal mover. *Samson Agonistes,* though offering a unique opportunity to study the temporal adjustments of prophetic drama, is possibly the last in a series of poems that strain language and form to imitate the divine complexities of time.

Christian history moves in a linear sequence, allowing for the causal reasoning of Christian historians and Christian scientists. But the sequence is complicated by the divine art of typology—a logic of temporal phenomena more suited to the eternal perspective of the holy prophet. When Moses strikes the rock, an action is begun which will not be complete in time until Christ bleeds on the cross; in eternity Christ is always on the cross. Having escaped from sequence, the Old Testament instant hovers perfected in eternity while the motions of time proceed toward its unveiling. Eternity folds up history. Christian typology, filling the instant with past and future events, contracts linear time; the future is in the present, the conclusion is in the premise. A human artist who would measure time in this way must, like the prophets of the Old Testament, violate the sequential understanding of time embodied in human logic and human language. He must prevent time from assuming "its own proportions / silently, of its own properties." Language is the natural medium of time-serving historians and scientists. Constructed about an Aristotelian conception of time, our language is most comfortable when recording chronological events and developing sequential arguments. Much of the creative intensity in Milton's poetry is necessarily directed toward the defeat of natural expression; his words labor to accommodate an eternal perspective. No *carpe diem* poet, no ordinary divine poet, he dissolved and reordered our literary language to express a prophetic understanding of time fundamentally antipathetic to language itself.

Milton first imitated the typological contraction of time in the prophetic masque of the Nativity Ode. The limited span of clock-time between the Incarnation and the approaching Epiphany absorbs previous time and adumbrates future time. Adhering to a pattern of irregular tenses, it is a poem about cessations and beginnings. The pagan oracles cease, the pagan gods flee, the curse of the Fall is lifted. But redemption, peace, bliss, and judgment now begin. The end "now begins," for the Incarnation, revealing Christ, reveals the Last Judgment as well. Controlling the pagan gods assumes the final binding of Satan; the old dragon is already "wroth to see his Kingdom fail" (l. 171). Since the full and perfect bliss is within this joyous beginning, the tree within the seed, Milton presents the sunrise "On the Morning of Christ's Nativity" as if it were a sunset:

> So when the Sun in bed,
> Curtain'd with cloudly red,
> Pillows his chin upon an Orient wave. . . .
> [Ll. 229–31]

"Orient" means "east" and Christ is, traditionally, *Filius Orientis*.[11] But the "sun in bed" with pillowed chin unmistakably suggests the dying sun of the west. The end and the new beginning seem to occur at once.

"Upon the Circumcision" is also about a single event conceived of as both a beginning and an end. The mathematically central lines of the poem, contracted spatially, speak of contracted time:

> Alas, how soon our sin
> Sore doth begin
> His Infancy to seize!
> [Ll. 12–14]

The first half of the poem goes back in history to relate the Circumcision to the Nativity. Milton shows how the joy of the first event comes to an end in the sorrow of the present event. After the painful and sorrowful beginning at the center of the poem, the last half moves forward in history to consider the typological relationship between the Circumcision and the Passion. "This day" (l. 26) opens out in both directions of time to include other days, acting as a container for time past and time future. Martin Luther wrote: "All the created orders are masks or allegories with which God paints his theology; they are intended as it were *to contain* Christ." [12]

[11] See Herbert Grierson's note to Donne's "Hymn to God my God, in my sickness" in *The Poems of John Donne* (Oxford: Clarendon Press, 1912), II, 248–49. This name for Christ derives from the Vulgate version of Zech. 6.12, "Ecce vir oriens nomen ejus."

[12] Quoted in E. M. Carlson, "Luther's Conception of Government," *Church*

The created world figures forth the incarnate Christ, holding the eternal within the temporal. But George Wither defined one aspect of biblical metaphor as the confusion of "container and thing contained" (p. 103). The incarnate Christ of this poem, contained by time, is also a container. He "Emptied his glory, ev'n to nakedness" (l. 20) in order to receive "the full wrath" (l. 23) of divine justice. The Circumcision, then, is the moment in time when Christ "sore doth begin" to receive this wrath. In eternity, though, he already receives it fully. The poem juxtaposes the two perspectives. The Circumcision contains the beginning and the end of the life of Christ, a midpoint between joy and sorrow. Two events mysteriously converge in the climactic and anticipatory event of "This day."

Milton's poems are often about events framed by other events that occur outside the formal bounds of narrative time. Similarly, the action of creating the poem is often an event framed by other creative events. "Lycidas" takes place in a single day; the song is sung while the sun "stretch't out all the hills" (l. 190). The opening words, "Yet once more," indicate the repetition of past actions and the closing words, "Tomorrow to fresh Woods, and Pastures new," adumbrate future actions. As the beginning absorbs the past of the singer, the end suggests his future. The narrator of "The Passion" refers to his creation of the Nativity Ode, and the events of both these poems are contained within "Upon the Circumcision." All three poems, and "Lycidas" as well, maintain the unity of time exemplified in classical drama. But they imitate moments of historical density—something in past time comes to an end, something in future time begins to appear. With the exception of the Nativity Ode, their creation is itself such a moment of transition.

Milton's poems are curiously anticipatory and, in a special way, incomplete. Often the reader is led, through proleptic ironies, to expect a fulfillment; but the fulfillment, when it comes, turns out to be yet another anticipation. The events of the poems move outside the temporal frames of art. *Paradise Regained* proceeds inexorably to the moment on the pinnacle when Christ stands against the Adversary. Yet this moment, this fulfillment of anticipation, is partial. The ultimate contest between these two will happen in another time,

---

History, 15 (Scottsdale, Pa.: American Society of Church History, 1946), p. 260.

in another place. But the partial is also complete: that ultimate contest has already happened, fully contained in the typological moment on the pinnacle.[13] The poem is equally centrifugal and centripetal. The climactic action becomes another anticipation, moving the reader outside the poem, beyond the frame of narrative time, if he wishes to contemplate the ultimate fulfillment. But the same action tends to draw that ultimate fulfillment within the temporal frame of the poem. Milton marks off a small frame of clock-time only to show that time rightly conceived cannot be framed, cannot be measured in the strict sequence of motion following motion.

Paradise Lost is Milton's fullest imitation of the Bible, and therefore the least centrifugal of his poems. Anticipations find their fulfillments. To elucidate fully a single event, the Fall, the epic presents all of human history and eternal "history" from the Exaltation to the Last Judgment. The first revelation of Christ and the creation of "New heav'ns, new Earth" (XII.549) circumscribe in eternity the fixed historical time between the Fall and the Apocalypse. Tasso advised the epic poet to be "careful in his descriptions of . . . the sunrise, the sunset, midday, midnight, the seasons of the year," and recent critics have explored the complex representations of time in the epic, particularly the function of Miltonic "noon" in a detailed scheme of symbolic astronomy.[14] Both midday and midnight, noon organizes the epic action. The Exaltation, the first arrival of Satan in Eden, the arrival of Raphael, the Fall, and the Crucifixion take place at midday. The revolt of Satan, the first temptation of Eve, and the second arrival of Satan in Eden take place at midnight. As-

[13] For expansions of this point, see Northrop Frye, "The Typology of *Paradise Regained*," *MP*, 53 (1956), 227–38; Lewalski, *Milton's Brief Epic*, pp. 133–63.

[14] The remark by Tasso appears in Gilbert, p. 490.

On noon in *Paradise Lost*, see Jackson I. Cope, *The Metaphorical Structure of* Paradise Lost (Baltimore: Johns Hopkins Press, 1962), pp. 130ff.; Albert R. Cirillo, "Noon-Midnight and the Temporal Structure of *Paradise Lost*," *ELH*, 29 (1962), 372–95; Philip Brockbank, "'Within the Visible Diurnal Spheare': The Moving World of *Paradise Lost*," in *Approaches to* Paradise Lost, ed. Patrides, pp. 199–222, and the introduction to the epic by Alastair Fowler in *The Poem of John Milton*, ed. John Carey and Alastair Fowler (London: Longmans, 1968), pp. 443–50. In seventeenth-century English, the word "noon" could refer to midday and midnight.

The best treatment of Milton's philosophy of time is Laurence Stapleton, "Milton's Conception of Time in *The Christian Doctrine*," HTR, 57 (1964), 9–21. See also the citations in Patrides, *Milton and the Christian Tradition* (Oxford: Clarendon Press, 1966), pp. 128–30.

sociated with midnight, Satan is also connected with the eclipsed sun. He "stood like a Tow'r" with "Glory obscur'd," like the sun "from behind the Moon / In dim eclipse" (I.591–97). After his successful adventure in Eden, the planets shift alignments and for the first time suffer "real Eclipse" (X. 413). Among the heavenly bodies really eclipsed is Satan himself, as he ironically indicates when telling his followers that Christ "hath to himself ingross't / All Power, and us eclipst" (V.775–76). To explain this structural principle, critics have referred to the Platonic "Great Year"–beginning and ending with a universal noon of perpendicular alignments–and to the Psalm tradition of the *daemonium meridianum,* that noontime devil who comes disguised in light at the time of greatest appetite and greatest sloth. Whichever tradition applies, it seems clear that this astronomical pattern defines the relationship between opposites. In the *Artis Logicae* Milton devoted a chapter to *adversa,* those contraries "absolutely diagonally adverse": "direct opposition, the most complete, is to be understood, such as that between two points of the diameter of the same circle" (CE XI, 131). There are two kinds of *adversa,* those in the same genus, such as black and white, and those in opposite genera, such as good and evil. By this measure Christ and Satan would seem to be *adversa* of the second kind. But may they not, in fact, occupy the same genus? During their morning prayers Adam and Eve address the planet Venus:

> Fairest of Stars, last in the train of Night,
> If better thou belong not to the dawn,
> Sure pledge of day, that crown'st the smiling Morn
> With thy bright Circlet, praise him in thy Sphere
> While day arises, that sweet hour of Prime.
> [V.168–71]

Lucifer, "Fairest of Stars," is of course associated with Satan, but also with Christ, the identity of the Evening and Morning Stars being to this day a common emblem of the Resurrection. Satan, no less than Christ, is a son of God and *filius orientis.* The language here seems calculated (though not by Adam and Eve) to reveal the double nature of this single star, "last in the train of Night" suggesting Satan and "Sure pledge of day" suggesting Christ. The large irony of *Paradise Lost* is that Satan, defeating his own purposes, does indeed participate in the universal praise of God. It may be that the physical symmetry of noon, the radiant sun of Christ and the eclipsed sun of Satan, positions *adversa* of the same genus opposite each other on the diameter of a single imaginative orbit. The sun at midday is Christ, the sun at midnight is Satan. Though adverse, both moments occur at "noon."

Noon also organizes the dramatic action of *Samson Agonistes*. In his note "Of that Sort of Dramatic Poem which is call'd Tragedy," Milton observed that his tragedy "after the ancient manner" follows the classical unity of time: "The circumscription of time wherein the whole Drama begins and ends, is according to ancient rule, and best example, within the space of 24 hours." The "circumscription" of *Samson Agonistes* begins with the "day-spring" of the festival day and ends just after the destruction of the temple at high noon of this day. But Milton creates, through metaphor, an imaginative time running counter to the measures of sequential dramatic time. In the opening soliloquy, Samson defines his blindness as if it were noontime, not morning: "O dark, dark, dark, amid the blaze of noon" (l. 80). His present a dark noon, Samson often characterizes his former life with the word "prime" and its Latin associations with morning. He can no longer apprehend light, "the prime work of God" (l. 70) and "prime decree" (l. 85). Dalila is, he says, the "prime cause" of the dark noon he suffers now (l. 236). She betrayed him in "her prime of love" (l. 388). In the middle of the drama, the Chorus laments the contrarious hand of God toward His champions:

> Yet toward these, thus dignifi'd, thou oft,
> Amidst their height of noon,
> Changest thy count'nance and thy hand, with no regard
> Of highest favors past
> From thee on them, or them to thee of service.
> [Ll. 682–86]

Here Samson's heroic past is metaphorically another noon. The passage suggests two associations with midday. It is, in the tradition of the *daemonum meridianum,* a time of danger and prideful indulgence. But noon is also the metaphorical time of "highest favors," a time of ripeness and maturity, a season for the fulfillment of supposedly destined actions. Destroying the temple at the genuine noon of dramatic time, Samson has in fact "fulfill'd" (l. 1661) the prophecies of his birth and "Fully reveng'd" himself (l. 1712). Noon is *kairos*—a moment of crisis at which one either rises or falls.[15]

Imaginatively, the drama of Samson's life moves from noon to noon. He begins, in this metaphorical astronomy, at noontime eclipse:

> O dark, dark, dark, amid the blaze of noon,
> Irrecoverably dark, total Eclipse
> Without all hope of day!
>
> [Ll. 80–82]

> The Sun to me is dark
> And silent as the Moon,
> When she deserts the night,
> Hid in her vacant interlunar cave.
>
> [Ll. 86–89]

But the "contrarious" ways of God ironically unite opposites. This noon of fallen darkness becomes, at the climax of the drama, a noon of risen day. The end is, as the Chorus says, "destruction at the utmost point" (l. 1514). Samson begins the drama associated with the satanic eclipse of *Paradise Lost*, but he ends in glorious splendor, his fiery virtue roused in the blaze of the noonday sun.

The famous passage of metaphorical transformation, defying the rigors of dramatic time, represents the switching of polarities:

> But he though blind of sight,
> Despis'd and thought extinguish't quite,
> With inward eyes illuminated
> His fiery virtue rous'd
> From under ashes into sudden flame,
> And as an ev'ning Dragon came,
> Assailant on the perched roosts,
> And nests in order rang'd
> Of tame villatic Fowl; but as an Eagle
> His cloudless thunder bolted on thir heads.
> So virtue giv'n for lost,
> Deprest, and overthrown, as seem'd
> Like that self-begott'n bird
> In the *Arabian* woods embost,
> That no second knows nor third,
> And lay erewhile a Holocaust,
> From out her ashy womb now teem'd,

[15] Kermode provides a brilliant introduction to *kairos* and *chronos* in renaissance literature (*Sense of an Ending*, pp. 46–64).

> Revives, reflourishes, then vigorous most
> When most unactive deem'd,
> And though her body die, her fame survives,
> A secular bird ages of lives.
>
> [Ll. 1687–1707]

I think these lines are the greatest Milton ever wrote. To experience their full power, one should begin with simple matters. We know from the Messenger's account that the action begins with Samson "bow'd" and "straining all his nerves," exerting all his strength from the very beginning. The whole action is continuous, swift, and perfect. But in the telling, this instantaneous flow of power is remarkably prolonged. The first description of the moment seems to be completed with the "Dragon" simile. Yet the conjunction "but" in line 1695 introduces an alternative simile, redescribing the same moment. Then the passage breaks at the mathematical center, line 1696, and the Phoenix simile loops back in time to describe the moment yet once more. What appears to be a break, however, is actually a linguistic and temporal expansion: the Phoenix simile is already present in "His fiery virtue rous'd / From under ashes into sudden flame," the past tense of which occurs before the dragon and the eagle have been introduced. The opening allusion to the Phoenix is fragmented and dispersed in the "Dragon" and the "Eagle," then reconstituted toward the end of the passage. It is as if the instant will not pass, the moment will not fall back into history. Though we experience the passage sequentially, we have the impression that everything happens and rehappens simultaneously. We are prisoners of an unnatural instant.

One function of the movement from "Dragon" to "Eagle" is to dramatize the meaning of "With inward eyes illuminated." The word "Dragon" derives from a Greek root meaning "one who sees," especially one whose piercing look commands attention.[16] Thus Samson, an "ev'ning Dragon," begins the passage between midnight and midday, darkness and light, blindness and seeing. "But they that wait upon the Lord shall renew their strength; they shall mount up with wings as eagles" (Isa. 40.31). As an "Eagle" Samson is able, according to renaissance folklore, to stare directly into the sun. And indeed, the eagle of this passage brings down

[16] Lee Sheridan Cox, "The 'Ev'ning Dragon' in *Samson Agonistes:* A Reappraisal," *MLN,* 76 (1961), 577–84. Noting the etymological pun, Cox proceeds to offer an excellent analysis of the sight imagery in the drama.

"cloudless" thunder. In *Areopagitica* Milton associated Samson with this legend about the eagle and also confused the sex of his "strong man" just as the female Phoenix ("her ashy womb") confuses the sex of Samson. The prose of *Areopagitica* is one convenient gloss on the metaphors of this climactic passage:

> it betok'ns us not degenerated, nor drooping to a fatall decay, but casting off the old and wrincl'd skin of corruption to outlive these pangs and wax young again, entring the glorious waies of Truth and prosperous virtue destin'd to become great and honourable in these latter ages. Methinks I see in my mind a noble and puissant Nation rousing herself like a strong man after sleep, and shaking her invincible locks: Methinks I see her as an Eagle muing her mighty youth, and kindling her undazl'd eyes at the full midday beam; purging and unscaling her long abused sight at the fountain itself of heav'nly radiance; while the whole noise of timorous and flocking birds, with those also that love the twilight, flutter about, amaz'd at what she means, and in their envious gabble would prognosticat a year of sects and schisms. [CE IV, 344] [17]

As the metamorphosis of the drama begins with a "Dragon," so this prose passage begins with the metaphor of a serpent "casting off the old and wrincl'd skin of corruption." But this metaphor is not cast off until the appearance of the eagle "unscaling her long abused sight." So Samson progresses from an "ev'ning Dragon" to an eagle, leaving the company of those birds in *Areopagitica* "that love the twilight." Become an eagle, the hero is illuminated with "undazl'd eyes at the full midday beam." Though he is "one who sees" at "ev'ning," Samson sees more perfectly at noon. The eagle can see noon itself and attacks those "tame villatic fowl" in love with the half-light of evening. As the noble nation is "rousing herself like a strong man after sleep," so the strong hero of *Samson Agonistes* is "rous'd" and awakened into activity. As the "timorous and flocking birds" of *Areopagitica* stand—in a splendid phrase—"amaz'd at what she means," so Samson has promised that this moment between the pillars "with amaze shall strike all who behold" (l. 1645). In a large body of work filled with suggestive correspondences, this one is perhaps the most remarkable. The ways of truth "in these latter ages" eventually appear as the ways of truth in former

[17] I am hardly the first to note this parallel. See, for example, Kenneth Burke, *A Rhetoric of Motives* (Berkeley: University of California Press, 1967), pp. 3–5.

ages. Those "timorous and flocking birds" who failed to understand the English destiny eventually appear as the "tame villatic fowl" who oppose the Hebrew destiny. The prophetic vision of *Areopagitica* becomes the climactic action of *Samson Agonistes*—but the providential agent is no longer an entire people. In the second avatar God places His strength in the one just man. The English nation of 1644, likened to a strong man with "invincible locks," metamorphoses into the solitary Samson trying to free the nation that betrayed him to their common enemies. In 1644 the inspired pamphleteer thought he saw a vision of impending triumph for his awakened country. That prophetic optimism ultimately wore the guise of tragedy. In *Samson Agonistes* only one man sees at noon.

But the progression toward better seeing is simultaneous with another and more important movement. The mysterious "ev'ning Dragon" cannot be explained as simply an etymological pun. Critics have assumed that the "Dragon" is, in this context of many birds, a large and bulky serpent with relatively short wings. The essential contrast, then, is between the fierce monster and the "tame villatic fowl" that he assails. This rather marginal bird then becomes an "Eagle" capable of more soaring flight. However, there is another context here which suggests that we should not be thinking primarily of a reptilian dragon. In the earlier description of this divine violence, the comparisons progress from an earthquake to a storm. The roof falls "with burst of thunder / Upon the heads of all who sat beneath" (ll. 1651–52). This storm reappears in the great Semichorus, for after Samson "came" as an "ev'ning Dragon," he "as an Eagle / His cloudless thunder bolted on thir heads." In renaissance meteorology, a comet often presaged the coming of a storm.[18] So with this passage. The "ev'ning Dragon" is almost surely the *draco volans* or "fire-drake," a comet seen often over the Thames.[19] Notice the grammar here:

[18] Svendson, pp. 86ff.

[19] William Fulke discusses the *draco volans* in *A Goodly Gallery* (1563), reprinted in *The Frame of Order*, ed. James Winney (London: Allen and Unwin, 1957), pp. 167–68. There is a reproduction of a renaissance woodcut depicting the *draco volans* in Svendsen, p. 89; see also Cirillo, pp. 390–91. Neither critic relates the "ev'ning Dragon" to the renaissance fire-bird. At long last this old puzzle text has been clarified by Edward W. Tayler in "Milton's Firedrake," *Milton Quarterly*, 6, No. 3 (1972), 7–10. He uncrossed the crucial crux, and my own discussion is fully in his debt.

His fiery virtue rous'd
From under ashes into sudden flame,
And as an ev'ning Dragon came. . . .
[Ll. 1690–92]

The tenor of this vehicle is "into sudden flame"—"as an ev'ning Dragon" is a simile about the unexpected appearance of the "fiery virtue." So Samson, a *draco volans*, flames suddenly as the firebird which portends the storm "bolted" down by the eagle. The warning and the fact, the prophecy and the fulfillment occur at virtually the same time in this contracted history of divine bad weather. As the classical bird of Jove, the eagle can deliver the lightning of the Thunderer without being harmed by this fierce fire.[20] In *Paradise Lost* the eagle appears during an eclipse as the first carnivorous hunter:

Nature first gave Signs, imprest
On Bird, Beast, Air, Air suddenly eclips'd
After short blush of Morn; nigh in her sight
The Bird of *Jove,* stoopt from his aery tow'r,
Two Birds of gayest plume before him drove. . . .
[XI.182–86]

When combined, the fiery comet and the bird immune to meteorological fire comprise the Phoenix, that "self-begott'n bird" risen newborn from its own flame. This mysterious bird seems, before its revival, "In the *Arabian* woods embost." The word "embost" applies to the hunted animal driven into hiding. But Samson, reborn an eagle, changes from hunted to hunter and swoops down upon his prey bearing the divine fire. He is the hunter who traps his victims by pretending to be trapped himself; the calm before the storm is the cunning of heaven. From "ev'ning Dragon" to "Eagle," the emblems

[20] See Svendsen, p. 100. We retain this classical notion in the emblematic eagle of the United States often reproduced on military posters and patriotic letterheads.

The eagle of *Areopagitica* appears as an emblem of resurrection, another association clarified and perfected by the final bird of the passage in *Samson,* the Phoenix. Augustine, in *Expositions on the Psalms* (*NPNF,* VIII, 505–6), tells how an aged eagle cannot open his mouth because his beak curls over. Thus he breaks this obstacle on the "rock"—on Jesus. Augustine concludes: "And indeed the youth of the eagle is restored, but not into immortality, for a similitude hath been given, as far as it could be drawn from a thing mortal to signify a thing immortal" (p. 506). Insofar as its regeneration lessens the difference between symbol and meaning, the Phoenix is a more exact emblem of immortality.

The biblical eagle may also be found in Jer. 48.40, 49.22, and Hab. 1.8.

progress toward better seeing and also toward the assailant storm of God.

Finally, as the Phoenix, Samson internalizes and embodies the sun. His heroic action synchronizes metaphorical time with real time, metaphorical astronomy with real astronomy. The Phoenix, ancient symbol of the sun, traditionally revives at noon.[21] In *Paradise Lost,* Raphael arrives in the garden at high noon and appears to the Edenic birds as a Phoenix "gaz'd by all":

> till within soar
> Of Tow'ring Eagles, to all the Fowls he seems
> A Phoenix, gaz'd by all, as that sole Bird
> When to enshrine his reliques in the Sun's
> Bright temple, to *Egyptian Thebes* he flies.
> [V.270–74]

Like the Phoenix, Raphael draws the gaze of all, and this command of attention helps to explain why the Phoenix-like Samson is appropriately an etymological "Dragon" as well. Even the birds of Jove pay attention. Associated with Egypt in *Paradise Lost* and the *"Arabian* woods" in *Samson Agonistes,* the Phoenix is an eastern bird. Raphael arrives from the east, and an entranced Adam speaks of his arrival as the creation of a new temporal measure:

> Haste hither Eve, and worth thy sight behold
> Eastward among those Trees, what glorious shape
> Comes this way moving; seems another Morn
> Ris'n on mid-morn. . . .
> [V.308–11]

The bright angel flies from the east as if another sun. But the earlier comparison between Raphael and the Phoenix compresses the two suns into one symbol. Flaring suddenly, rising "on mid-noon," the mythical eastern bird "dawns" at noon. Similarly, the hero of *Samson Agonistes* "Revives, reflourishes" in his most perfect form. Acting amid the blaze of noon, "His fiery virtue rous'd," the awakened Samson flames suddenly as an emblem of the noontime sun itself. He is in a

[21] Cirillo, pp. 388–90. On the Phoenix in *Paradise Lost,* see also Geoffrey Hartman, "Adam on the Grass with Balsamum," ELH, 36 (1970), 180–92. Roger Wilkenfield treats the Phoenix of *Samson* in "Act and Emblem: The Conclusion of *Samson Agonistes,"* ELH, 32 (1965), 160–68. Sir Thomas Browne summarizes many of the legends about this bird in his *Pseudodoxia Epidemica,* in *The Works of Sir Thomas Browne,* ed. Geoffrey Keynes (Chicago: University of Chicago Press, 1964), II, 191–97.

moment reborn complete, like a sun rising at once to the center of the sky. He dawns at noon, as noon.

When a narrated action begins with a reference to "ev'ning," we naturally expect the temporal references to proceed in the direction of night. But here is a miracle. At the noontime climax of *Samson Agonistes,* the metaphorical day runs backwards from evening to dawn. As the old Phoenix "dies" into youth, the natural sequence of time reverses itself. The passage progressively recreates the sun, resurrecting Samson from the satanic eclipse at which he began the play. He begins in a twilight "ev'ning" state between midday and midnight and ends at the dawning height of noon:

> O dark, dark, dark, amid the blaze of noon,
> Irrecoverably dark, total Eclipse
> Without all hope of day!
>
> [Ll. 80–82]

In light of the great Semichorus, these words acquire an astounding irony. Though Samson cannot know what he means, the reader stands amazed at what he means. The dawning noon between the pillars does in fact eclipse this inactive, blind, bound, depressed Samson. As in *Paradise Lost,* the eagle hunts his prey during an eclipse. Samson, in his moment of darkest despair, ironically defines his noontime height of glory. During that last moment, Samson, like the metaphorical day and like the Phoenix, instantaneously recovers his youth:

> Yet toward these, thus dignifi'd, thou oft,
> Amidst their height of noon,
> Changest thy count'nance and thy hand, with no regard
> Of highest favors past
> From thee on them, or them to thee of service.
>
> [Ll. 682–86]

Imaginatively, the life of Samson returns to the "height of noon" and "highest favors" from which he fell. He has moved forward only to rediscover his past. From the high noon of his fall, to the dark noon of his eclipse, to the dawning noon of his rebirth, Samson steers his zenith.

With the full appearance of the anticipated Phoenix, the passage, recapitulating the movement of the entire drama, arrives at paradox. As Samson "revives," he also dies. He is reborn in an ashy womb which is, if you will, both anal and vaginal. The verb "rous'd" in line 190 may be either active or passive, for at this point there is no longer any difference between the will of Samson and the will of God. "Dire necessity" is inseparable from "my own accord," and the champion acts both freely and obediently. Retroactively from this moment, the word "or" in *Samson Agonistes* acquires the new meaning of "and."[22] Alternatives collapse into harmony. The two pillars Samson stands between and topples are virtually emblematic of the various either-or alternatives posed in the drama. Manoa distinguishes between self-preservation and suicide (ll. 503–20), yet Samson, like the Phoenix, is at once "self-begott'n" (l. 1699) and "self-killed" (l. 1664). The Chorus distinguishes between the military "winged expedition" of active heroes and the inner fortitude of patient saints (ll. 1271–91). "Either of these is in thy lot," the Chorus concludes (l. 1292). But the Phoenix is "vigorous most" when "most unactive." Champion and saint, Samson exemplifies both patience and activity during his "winged expedition." "Living or dying," the Chorus declares (l. 1661), Samson has fulfilled the promises at his birth. The Phoenix makes these alternatives compatible.

The radical irony of the play is that Samson, in noontime eclipse, is also steering his height of noon. His captivity, his blindness, his humiliation result in his triumph. The "guiding hand" of the first line becomes the hand of the Philistine officer and the hand of God, the two acting inseparably as one. Even the wiles of Dalila move in strange harmony with the unsearchable ways of providence. Samson complains that his nature is "In all her functions weary of herself" (l. 596). This tired, feminine nature foreshadows the Phoenix. "Deprest," the mysterious bird revives to the height of creative and destructive vigor. Despair is the condition of heroic glory. Despair leads to repair. The three transformations at noontime suggest the source of these ironies. The *draco volans* adumbrates the eagle with fire in its talons, and the eagle unharmed in this fire adumbrates the Phoenix. As the linguistic past contains the linguistic future, so the future retains the past. The seeing eagle with his "cloudless thunder" absorbs the seeing fire-dragon, and both are absorbed in the compressed symbolism of "that self-begott'n bird."

Time is the source of irony in *Samson Agonistes*. When the

[22] Joseph Summers, "The Movements of the Drama," in *The Lyric and Dramatic Milton*, ed. Summers (New York: Columbia University Press, 1965), pp. 157–60.

characters divide human actions into contrasting alternatives, they assume that time flows in the familiar sequence. One man cannot be both a military champion and a meditative saint, though one man could be first a champion and then a saint. Because instants follow instants and measure motions that follow motions, a man must choose to perform one action at a time. He is "unactive" at one moment and "vigorous" at another. He "despairs" at one moment and "repairs" at another. In sequential time, alternatives appear mutually exclusive. But as the real day stands poised at noon, the metaphorical day begins at evening and ends at dawn. In his *Didascalicon,* Hugh of St. Victor explained why the study of the Bible must begin with the New Testament:

> The same order of books is not to be kept in historical and allegorical study. History follows the order of time; to allegory belongs more the order of knowledge, because . . . learning ought to take its beginning not from obscure but from clear things, and from things which are better known. The consequence of this is that the New Testament, in which the evident truth is preached, is, in this study, placed before the Old, in which the same truth is announced in a hidden manner, shrouded in figures. It is the same truth in both places, but hidden there, open here, promised there, shown here.[23]

The prophetic books of the Old Testament were sealed because they could not be understood until the coming of Christ, who broke open the seals. The student of the Bible must read backwards in order to read forwards, measuring time from new to old in order to comprehend the sequence of history from old to new. Similarly, the reader of *Samson Agonistes* must apprehend the drama in both *ordo temporis* and reversed *ordo cognitionis.* After the end, the beginning is clear. If a given stretch of time is measured simultaneously from past to future and from future to past, the two measures inevitably meet at a moment in the center and fill that moment with the knowledge of all given time. Noon is dense with morning and evening. The reader of *Samson Agonistes* is offered the perspective of simultaneity—the vision of prophecy. We are not unduly surprised that the eagle absorbs the dragon, that the past of Samson somehow explains and makes possible his present. Samson rises only because he fell to Dalila. It is the familiar paradox of the fortunate fall. But measure the

[23] *Didascalicon* VI.6, trans. Jerome Taylor (New York: Columbia University Press, 1961), p. 145.

day from evening to morning as well: the dragon contains the eagle, and the man Samson will be somehow explains the man Samson is. At the "day-spring" of sequential dramatic time he lolls in obscure eclipse; at the dawn of reversed narrative time he stands divulged at the height of noon. Measuring dramatic time backwards, as the great passage suggests we should, Samson in eclipse was already at his noon, his future canceling and balancing his past. The eclipse amid the blazing noon and the height of blazing noon assume each other and cannot occur without each other. They happen, in imaginative time, at a single moment.

The treatment of noon in *Samson Agonistes* questions the completeness of previous explanations of Miltonic noon. The Great Year of Plato would not seem of much interest to readers of this drama, and the *daemonio meridiano* of only limited interest. Samson has some devilish characteristics, I suppose, and however we wish to interpret the "ev'ning Dragon," some degree of Satanic association would appear unavoidable. At least once Samson ironically imitates Satan and Comus, those inveterate tempters: "The way to know were not to see but taste," he tells Harapha (l. 1091). But we cannot damn him for a jest. The only passage that evokes the tradition of noontime temptation is the Choral speech about favors withdrawn at noon. They refer in this speech to an earlier statement about the wheel of fortune:

> O mirror of our fickle state,
> Since man on earth unparallel'd!
> The rarer thy example stands,
> By how much from the top of wondrous glory,
> Strongest of mortal men,
> To lowest pitch of abject fortune thou art fall'n.
> [Ll. 164–69]

Thus Samson falls from his first "height of noon." The drama, though honoring the metaphor, repudiates this crude *De casibus* moralizing. The Chorus separates rising from falling, whereas the life of Samson finally unites them in simultaneity. The Chorus measures time in one direction only. What of the awakened noon of the Phoenix?

The use of noon as a structural and thematic principle in *Samson Agonistes* comprehends the Great Year, the noontime devil, and a traditional association vastly more available than either of these. Following the New Testament, renaissance divines often spoke of biblical history as a single metaphorical day. In the usual formulation, Christ is the *sol justitiae* of Mal. 4.2 whose gospel light begins a new day for Christian man. "I am the light of the world," Christ said. Hence the life of Christ often appeared in religious writing as a biblical "dawn" or "sunrise." The adjective "dark" was regularly applied to Old Testament events in contrast to the "light" of New Testament events. Figures under the old dispensation, wrote William Tyndale, have only "a starlight of Christ," although some few enjoy "the light of broad day, a little before the sun-rising." [24] The metaphor assumes the Hebraic definition of "day" found in Genesis, where the evening and the morning compose the days of the Creation. Donne preached that the Bible, as the full compass of the Word, takes the form of one Hebraic day: "God's word . . . began in Moses, in darkness, in the *Chaos:* and it ends in Saint John, in clearnesse, in a Revelation. Here is the compass of all time, as time was distributed in the Creation, *Vespere* & *Mane;* darknesse, and then light: the Evening and the Morning made the Day; Mystery and Manifestation made the Text." [25] The fixed time between Creation and Apocalypse repeats in macrocosm the day between evening and morning. For English Christians, the easy possibilities of the words "sun" and "Son" made the metaphor all the more alluring. This pun, wrote the ecstatic Herbert, is the central glory of the English language.[26] The metaphor of the biblical day provided ready wit for numerous seventeenth-century poets. It gave imaginative coherence to a poem like Vaughan's "Cock-Crowing"—prophets, patriarchs, and preachers herald the gospel dawn.[27] The single

[24] *The Work of William Tyndale,* ed. Genase Duffield (Philadelphia: Fortress Press, 1965), p. 60. Tyndale remarks that some figures "express Christ, and the circumstances and virtue of his death so plainly, as if we should play his passion on a scaffold, or in a stage play" (p. 60). Samson acts in this drama.

The metaphor of the biblical day originated in the New Testament: "it is high time to awake out of sleep: for now is our salvation nearer than we believed. The night is far spent, the day is at hand: let us therefore cast off the works of darkness, and let us put on the armour of light" (Rom. 13.11–12). "Rous'd," Samson awakens "out of sleep" and, in moving from evening dragon to noontime eagle, casts off "the works of darkness." Cf. Ezek. 30.2–3; Isa. 49.8; John 8.56; 2 Cor. 6.2; 2 Peter 1.19, 3.12.

[25] *Sermons,* III, 206. Augustine associated "twilight" with knowledge of the creatures and "dawn" with knowledge of the creator (*City of God* XI.vii). Angels, however, enjoy a "noonday knowledge" of God (XI.xxix).

[26] See "The Sonne" in *Works,* pp. 167–68.

[27] Don Cameron Allen, in "Vaughan's 'Cock-Crowing' and the Tradition," *ELH,* 21 (1954), 94–106, cites a great deal of material bearing on the metaphor of the biblical day.

biblical day subsumed in evening the history of Israel and in morning the history of the Christian church. Many days formed one day.

Calvin, who was particularly fond of this metaphor, traced the simultaneous progress of the one day and the many days:

> The Lord held to this orderly plan in administering the covenant of his mercy: as the day of full revelation approached with the passing of time, the more he increased each day the brightness of his manifestation. Accordingly, at the beginning when the first promise of salvation was given to Adam it glowed like a feeble spark. Then, as it was added to, the light grew in fullness, breaking forth increasingly and shedding its radiance more widely. At last—when all the clouds were dispersed—Christ, the Sun of Righteousness, fully illumined the whole earth.[28]

But the metaphor has shifted. Here the beginning of time, not the gospel birth, appears (seemingly) as the first gleam of biblical dawn and the incarnation of Christ, who "fully illumined," as a biblical noon. Calvin, however, adapted the metaphor to eternity as well as time. In eternity, Christ always shines at full intensity; the biblical day in this passage is actually the slow withdrawal of "all the clouds" from the "Sun of Righteousness" ever at its zenith. The metaphorical sun does not progress through history, submitting to the measures of temporal motion. The clouds move, the sun is unveiled. Not a progress from dawn to noon, the biblical day is a continuous revelation of a single instant. Still, the movement from dawn to noon competed with the movement from evening to morning as the correct shape of the biblical day. The same writer might use both formulations. Donne, who wrote of "*Vespere* & *Mane*," also defined Christians as "the children of the day, for thou hast shined in as full a noon upon us as upon the Thessalonians." [29]

Calvin often referred to the gospel noon. "Now therefore,

[28] *Institutes* II.x.20. See also Tyndale, p. 59: "For all that were before Christ were in the infancy and childhood of the world, and saw that sun, which we see openly, but through a cloud, and had but feeble and weak imaginations of Christ, as children have of men's deeds, a few prophets except, which yet described him unto others in sacrifices and ceremonies, likenesses, riddles, proverbs, and dark and strange speaking, until the full age were come, that God would show him openly unto the whole world, and deliver them from their shadows and cloud-light, and the heathen out of their dread sleep of stark blind ignorance." Like Calvin, Tyndale was speaking of a stationary sun seen by certain Israelites through the moving clouds of time. The "cloud-light," of course, alludes to the appearance of God in Exod. 16.10, 19.19, 24.15–16, 34.5, etc.

[29] *Devotions upon Emergent Occasions* (Ann Arbor: University of Michigan Press), p. 92.

since Christ, the Sun of Righteousness, has shone, while before there was only dim light, we have the perfect radiance of divine truth, like the wonted brilliance of noonday."[30] Figures in the Old Testament cannot behold "the fullness" of light "as at noontime."[31] In the following passage, Calvin presented both formulations as interchangeable alternatives: "Christ calls himself the light of the world. Not that the fathers wandered like blind men in a mist, but that they had to be content with the light of the early dawn or with the moon and stars. We know how obscure the teaching of the Law was, so that it is truly called a 'shadow.' But when the heavens were finally opened by the gospel, then indeed did the sun rise; and when the risen sun gives light the full day comes."[32] When "the risen sun gives light," immediately "the full day comes." Christ dawns at noon. Depending on whether the gospel birth is a noon or a dawn, the Old Testament light is either "the light of early dawn" or "the moon and stars." Metaphorically, Christ must be the noon as well as the dawn of biblical day, because at noontime there are no shadows: when Christ rises in history, His full radiance dispels the typological "shadows" or *umbrae* of the Old Testament forenoon. The dawning noon of the gospels, then, implies the fulfillment of the shadowy types.

In *Samson Agonistes* the noontime astronomy defines a typological relationship. The heroic action contracts history into one dense moment. Like the long biblical day, Samson begins at "ev'ning," a "Dragon" harboring connections with both fallen darkness and Christian light. Then an eagle, he sees through all those clouds to the eternal "cloudless" face of noon. He sees through time. Rising at last in the image of a resurrected Phoenix, he adumbrates the dawning noon of the gospel. For an instant, Samson leaps out of the slow sequential day of biblical history, beginning to do what cannot yet be done. The hero stands poised at noon between Hebrew and Christian, anticipation and fulfillment, shadow and light. The great passage, beginning with a symbol of Satan and ending with a symbol of Christ, establishes a definitive alignment between type and anti-type.

So we come at last to the vexed question of Samson and Christ. Though the typological relationship argued by Krouse, Madsen, and others certainly exists, its correct formulation

[30] *Institutes* IV.viii.7. [31] *Commentaries,* pp. 94–95. [32] *Ibid.,* p. 144.

is, in part, a matter of emphasis and critical tact.[33] Those who dissent from this interpretation and argue that *Samson* must be read as a historical drama, Hebrew or Greek but definitely not Christian, use the word "historical" in a way which excludes the possible intentions of the author.[34] Much of the ironic comedy of *Paradise Regained* derives from the inability of Satan to understand how waiting is a part of acting, how the present contains the future, how time is complicated by eternal providence.[35] In the Bible an angel prophesies that Samson will "begin to deliver Israel out of the hand of the Philistines" (Judg. 13.5). But in *Samson Agonistes* the hero declares,

> Promise was that I
> Should Israel from Philistian yoke deliver. . . .
> [Ll. 38–39]

If we understand history as simply a temporal sequence, Samson does not "deliver" Israel when he pulls down the Philistine temple. But history is typological. Leaving with the Philistine officer, Samson cannot be certain whether this day will be "The last of me or no" (l. 1426). It is indeed the last of him—but not the last of him, for the word "or" comes to mean "and." The shadow of his act moves out of history, free from the yoke of sequential time, to be fulfilled in the full radiance of Christ.

Resistance of this typological interpretation has dwindled in recent years, overwhelmed by the persistent expression of scholarly certitude. Resistance, however, is not without virtue. Milton developed the Phoenix simile as if to discourage the easy identification of Samson and Christ. The bird "no second knows nor third." And in what sense is Christ "secular" for

[33] Krouse (esp. pp. 51–52) presented the case initially. Madsen, in "From Shadowy Types to Truth," *The Lyric and Dramatic Milton*, ed. Summers, pp. 95–114, accepts this view with many qualifications. These men are enemies in the same camp: differences aside, they agree that Milton wishes his reader to consider a relationship between his hero and Christ. Their disagreement, as Madsen realizes, is over the nature of typology.

[34] Sir Richard Jebb argued for the "Hebraic spirit" of the drama in "*Samson Agonistes* and the Hellenic Drama," *PBA* (1907–8), pp. 341–48, and was answered by W. R. Parker, *Milton's Debt to Greek Tragedy in* Samson Agonistes (Baltimore: Johns Hopkins Press, 1937). Parker maintained that the drama has a "Greek spirit." Roy Daniells, in *Milton, Mannerism and Baroque* (Toronto: University of Toronto Press, 1963), pp. 213–16, tries to synthesize the two views.

[35] See Frye, "Typology of *Paradise Regained*."

"ages of lives"? The word "secular," apart from its connection with *saeculo* and the centennial rebirth of the Phoenix, forbids any simplistic understanding of the mythical bird as an emblem for Christ. It will not suffice to catalogue hundreds of examples in which the Phoenix represents the resurrection of Christ. Nor can a critic prove that Samson-Christ typology, by virtue of its popularity in the seventeenth century, informs *Samson Agonistes*. Moreover, Samson quits himself "Like Samson" (l. 1710). The whole artistry of the play is in jeopardy here. If we read "Like Samson" as the equivalent of "Like Christ," we annihilate the historical and dramatic identity of the hero. The drama, no longer dynamic typology, freezes into static allegory: the central tradition of typological exegesis asserted the literal and historical existence of the types.[36] At no point can the name "Christ" replace, equal for equal, the name "Samson." Otherwise we cheapen the suffering and the triumph of the hero by denying him individuality and, literally, distinction. We trivialize the magnificent lines, "All is best, though we oft doubt. . . ." *Samson Agonistes* tries the limits of human doubt. Israel is fallen, captive, its destined deliverer in chains; by testing the strength of Samson, the drama tests the truthfulness of God. If "Samson" equals "Christ," this deep searching doubt is insignificant and insubstantial. The tragic suffering is reduced to ignorance. "God of our Fathers, what is man!" The line has no force at all, no power to move, if the man is Christ. Inevitably, the reader of an allegorical *Samson* will condescend to characters who suffer only because they do not understand the allegory.

The final glorious deed of Samson typifies both the Sacrifice of Christ, primarily an act of love, and the Last Judgment, primarily an act of vengeance. Samson the tragic actor plays the "pathos" or "Passion" of Christ. As the angel foretold, he offers himself as a sacrifice, a holocaust, to deliver Israel. But this similarity reveals a difference, for Christ offers Himself as a sacrifice to deliver all men from the metaphorical yoke of death, not the actual yoke of bondage. No sense of universal love either warms or sentimentalizes this nationalistic play. The grammar of the last passage conveys the separation as well as the identity of type and antitype. The singular "Champion," referring to Samson alone, yields to

[36] The orthodox conception of typology descends from Tertullian. See Auerbach, "Figura," in *Six Scenes from the Drama of European Literature*, pp. 29–37.

the plural "His servants," a form which includes in one communal name both Samson and the other unnamed servants before and after him. Protecting the integrity of his singular hero while grouping him with other heroes, Milton puns in the final line. The drama, expending "all passion," rehearses the "Passion" of the gospels. Between the pillars Samson first assumes the posture and attitude of the Crucifixion:

> He unsuspicious led him; which when *Samson*
> Felt in his arms, with head a while inclin'd,
> And eyes fast fix'd he stood, as one who pray'd,
> Or some great matter in his mind revolv'd.
> [Ll. 1635–38]

His head, bowed in weary despair through most of the drama, bows down again. But now Samson humbles himself voluntarily. Full of pride and strength, he chooses to incline before his God. This gesture foreshadowing the Crucifixion—arms spread, head bowed in voluntary humility—yields immediately to the "head erect" of Samson triumphant, a military deliverer. Humility passes to revenge, passivity to action. The hero of this tragedy more perfectly typifies Judgment than Sacrifice and glorifies himself more through wrath than love.[37] In "Lycidas," St. Peter bears two keys to the gate of heaven: "The Golden opes, the Iron shuts amain." Samson is closer to the iron judgment of the "dread voice" than to the golden love and "dear might of him that walk'd the waves."

The drama is fulfilled in hatred. Samson revives by exercising zealous contempt for Dalila and Harapha. He becomes impervious to the concerns of his father and his friends. Through most of the drama, his two characteristic emotions are lordly guilt and righteous scorn. A Nazarite, a man apart, he becomes for a time absolutely inviolable. When Dalila asks if she may "touch" his hand (l. 951), he threatens to tear her to pieces joint by joint—a moment which Northrop Frye rightly calls "one of the most terrible passages of all tragic drama." [38] When he consents to take the hand of the Philistine officer, Samson begins to speak with a new and special irony. His parting words to the Chorus and his address to the

[37] Barbara Lewalski also emphasizes the apocalyptic typology in "*Samson Agonistes* and the 'Tragedy' of the Apocalypse," *PMLA*, 85 (1970), 1050–62. However, there is precious little in the text to support her connections between Samson and the church, Dalila and the Great Whore of Babylon, Harapha and Antichrist.

[38] *Anatomy of Criticism*, p. 223.

Philistine assembly are designed in such a way that the human audiences will misunderstand and only the divine audience fully understand. He excludes himself from humanity. Sudden, irresistible, terrible, the rousing motions of God drive him beyond the world we know. Anne Ferry writes of this final Samson: "He has passed beyond the reach of all social and political relationships—with parent or wife, with friends, countrymen or enemies—to become now utterly 'separate to God.' . . . It is like a strange transformation into another order of being, no longer 'mutable,' as if he passed into the living body of God."[39] Progressively shedding all human connection, Samson arrives at his moment of calculated violence. The final action, though at once a sacrifice and a judgment, more powerfully evokes the military Christ of *Paradise Lost* and the warrior Zeal of *The Reason of Church Government*—the flashing chariot, the trampling wheels, the bruised and broken heads of the adversaries, the charioteer with fierce arresting eyes and head erect. As they hear the sound of the collapsing temple, Manoa and the Chorus unconsciously direct the reader to the proper typological fulfillment:

> *Manoa.* I know your friendly minds and—O what noise!
> Mercy of Heav'n! what hideous noise was that?
> Horribly loud, unlike the former shout.
> *Chorus.* Noise call you it or universal groan
> As if the whole inhabitation perish'd?
> Blood, death, and deathful deeds are in that noise,
> Ruin, destruction at the utmost point.
>
> [Ll. 1508–14]

The phrase "As if the whole inhabitation perish'd" explicitly identifies this catastrophe as a type of the Apocalypse. It is a time for men to implore the mercy of heaven. The "universal groan" also recalls the "wound" of the Fall in *Paradise Lost,* nature "sighing through all her Works" (IX.782–84).

The Fall, as Milton recognized early in his career, was the first event in human history to assume the form of tragedy. In the invocation to Book IX of *Paradise Lost,* the narrator announces that his epic must now become a tragedy:

> I now must change
> These Notes to Tragic; foul distrust, and breach
> Disloyal on the part of Man, revolt,

[39] *Milton and the Miltonic Dryden* (Cambridge: Harvard University Press, 1968), pp. 173–74.

And disobedience: On the part of Heav'n
Now alienated, distance and distaste,
Anger and just rebuke, and judgment giv'n,
That brought into this World a world of woe. . . .
[IX.5–11]

The tragic climax of *Samson Agonistes* recapitulates the tragic climax of *Paradise Lost,* except that Samson, having imitated our first disobedience, also takes "the part of Heav'n." A chosen man delivers the "Anger and just rebuke, and judgment giv'n." Because of his success, the "world of woe" that accompanies the tragedy of the Fall becomes "nothing but well and fair":

Nothing is here for tears, nothing to wail
Or knock the breast, no weakness, no contempt,
Dispraise, or blame, nothing but well and fair,
And what may quiet us in a death so noble.
[Ll. 1721–24]

Samson, like Heaven in *Paradise Lost,* becomes "alienated" in "distance and distaste"—he must remove himself from humanity so that he may deliver his "just rebuke." Once he has executed this judgment, other men take comfort in the fact that he, unlike Adam, has acted his tragic part in accord with God.

If the Fall was the first tragedy, the Apocalypse will be the last. As early as 1641, in *The Reason of Church Government,* Milton accepted the views of David Paraeus: the Christian tragedian could imitate St. John as well as Sophocles. Quaint to a modern reader, the precedent of Revelation justified the classical genre of tragic drama. This notion reappears in the preface to *Samson Agonistes:* "Paraeus, commenting on the *Revelation,* divides the whole Book as a Tragedy, into Acts distinguisht each by a Chorus of Heavenly Harpings and Song between." At the apocalyptic tragedy, the deliverance of just rebuke will be once again "the part of Heav'n." As Christ brings down the judgment in *Paradise Lost,* so he will preside over the Last Judgment, when in the words of the Nativity Ode, "The dreadful Judge in middle Air shall spread his throne" (l. 164). The tragedy of Samson stands between the two tragedies which circumscribe human history, its hero performing the part assigned to Christ at the Fall and the Apocalypse. After their catastrophe, Adam and Eve suffer, weep, and cannot rest. The catastrophe of *Samson Agonistes* divides the human actors into woeful sufferers and becalmed servants. As angels sing hallelujahs to the sound of harps, the final catastrophe will make this division both perfect and eternal, the woeful forever distinguished from the peaceful. Samson, then, begins to divide the children of Adam, and his tragedy poses one pair of alternatives that can never collapse into harmony:

> for God
> Nothing more certain, will not long defer
> To vindicate the glory of his name
> Against all competition, nor will long
> Endure it, doubtful whether God be Lord,
> Or *Dagon.*
>
> [Ll. 473–78]

This "Or" cannot be compromised. What the catastrophe of *Samson* divides, the Apocalypse will clarify once and for all.

The drama encompasses a single day. This "circumscription" of a human day connects typologically with the biblical "day of the Lord," foreshadowing the dreadful day of judgment at the end of time.[40] Clement of Alexandria commented on the word "today" in Heb. 3.13: "And this 'today' is extended day by day, so long as the word 'today' exists. Both the 'today' and the teaching continues until the consummation of all things; and then the true 'today,' the unending day of God, reaches on throughout the ages. Let us, then, ever listen to the voice of the divine Word. For 'today' is an image of the everlasting age, and the day is a symbol of light, and the light of men is the Word, through whom we gaze upon God." [41] The day of *Samson Agonistes* typifies "the consummation of all things" and is therefore an image of the true eternal day; the mortal day of dramatic time will run into "the unending day of God." In his *Confessions,* St. Augustine pondered the difference between time and eternity: "Thy yeeres neyther goe nor come; whereas these yeeres of ours, doe both goe and come, that (in their order) they may all come. Thy yeeres are in a standing all at once, because they are still at a stay: nor are those that goe, thrust out by those that *come,* for that they passe not away at all; but these of ours shall all bee, even when they shall not all be. Thy yeeres are one day; and thy day, is not *everyday,* but *today:* seeing thy *To day* gives

[40] See Isa. 11.13; Joel 2.31; Zeph. 1.14; Rev. 6.17.
[41] *Exhortation to the Greeks,* in *Clement,* p. 189.

not place unto *To morrowe,* nor comes in place of *yesterday.* Thy *To day* is Eternity."[42] To observe the classical unity of time, the Christian Milton circumscribed a day which is itself circumscribed by the eternal "To day" of God. As Samson moves through the metaphorical day that brackets biblical history, changing from an "ev'ning Dragon" to a rising Phoenix, he also adumbrates the eternal day that brackets this metaphorical day. Precisely at noon, the small circle of time within the drama becomes concentric with both the circle of history and the circle of eternity. This Christian tragedian observes the classical unity of time while also imitating the divine unity of time.

Such matters are not easily described in a temporal language which assumes its own proportions, arranging time into the familiar sequence of past, present, and future. I attempt this formulation because the complexities of time may serve to indicate the artistic difficulties that Milton confronted in the writing of *Samson Agonistes.* At the climax of his play, the dramatist clearly tried to escape from the temporal bonds of his chosen form. The clock-time of dramatic representation runs from "day-spring" to noon, then yields to a narrative time from "Sunrise" to noon. Depicting the moment between the pillars, the Semichorus shapes narrative time to the contours of prophetic vision. Of course they cannot apprehend what they have implied. At mysterious noon, when the classical unity of time is made to accommodate a Christian vision, the reader alone escapes from temporal sequence and comes to rest in prophecy. For its Christian audience, if not for its Hebrew characters, the encircled day of *Samson Agonistes* threatens to dissolve into the expanse of sacred history which, insofar as Samson typifies the Christ of the Last Judgment, threatens itself to dissolve into eternity—into eternity where consolation is complete and judgment irrevocable. Exactly how becalmed are we to be at this "fair dismission"? Milton resisted similar problems of typological diffusion in other works, recalling the audience of the Nativity Ode, with some hesitation and evident regret, from blissful contemplation of the Last Judgment to the moment distinctly at hand ("But wisest Fate says no") and concluding *Paradise Regained* with the return of Christ, just after another foreshadowing of the Last Judgment, to the privacy of his temporal existence. While

[42] Trans. William Watts (London, 1631), pp. 753–54.

consoling readers with the steady typological march toward shadowless joy, he also reminds them of the dark times still to be endured with the hard virtues of patience and fortitude: his poems often end by reaffirming the necessary labors of history. Here the artistic problem was to protect his hero from complete dissolution in Christ, his plot from complete dissolution in divine providence, his dramatic time from complete dissolution in static eternity. He had to avoid allegorical equations while still establishing connections between these events and eternal events. All the many "unconscious" allusions to the Crucifixion and Apocalypse, the glorious metamorphosis from dragon to eagle to Phoenix, push against the perimeter of the circumscribed human day. The historical integrity of the drama almost, but not quite, explodes. Milton was entirely successful in mediating between the sequence of history and the simultaneity of eternity. The issue of this mediation is a tragedy animate with contrary yet harmonious passions.

Though foreshadowing moments beyond its temporal frame, the drama contains many adumbrations and fulfillments coherently within itself. Time and again the characters unknowingly foretell the end of the play, often using the conjunction "or," which will, at the appearance of the Phoenix, also mean "and." These dramatic ironies bind together the internal actions of the play, working against the centrifugal force of the typological implications. Almost every line of the opening monologue contains an image or idea redefined or "fulfilled" by the end of the play. Samson believes himself "Scarce half" alive, "dead more than half" (l. 79). He lives on "half dead," "a moving grave" (ll. 100–102). The ashy womb of the Phoenix redefines this initial conjunction of life and death; Samson comes to see his death as a life, not his life as a death. Similarly, the "breath of Heav'n" becomes "secret refreshings" and finally "the force of winds" between the pillars; the "guiding hand" becomes the hand of the Philistine and the "guide" of Israel (l. 1428); the eclipsed noon becomes the dawning noon; Samson "the scorn and gaze" (l. 34) becomes Samson the scorner and gazer. Such adumbrations and fulfillments tend to close the small circle of dramatic action and resist the disintegration of Samson into Christ and time into eternity. If the climax draws the reader out of dramatic time and into prophetic time, it also pulls him back into dramatic time, back with new understanding to the moments he misunderstood before.

The New Testament God resides in the heart. Whereas before He wrote the Law on stone tables, now He writes on the fleshly tables of the heart. He judges internal thoughts as if they were external actions: the covetous man commits adultery in his mind. The God of this play is "our living Dread" (l. 1673), and He demands obedience to the external law. With the approval of the Chorus, Samson insists on the dietary strictures of this God. Yet the same God prompted Samson to disobey the external law in his marriage choices, an "exemption" which the Chorus also defends. The climactic action is inseparably mental and physical. Samson stands "as one who pray'd, / Or some great matter in his mind revolv'd" (ll. 1637–38). Here the mind and body converge as they do in the medicinal theory of catharsis. Faith moves the mountain. There is "some great matter" revolving in his "mind"—Samson apparently tears down the pillars in his head.

Though the mind and body both "act" at the climax, they are distinguished throughout the play. Samson often mourns his failure to conjoin "strength" and "wisdom," assuming in such speeches that the two powers can exist apart from each other. Alternatives do indeed collapse. The conjunction "or" eventually means "and." But this harmonious perspective exists for just an instant, at noon. Because we understand the dramatic alternatives only in retrospect, their initial separation remains. The drama moves in sequence to the perspective of simultaneity. "And" pulls together what "or" pulls apart. The reader must feel the pull in both directions. *Samson Agonistes* dramatizes, in the life of its hero, the "brotherly dissimilitudes" of *Areopagitica*.

The marginal commentary of the Geneva Bible informs the reader of Judges that in biblical language the sign does not equal the thing signified. The strength of Samson, we are told, was not really vested in his mighty locks: "Not that the strength lay in the hair, but that the cutting off of his hair was the breaking of the Vow of Nazariteship." [43] Here is precisely the kind of reading that Milton, I expect, tried to discourage in *Samson Agonistes*. The "living Dread" did indeed hang the strength of Samson externally in his hair:

[43] This note is next to Judg. 16.17.

God, when he gave me strength, to show withal
How slight the gift was, hung it in my Hair.
[Ll. 58–59]

Shall I abuse this Consecrated gift
Of strength, again returning with my hair. . . .
[Ll. 1354–55]

And I persuade me God had not permitted
His strength again to grow up with his hair
Garrison'd round about him like a Camp
Of faithful Soldiery, were not his purpose
To use him further yet in some great service. . . .
[Ll. 1495–99]

The strong man is physically strong, and his strength resides, like "faithful Soldiery," in his hair. Samson labors under the old dispensation. It is equally true that the temple falls in his mind, that his "faithful" strength is internal, mental, and spiritual. If, like the Genevan commentators, we construe alternatives and choose between them, then Old Testament Israel vanishes like an unbodied illusion. Once we separate, it will not be long before Samson becomes the Savior and the living Dread dissolves in love. A critic has recently written that Milton "of course intended Samson's bodily strength and the physical dimension of his final act to be only signs of his spiritual state." [44] This reader is in danger of constructing an allegory, and if he does, he will be left with no drama at all. Because the physical strength and physical action of Samson are "only signs," he must conclude that the hero never really suffered from blindness, from Philistine chains, from the debasing labor of a beast. No doubt the death of an entire Philistine city was "only a sign" of its spiritual corruption. Having divided what the language actually says from what the language actually means, this critic argues that *Samson Agonistes* is "centrally concerned, not with Samson, but rather with the way in which the Old Testament hero's story could be made to figure forth the nature of spiritual strength and insight, and of the kind of activity needed to achieve these objectives." [45] He uses "figure forth," the language of typology, but the phrase "not with Samson" indicates that he

[44] Franklin R. Baruch, "Time, Body, and Spirit at the Close of *Samson Agonistes*," *ELH*, 36 (1969), 328.
[45] *Ibid.*, p. 319.

is speaking of an allegory. Though Milton calls his hero "Samson," and Samson says that God hung physical strength in his hair, this critic is explicating an allegorical drama about Christ and the new dispensation wherein the dramatic time of *Samson Agonistes* exists only to pont away from itself. A dumb show.

The dramatic action is almost absorbed in those two great watersheds of time, Crucifixion and Apocalypse. But the catastrophic wound also pulls the reader back toward the woeful tragedy of the Fall. Samson recalls Adam in his relations with Dalila and he begins the drama in satanic eclipse. A "witness" in two senses, he is imperfectly the martyr. Hobbes, an acute man with definitions, realized that "a *Martyr* is (to give the true definition of the word), a Witnesse of the Resurrection of Jesus the Messiah" (p. 529). To this purer martyrdom, Samson cannot aspire. He begins the play with "choice of sun or shade" (l. 3). At noon he is aligned with eternal noon, rising as the Phoenix, but he also moves as a dragon through shadowy evening. All that is shadow distinguishes him from Christ and allies him with Adam, all that is sun separates him from Adam and identifies him with Christ. When his noon declines, the great moment past, Samson returns "Home to his Father's house" and finds his ultimate "shade":

> there will I build him
> A Monument, and plant it round with shade
> Of Laurel ever green, and branching Palm,
> With all his Trophies hung, and Acts enroll'd
> In copious Legend, or sweet Lyric Song.
> [Ll. 1733–37]

The father speaking is an earthly father. He will create "shade" by interposing green leaves between the sun and a grave. Samson rests at last in the shadow of death. Beginning as a moving grave, he ends in a real grave.

This passage deliberately evokes the classical symbols of immortality—the "Laurel ever green," the graveyard "Monument," the heraldic "Trophies," the undying fame in literature and art. The reader understands the ironic difference between what Samson has done and what Christ will do. In a future known only to him, the Sun of Righteousness will appear and, fully radiant, open wide the monuments of men. He will illuminate the typological shadows and His shade will be the everlasting rest of the saints. He will bring the promise of life to the dying. Then the nuptial choirs of the Lamb will one day replace our human legends and sweet songs of remembrance; in the final tragedy, the role of the human chorus will pass to angels. "Nothing is here for tears," this Chorus states (l. 1721). In another time, in another place, angels may wipe the tears forever from their eyes. The promised actions of the surviving characters constitute an earthly, fleshly, classical, unconscious parody of the eternal consolation yet to appear in time. This earthly father can promise Samson only a gentle burial and immortality in the memory of men. Merely his "fame survives" under the sun. But the reader has seen the future gather at noon and the design of history begin to unfold. The perspective of eternity, where consolation already exists, dawning forever at noon, reveals to him the delicate irony of the last speeches. "All is best, though we oft doubt / . . . And ever best found in the close." It is neither the best nor the close. Risen on his noon, Samson ends the drama in shade and death. He falls to the curse of Adam. History as a sequence reasserts itself. The reader confronts, not an allegory of paradise, but an irony of prophecy.

The Phoenix foreshadows the resurrection and afterlife, the coming freedom from death. "A secular bird ages of lives," the Phoenix is divine for rare moments of dazzling intensity. Like the "Laurel ever green," this mythical bird is a classical allusion, a vehicle bound in time, a symbol with a literary past. It was indeed a secular bird until Christian authors filled the old Ovidian myth with new significance. Though the Phoenix gives meaning to Samson, Christ is the sum of all significance and gives meaning to the Phoenix. Both Samson and Christ die in order to live, and both are therefore possible tenors for this classical vehicle. Yet what Samson does for a moment in time, Christ does forever in eternity. Christ stands forever at noon, revealed to men as the clouds of time pass by. Samson is the more suitable tenor. He more truly resembles this habitually secular, momentarily divine Phoenix: and therein lies the precise imperfection of the shadowy type in relation to the truth. The noon of *Samson Agonistes,* having touched eternity, declines into the shadow of death and is itself but the *umbra* of Christian life.

The satisfactions of this incomparable work are not dramatic in any usual sense. A reader enjoys the unsaid, the misunderstood, the merely implied—all that intimate, busy silence. His fundamental and unique satisfaction radiates from the irony of precise definition. Milton wrote a Christian tragedy "after the ancient manner" which really turns on the irony of irony itself. *Samson Agonistes* indicates the exact difference between human and divine audiences, between the ironic perspective of man and the ironic perspective of heaven. If human action in this *theatrum mundi* is a spectacle for God, angels, and prophets, then each single drama is inevitably ironic. Viewing all the shows of time, heavenly spectators would be appreciative of an extraordinary dramatic irony. Any given plot would take shape in the presence of every other plot. God is the author of history, but He understands history from the pinnacle of eternity—His creative mode is necessarily ironic. God sees His end in all beginnings. Creating a tragic drama about human action, Milton imitated this extraordinary perspective in what appears to be—but what is not—the familiar dramatic irony of classical and renaissance tragedy. The irony begins familiarly enough. As dramatic time moves like a clock toward noon, *Samson Agonistes* disposes its fit readers toward the coming catastrophe, the destined triumph. Words and events cannot be fully understood without reference to the dramatic future; the "guiding hand" of the first line leaps forward in time to the hand of the Philistine, guiding Samson to his destiny as it guides the reader to a perception of simultaneous action. This dramatic irony, operative throughout most of the drama, is in kind no different from the ironic foreshadowings of, say, *Othello*. It is an irony appreciated by those spectators who already understand the end, those spectators willing to forego the time-bound pleasures of suspense. In retrospect, Manoa and the Chorus share the ironic comprehension of this tragic day:

> all this
> With God not parted from him, as was fear'd,
> But favoring and assisting to the end.
> [Ll. 1718–20]

They realize that God assisted Samson despite His apparent absence, that He guided the blind hero from the very opening lines of the play; God only "seems" to hide His face. They realize that, in the long view of providence, "or" meant "and." But these are the quotidian ironies of a single day, a single plot. Locked in dramatic and historical time, the Israelites cannot fully appreciate either their Lord or their champion. In this Christian tragedy the distance never closes between the ironic perspectives of the audience within and the audience outside.

Uncontrollable and unsearchable, the God of *Samson Agonistes* refuses to accommodate Himself to the human categories of sequential time, causal action, and familiar dramatic irony. The form of His action does not lend itself to the Aristotelian tragedy. A temporal audience perceives dramatic irony when they see one plot all at once; a divine audience perceives the final and exquisite irony of seeing all plots all at once. Circumscribing one Hebrew day, the prophetic dramatist folded eternity into noontime. At noon the clock-time of a dramatic plot, a human life, runs into eternity: Samson is guided right out of time, his motions blending inseparably with the timeless motions of God. Noontime can only be measured from eternity. At this moment conventional dramatic irony, operating within the bounds of a single plot, bursts from the plot of *Samson Agonistes* into the providential plot of all history. This is dramatic irony with a vengeance. Readers of *Samson Agonistes* escape the earthly theatre of Sophocles and Shakespeare to sit down with angels and prophets. They rise to appreciate the spectacles of heaven, apprehending the irony of a single tragic day cross-referenced with the tragic Fall, the tragic Crucifixion, the tragic Apocalypse—cross-referenced, that is, with the full shape of time. Their perspective enlarged to include the frame of history itself, Christian readers complete the dramatic irony of the Israelite audience as Christ, loving servant and dreaded judge, ironically completes the act of Samson. Dramatic irony in the theatre of the human tragedian is reborn as providential irony in the prophetic theatre of God. Milton adapted tragic drama "after the ancient manner," most intractably temporal of all literary forms, to the eternal vision of prophecy.

Conclusion

LITERARY MEN of the renaissance were long concerned with whether poetry must be, could be, or should be a human art requiring various proportions of natural talent, skilled craftsmanship, and humanist learning. Poetry so conceived might treat of divine subject matter, but its creation was unquestionably secular. The art of the linguistic craftsman posed no mysteries; poets strained and studied to achieve their calculated effects, fashioning their imitations for the sophisticated pleasure of a human audience. This conception left poetry vulnerable to attack from those who believed that art corrupted nature and subject to neglect by those who scorned the unquestionably secular. It also contradicted ancient authority, poets having inherited a tradition of divinely inspired verse. But the literary man could not appeal to this tradition without confronting yet another contradiction, for the god of those divinely inspired poets was no longer divine. If poetry were to protect its ancient heritage, the forms of Apollo would have to accommodate the meanings of the Holy Spirit. Biblical prophecy offered the necessary alternative to pagan inspiration. So the literary man labored to distinguish the vatic Apollo from the poetic Holy Spirit as the early Fathers had labored to distinguish the oracular Apollo from the prophetic Holy Spirit. Usually he made this division with noticeable reluctance. When a Christian literary critic presents Ovid and Spenser as examples of celestial instruction operating in the sphere of poetry, when he cites David and Virgil as divine singers, one can only conclude that his mind is arranged about a fundamental ambivalence: he honors his God no more than he honors the culture of another god. The distinction might compromise its maker in other ways. The escape from secular art could be too perfect, disavowing altogether the virtues of natural talent, skilled craftsmanship, and humanist learning. The escape from secular prejudice could also be too perfect, exalting the inspired modern poet as an arrogant modern heretic. Finding their way in these treacherous issues, renaissance poets and critics defined themselves largely through their attitude toward divine inspiration.

Renaissance Protestants were even more attentive to the significance of divine inspiration. In the late Middle Ages the authority of Old Testament prophecy had justified the scientist, the philosopher, the mystic, and the exegete; divine illumination had authorized various types of the *via contemplativa.* But Luther and Calvin, reinvigorating the old tradition of prophetic exegesis, characterized the Spirit as a more passionate mover. Residing in the holy man and not in his institution, the Spirit prompted these men to oppose an established church. They preached the vernacular Bible sustained by the arresting and comforting precedents of holy prophecy, the trials of Isaiah and the power of lonely Micah. Their followers, combining the apocalyptic disposition of Luther with the radical epistemology of Calvin, extended the motions of the Spirit to politics. The evangelist who inherited the prophetic office of Christ came to identify with the denouncing prophets of the Old Testament. God armed those Hebrews against wicked kings. Clothed in their ancient justice, Protestant preachers became orators for revolution. Eventually the Spirit prompted some holy men to oppose even Protestant establishments. The psychological postures of Old Testament Israel reappeared in the public life of a troubled Europe.

English poets and Protestants acted more or less in accord for over a century. Hoping to glorify the monarch and dignify the language, the movement for divine poetry complemented the Protestant programs for translating the Bible—Wyatt and Sidney were among many sixteenth-century poets to translate the Psalms.[1] A public favorably inclined toward the vernacular Bible naturally tolerated the programmatic redemption of the native muse. It was conventional for a poet to begin his career writing of love and then, studied in the ways of treachery, compose a poem bidding farewell to false love; the chastened poet, weary of lustful passion, vowed to write of God.[2] Though the books of poets doubtless took this

[1] Lily Bess Campbell discusses the poetry of biblical translation in *Divine Poetry and Drama,* pp. 20–73.

[2] At the beginning of the sixteenth century Wyatt bid farewell to false love in a number of his lyrics, perhaps the best of which is "Farewell love and all thy lawes for ever." The poet "lusteth no longer rotten boughes to clymbe" and indeed, he concluded his literary career with the publication of the *Penitential Psalms.* At the end of the century Philip Sidney, author of "Leave

shape more often than the lives of poets, the popularity of the convention is itself revealing. Art could be what life could not. The literary public delighted in the drama of religious and artistic conversion, savoring the contrite verses of the sonneteer who, but a few poems ago, was a dedicated sinner; once humiliated before his lady, the fashionable sonneteer discovered humility before his God. The essential harmony of art and religion continued into the seventeenth century. King James sponsored the translation of the Bible and was, more than anyone else, responsible for the popularity of Du Bartas in England.[3] But during the Revolution, English Protestantism divided, and the inevitable consequence was the division of the English tradition of divine poetry. Unlike Protestantism, which survived its fragmentation, devotional poetry all but disappeared from the vital center of English culture after the Civil War. In England the sacred poet had often been vague about divine inspiration and usually had written without the explicit prompting of God; ultimately he lacked inspiration of any kind. Satire, an outgrowth of political prose, became the dominant mode of English verse. By the eighteenth century divine poetry was, with few exceptions, the bedtime hobby of the country parson and the village vicar—none so accomplished as George Herbert and Robert Herrick. By then it was indeed "an age too late." John Milton lived during the time of transition. He prepared himself to be a divine poet during the reigns of James I and Charles I; he wrote his major divine poems during the reign of Charles II. In his own terms he understood the transition: Urania would find few readers fit in his late age. Uniting the inspiration of poets and Protestants, he became a prophet of unique capacities.

Milton believed himself divinely inspired. He dedicated his youth to becoming a sacred singer distinct from common men by virtue of his favored office. In the Nativity Ode his Heavenly Muse "divided" with angels and his inspired voice joined with the voices of Old Testament prophecy to dispose all nature toward the advent of Christ; in "Lycidas" the

me O Love," fulfilled the promise of that poem and died while translating the Psalms. The career of his more talented friend, Fulke Greville, followed a similar pattern, moving in *Caelica* from love poems to devotional poems. Numerous lesser figures participated in this popular drama of artistic redemption. The major example of religious penance, in art as in life, was of course John Donne.

[3] See Campbell, *Divine Poetry and Drama,* pp. 74–92.

apocalyptic and Protestant voice of Peter foretold the reformation of the Reformation. He chose to write about moments of historical density, imitating the art of God in the temporal art of men. The shifting tenses, the rising and setting sun of the Nativity Ode, the balanced structure of "Upon the Circumcision," the redefinition of time at the conclusion of "Lycidas"—these are all efforts to express prophetic knowledge in sequential language. His need to accommodate divine inspiration, the source of this knowledge, dictated his sense of poetic form. Speakers had to be separated from their creations, heard in dialogue with heavenly powers. "The Passion" strayed from landscape to landscape, vision to vision, unable to make connection with God or with His sense of typological action. Inspired by merely human motives, the act of creation might never find an end. Double frames made a place for the Heavenly Muse to enter the poem and establish the prophetic authority of the poet. As we learn from the devout prayer of its first four stanzas, the Nativity Ode could not have been written without inspiration—the poem itself is proof of an answered prayer. For this prophetic artist, the power to create assumed the power to explicate history with divine sanction.

After experimenting with the court masque and with narrative frames, Milton planned a tragedy about the Fall. The drafts for this unrealized project suggest the difficulties of a sacred poet confronting a largely secular audience. Uncertain whether to reveal or withhold the vision of prelapsarian innocence, Milton wavered between the denouncing prophet and the accommodating angel. It is highly probable that he equated the audience of his unwritten tragedy with the nation itself; in *The Reason of Church Government* tragic drama, not epic, may be more "doctrinal and exemplary to a nation." If his countrymen were worthy of new revelation, Milton hoped to provide definitive religious art. He understood that his inspiration could be no greater than what England deserved. Inspired national poetry was a gift of God, a mark of His special favor. The Lord chose sacred singers from among the poets of great nations. Lacking the adornment of an inspired poem, neither a people nor their language could lay claim to the highest honor; when a mother tongue bore no fruit, the men who spoke that tongue were immature in the eyes of God as well as in the eyes of posterity. Milton prepared himself to fulfill the long dream of English poets: "I apply'd my selfe to that resolution which *Ariosto* follow'd against the perswasions of *Bembo,* to fix all the industry and art I could unite to the adorning of my native tongue; not to make verbal curiosities the end, that were a toylsom vanity, but to be an interpreter & relater of the best and sagest things among mine own Citizens throughout this Island in the mother dialect. That what the greatest and choycest wits of *Athens, Rome,* or modern *Italy,* and those Hebrews of old did for their country, I in my proportion with this over and above of being a Christian, might doe for mine" (CE III, 236). Because he was a true Protestant Christian, his "proportion" would be "over and above" the inspired national verse of Greece, Rome, Italy, and even Israel. As Protestant England exceeded Old Testament Israel, so Milton would exceed the Israelite prophets. But for twenty years he imitated the temporal duties, not the visionary pleasures, of these zealous denouncers, fighting with righteous hatred to secure the future of a great nation. When, blinded in the defense of liberty, he returned to inspired poetry with a fuller sense of divine favor, his nation had proved itself unworthy. His earlier conception of great national poetry, formed in an age of high expectation and relative tranquillity, required severe modification in this later age.

In *Paradise Lost* Milton dramatized the progress of his own inspiration, merging the conventions of epic invocation with the theology of prophetic experience. But the prophet displayed no national pride; his epic did not emerge as an enduring monument to the literary and political maturity of Cromwellian England. The failure of his countrymen would not, as he feared, preclude the Lord from granting revelation to an English prophet, but would prompt Him to define a community of solitary exiles dissociated from the barbaric communities of history. True poetry, like true politics, was vested in the types of Abdiel. Surrounded by evil tongues, the inspired poet spoke his words like Abdiel defying the legions of Satan—except that Milton, acting in a prophetic theatre, avoided direct confrontation with an audience. Urania solved the difficulty of the fit and unfit reader. His only acknowledged auditor, she drives far off the murderous "Revellers" even as her answerable style drives far off the fallen connotations of the very word "revels." The poem arrives at its final lines to become whole and complete, a body of harmonious sound safe from the fate of dismembered Orpheus.

Milton reworked in the higher context of divine inspiration all of the traditional aims of the sacred poet in England. He reformed the secular tradition, imitating its conventions while rejecting its conventional morality. He justified the ways of a monarch—not Elizabeth or James or Charles, but God the Almighty and Universal King. He adorned the native tongue, submitting the English language to a heavenly poet in order that its words, tones, and styles might be returned to the fit Englishman purged of disharmony. He distinguished with great care between classical and Christian inspiration, praying to the divine "Meaning" as he spoke the pagan "Name." His rearrangement of the nationalist aesthetic amounted to a judgment. The inspired Protestant epic was, in its proportion, "over and above" all previous national literature. As time dissolved the old motives of the divine poet, Milton protected his ambition by removing those motives from history. Abraham Cowley, depleted by the thievery of time, had found himself studying the "Art of Oblivion"—to avoid his fate John Milton pursued the art of eternity. The blind prophet soared beyond the reach of change. He wrote with heavenly language of the ageless Argument of an eternal King and found his audience in men of unfallen virtue. His poem about the happy garden emerged as a fortress in history, guarded on one side by an eternal creator and on the other side by a timeless reader. So enclosed, *Paradise Lost* escaped from the touch of an age too late.

The epic is offered as another Testament. Writing with prophetic inspiration higher than "those Hebrews of old," Milton assumes divine authority for every word, every event in *Paradise Lost* that does not appear in Scripture. His prophetic song fills in the hypotactic transitions of Genesis with an inspired parataxis, representing the conceptual logic of events missing in the account of Moses.[4] It is a fresh revelation, a Christian fulfillment. Milton unfolds cause and effect instead of isolate events:

> say first what cause
> Mov'd our Grand Parents in that happy State,
> Favor'd of Heav'n so highly, to fall off
> From thir Creator, and transgress his Will

[4] This paragraph owes much to the brilliant and influential treatment of Old Testament hypotaxis in Erich Auerbach's *Mimesis,* trans. Willard Trask (Garden City: Doubleday, 1957), pp. 124–51.

> For one restraint, Lords of the World besides?
> Who first seduc'd them to that foul revolt?
> [I.28–33]

He first asks the Heavenly Muse to speak of "cause." Moses had told the effect:

> That Shepherd, who first taught the chosen Seed,
> In the Beginning how the Heav'ns and Earth
> Rose out of Chaos. . . .
> [I.8–10]

In the biblical account "how" is simply the fact. The discrete sentences of Genesis, joined together by the alogical conjunction "and," reveal actions disconnected in time and cause. In the beginning God created heaven and earth—but *Paradise Lost* reveals "how" that beginning came about. The first question addressed to the Heavenly Muse is the question of a man who had read Genesis and wishes to know more. It is the question of a man ready to surpass the revelation of Moses, to extend and perfect the Word through his prophetic office. Milton asks to become the official historian of eternity. God seems to answer him.

The prophet discovers his power as the flight proceeds. His Heavenly Muse instructs him, illuminates him, and protects him, responding to his prayers with answerable style. From the very beginning he is both humble and quietly commanding. There is no shrill solicitude. "Instruct me, for Thou know'st" has not the least trace of pleading; the Muse is the correct instructor, and her instruction is correctly due him. The moment of severest pressure comes during his address to light in Book III, for here the blind prophet confronts the anguish of those who serve at the same time he begins the bold, presuming flight to the court of God. He demands the most of himself as he demands the most of God. Unwilling and unable to conceal himself, he permits his anguish free expression. The blind man has been denied the images of God in nature—denied the freshness of the turning seasons, the surpassing beauty of the human face. Though the blind man continues to worship the God of Light, requesting the compensatory vision of a holy prophet, he expresses a position beyond all compromise: without an inner light, blindness is utterly intolerable. We feel that even the refusal of God could not modify this necessary and radical condition. "So much the rather thou Celestial Light / Shine inward." Because of his daring integrity—man as well as man of God—we understand with irrefutable force that to serve is not indeed to be servile. He commands his tone, his humanity and his God. One of the most powerful achievements of *Paradise Lost* is the deliberate, enormously poised demeanor of a narrator who recognizes full well his boldness. Having studied the lesser flights of Moses, Virgil, Bellerophon, Orpheus, the blind classical sages, and even Satan, he fashions his prayers with perfect precision, always requiring the requisite guidance, the necessary protection. Throughout his dangerous flight the epic poet remains poised but intense, holding the rare pitch of tautness between strain and slack. He is tuned. In the last words of the final invocation he lists the possibilities for failure. Temporal circumstances may defeat the greater endeavor "if all be mine"—but the next line, initially subordinate to the conditional "if," ends with a reassertion of his guiding truth: "Not Hers who brings it nightly to my Ear." Defeat is both possible, "if" the poem is all his, and impossible, for she "brings it nightly" to his ear. The prophet, fearing excess and still assured, allows for what he cannot allow for. His conditional "if" both is and is not contrary to unquestionable fact. As the poem continues and concludes, readers stand witness to the realizing of the will of God in the completed mission of an authentic prophet. He represents his composition of *Paradise Lost* as an action performed "now" so that we may testify not only to the authenticity of the finished work but to the grace of the finishing. The narrator is the precise opposite of Satan "distract" with "horror and doubt." Singing before his God, Milton composed himself.

Though experienced as motion, life is understood as motive. We know a man when we recognize his passions. There need not be an identical correspondence between knower and known, since we understand so well the person who detests the things we love; a man is truly incomprehensible when we feel mere indifference toward his purposes. One expression of our sympathy for recognizable passion bears upon the relationship between an author and his characters. However they may sometimes protest, writers do not invent what is entirely incomprehensible to them; literary characterization inevitably rests on a conception of human motive intelligible to the literary creator. A passionate man, Milton was "Smit with the love of sacred Song" (III.29). His fundamental "love" embodied a number of assumptions about the mind—embodied a complete and detailed psychology in which artistic success, spiritual accomplishment, and mental health were virtually indistinguishable. As he understood himself with the psychological assumptions of prophetic experience, it was perhaps only natural that Milton should understand other minds as either violating or creating the psychic conditions that allowed for the inspiration of God. The inner configuration of the inspired mind became a major factor in the creation of his various heroic and unheroic characters. Studying these great figures, both in agony and in repose, we perceive something of how Milton came—old, blind, unheeded—to his abundant recompense.

In his opening soliloquy Samson compares "restless thoughts" with hornets and treats the hornets as an invading army:

> Ease to the body some, none to the mind
> From restless thoughts, that like a deadly swarm
> Of Hornets arm'd, no sooner found alone,
> But rush upon me thronging, and present
> Times past, what once I was, and what am now.
> [Ll. 18–22]

He has lost all sense of destined action. The hornet, biblical symbol of the scourge of God (Deut. 7.19–21), becomes for Samson a scourge of guilt; unable to lead an army against the Philistines, he leads an army of remorse against his mental "Ease." The thronging hornets "present" the violent disjunction between his past and his present, his inspired victories and his abandoned captivity. They attack when he is "alone," solitary and without his God. Once he had to suffer another kind of "swarm":

> How counterfeit a coin they are who friends
> Bear in their Superscription (of the most
> I would be understood); in prosperous days
> They swarm, but in adverse withdraw thir head
> Not to be found, though sought.
> [Ll. 189–93]

Both false friends and restless thoughts assault the inner quiet of the mind. They swarm the mental surface, sealing off the tranquil paradise within.

The Christ of *Paradise Regained* complains:

> O what a multitude of thoughts at once
> Awak'n'd in me swarm, while I consider

> What from within I feel myself, and hear
> What from without comes often to my ears,
> Ill sorting with my present state compar'd.
> [I.196–200]

This passage recreates with a difference the simile of the hornets in *Samson Agonistes.*[5] As Samson's "swarm" presents the difference between what he was and what he is, Christ's "swarm" presents the difference between what He will be and what He is—"What from within I feel myself" must refer, as the entire poem makes clear, to the great work about to begin. Christ is threatened with impatience, tempted to violate the schedule of eternity. His words unfold the connection between counterfeit friends and restless thoughts in *Samson Agonistes.* "What from without comes often to my ears" is the babble of urgent tongues, the constant pressure of impatient men. The psychological "swarm" is the hum of confusion when outward demands conflict with inner demands; the mind cannot escape the sensory pressure to enjoy its quiet center. Solitary, Christ evades this nervous confusion in the wilderness:

> The while her Son tracing the Desert wild,
> Sole, but with holiest Meditations fed,
> Into himself descended, and at once
> All his great work to come before him set. . . .
> [II.109–12]

Descending into himself, Christ apprehends His future all at once. Though impatient babble reappears in the figure of Satan, He remains "unmov'd," at rest, at ease with His own future. Like Christ, Samson begins the drama in solitude,

[5] It is interesting to entertain (though folly to prove) the possibility that the publication of *Samson Agonistes* and *Paradise Regained* in one volume (1671) was no accident: the two works complement each other almost as perfectly as "L'Allegro" and "Il Penseroso." Both Samson and Christ seem inactive throughout their dramas, then finally, in an emblematic moment defined by a burst of successive similes, perform a single physical action. Both are led by the "motion" of God (*PR* I.290). Both works deal with the concept of rest. In *Paradise Regained,* true rest is defined by the difference between Satanic and heavenly banquets, and false rest by Christ's "vain" attempt to sleep while Satan exercises his black magic (IV.397–438). There have been several efforts to relate the three visitors of the drama to the temptations of *Paradise Regained;* see, for example, the discussion of the "triple equation" in Krouse, pp. 125–33. Moreover, Samson is the type and Christ his antitype. Because of their relationship to events outside their frames of art, both works are ironic. But to compare Samson with Christ is to discover the ironies of the drama, whereas to compare Christ with Samson is to discover what is not ironic in the brief epic.

free from the swarm of counterfeit friends. But having evaded the false tongues, he descends into the swarm within. His guilty mind feeds on itself with poisonous stings, an ironic version of Christ "with holiest Meditations fed." Seeing between the pillars, moving in accord with the healing motions of God, Samson finally discovers a kind of "Ease" and "at once / All his great work to come before him set." The restless swarms are obstacles to prophecy.

Milton represents the origin of psychological "dis-ease" in *Paradise Lost*. The curse of first disobedience extends beyond physical labor to the restlessness of the mind. Our fallen parents may sit down, "but not at rest or ease of Mind" (IX.1120). They become indecisive. Quarreling, they are unable to sort out alternatives and rest in a chosen future: "And of thir vain contest appear'd no end" (IX.1189). Later, having confessed his disobedience in the first fallen prayers, Adam follows Michael to the Mount of Speculation hoping to "earn rest from labor won" (XI.370). He seems to know by instinct that rest for fallen man is only possible in opposition to physical and mental labor. Ultimately he and Eve are free to choose "Thir place of rest"—"rest" appears to be merely a place, an interlude between labors, and the emphasis falls on the mental activity of choice. But God lessens the possibility of endless restlessness, for through the long wandering journey of history man eventually regains "the blissful Seat." Adam is assured by Michael that "second Adam" will guide "long wander'd man" to "an eternal paradise of rest" outside of time (XII.313–14); death is one cure for the restless labors of choice. However, this "eternal paradise" has its analogue in history, in the mental "paradise within thee, happier far." And the blissful inner garden, where "ease of mind" can be reachieved, is associated with the prophetic understanding of time.

The attentuation of fallen restlessness begins with the contrite prayers inspired by "Prevenient Grace": "See Father, what first fruits on Earth are sprung / From thy implanted Grace in Man" (XI.22–23). Responding to this confession of our first disobedience, God creates prophecy as theological therapy for the weaknesses of guilt:

> Yet lest they faint
> At the sad Sentence rigorously urg'd,
> For I behold them soft'ned and with tears
> Bewailing their excess, all terror hide.

> If patiently thy bidding they obey,
> Dismiss them not disconsolate; reveal
> To Adam what shall come in future days,
> As I shall thee enlighten, intermix
> My Cov'nant in the woman's seed renew'd;
> So send them forth, though sorrowing, yet in peace.
> [XI.108–17]

Properly speaking, the divine gift of consolation for the fainting pair is not the Atonement of the New Testament. It is the *promissio* of this redemptive future that saves Adam and Eve from psychological disease: His prophecy is our peace. Acting with Michael in a prophetic masque, Adam measures "the Race of time / Till time stand fixt" and understands that long typological drama in which he bears the figure of "second Adam." The mitigation of restlessness proceeds simultaneously with the prophetic comprehension of time. Because he discovers a "paradise within," Adam may carry his innocent past and his gospel future with him as he leaves Eden in the fallen present. Our inspired parents enter history "sorrowing" over all the disobediences of time, "yet in peace" with the ultimately merciful response of God. Theirs cannot be, in any simple sense, a "happy" Fall. God uses the doubly negative "not disconsolate," for fallen minds will suspend the opposites of sorrowful labor and peaceful rest in harmonious disharmony. But their "wand'ring steps," potentially aimless and indecisive, are guided by "Providence." Insofar as knowledge of the shape of time allows the unfainting children of Adam to "stand fixed," balancing their irresolute "wand'ring" in the immediate with the resolved patterns of "Providence," prophecy mitigates the burden of decision. Man may join his ends to the revealed ends of God, making his destiny his choice.

In *Paradise Lost,* then, God invents prophecy to complete the process begun with the first fallen prayers, revealing to Adam that the apparent discontinuity of his time is in fact the initial act of a providential drama. Milton knew that the divine poet, like all the champions of God, would have to recreate this original paradigm—one began a sacred song with "devout prayer" to the Holy Spirit. The swarms of restless thoughts that beset Samson with deadly force and Christ with modest annoyance must be understood as impediments to prayer, barriers between the laboring mind and the inspiration of God. Samson and Christ, like fallen Adam, must escape from the immediate contrast between "now" and another time, the present self and another self in the past or future. Driven by such disjunctions, the troubled hero may act too quickly or retire too soon. For those who must choose to act in a providential drama, restless nonsense threatens the prophetic apprehension of continuous time. Assaulting the mind with inconclusive motion, insect "swarms" perpetuate a confusing moment and obscure the peaceful gift of time rightly understood.

We find the prototype of psychological swarming in the dramatic action of *Paradise Regained.* Insects—those archetypal pests, those ancient lords of irritation—reappear once more to define the contest between Christ and Satan:

> But as a man who had been matchless held
> In cunning, overreach't where least he thought,
> To salve his credit, and for very spite
> Still will be tempting him who foils him still,
> And never cease, though to his shame the more;
> Or as a swarm of flies in vintage time,
> About the wine-press where sweet must is pour'd,
> Beat off, returns as oft with humming sound;
> Of surging waves against a solid rock,
> Though all to shivers dash't, th' assault renew,
> Vain batt'ry, and in froth or bubbles end;
> So Satan . . .
>
> [IV.10–21]

Comparing the dauntless pestering of Satan to a "swarm of flies," Milton implies that Christ's earlier victory over the psychological "swarm" was, in effect, the victory over Satan. When he descended into himself and organized his future, Christ became a fixed rock against which all kinds of devilish flux might beat themselves to froth. He beat the devil by evading the swarm of nonsense and temporal confusion. *Summa propheta,* Christ made his peace with time. The struggle against interior restlessness is, for Milton, the struggle against Satan.

Natural man lost his physical and mental "rest" with the Fall. As he labors to recover that lost rest, he must defeat his Tempter. Satan is the very essence of inner motion, a dark angel of fear and desire similar in many ways to Hobbesian man: "For there is no such thing as perpetuall Tranquillity of mind, while we live here; because life it selfe is but Motion, and can never be without Desire, nor without Feare, no more than without Sense." [6] The Miltonic devil is constantly "distract" with "horror and doubt" and tormented with "fierce desire" that "unfulfill'd with pain of longing pines" (IV. 509–12). Satan is always agitated, always reexamining his motives, always reaffirming his purposes, endlessly making and remaking the same decision. Though without rational motive, his motion is incessant. He resolves to fight against God in Heaven—decides again in Hell, again before the earthly sun, again when he sees Adam and Eve embrace, again when he returns to Eden, and yet once again when he discovers the solitary Eve propping flowers. He is forever himself, Hell from the moment he conceives Sin; in *Paradise Regained* he continues with his pestering insistence. All of his frantic self-examination is really in the service of his essential immobility. The Miltonic God, however, acts with absolute resolve:

> So spake th' Almighty, and to what he spake
> His Word, the Filial Godhead, gave effect.
> Immediate are the Acts of God, more swift
> Than time or motion, but to human ears
> Cannot without process of speech be told,
> So told as earthly notion can receive.
>
> [VII.174–79]

He compresses the human sequence of deliberation, choice, will, and deed into an instant. The Christ of *Paradise Regained* adopts this divine resolution as he descends into himself "and at once" reschedules his time in harmony with an eternal clock. Samson much less perfectly imitates this resolution as he is motioned toward the Philistine temple and changes his mind with a sudden decisiveness. Nearing the fullness of time, Samson before the Philistines knows when to wait, when to rest, when to speak, when to perform. He is an actor who knows his play. Catastrophe bides its time. A fallen hero who could find "Ease to the body some, none to the mind" ultimately finds ease for the mind in the purgative labor of the body. He and his Lord have resolved to strike.

The themes of rest and restlessness are not uncommon in seventeenth-century literature. The pastoral eclogues, the many books on gardening, the tradition of the *hortus conclusus*, the classical ideal of *otium* and country solitude—all emphasize the possibilities for rest, refreshment, and quiet

[6] Hobbes, pp. 129–30.

in this busy life. But Puritans, with their commitment to work, tended to reserve this ancient concept for the afterlife. In *The Saints Everlasting Rest,* Richard Baxter argued that only the saints in heaven could find genuine ease; with regard to this life, at least, the Puritan had an unexpected ally in Thomas Hobbes.[7] For Milton a series of assumptions about interior motion, restful and restless, became the psychological center of a theory of prophetic inspiration. Patristic writers had acknowledged a sublime calm in the inspired mind. Extending and complicating this guiding principle, Milton characterized both the great man of *Samson Agonistes* and the greatest man of *Paradise Regained* as having to withstand a swarming confusion, a busy bustle of nonsense, to achieve an inner resolve which sets their great works before them. In *Samson Agonistes* insect swarms, restless and counterfeit, prevent the hero from apprehending a purposeful continuity of action in the past, present, and prophetic future. As motions cure motions, Samson eludes the contrast between "what once I was, and what am now," precisely the hateful contrary that beseiged Adam after his primal disobedience, and performs his prophetic action with knowing assurance. In *Paradise Regained* Christ enacts the resolution of Samson in two instants, one of prophetic apprehension and one of temporal fulfillment. His antithesis is the restless Satan. Incapable of prophetic understanding, Satan works to stuff time with frenzied activity. To this extent the Miltonic devil represents the endless motions of an unhealthy restlessness proceeding, in men and fallen angels alike, from guilt. Turmoil is the hard armor of his closed mind. The quintessential protection against this resolvedly irresolute devil is prophetic knowledge: what distinguishes the man of God is his unfragmented sense of how to act in time. Plato would have agreed that, in order to know itself, the rational soul must elude the sensory given; true knowledge requires escape from the motions of temporal experience. But when he spoke of divine inspiration, Plato described the afflated mind as unconscious, furious, frenetic. Reaffirming the patristic strategy, Milton adapted Platonic

[7] Stanley Stewart considers the *hortus conclusus* as an ideal of rest in *The Enclosed Garden* (Madison: University of Wisconsin Press, 1966) and Maren-Sophie Røstvig the clasical theme of country retirement in *The Happy Man* (Oslo; Norwegian Universities Press, 1962). Baxter discusses the "sin and folly of expecting rest here" in chapter 10, "The Saint's Rest is not to be expected on this earth," of *The Saints Everlasting Rest,* ed. Benjamin Fawcett (Charleston, 1811), pp. 180–200.

notions about rational knowledge to the psychology of divine inspiration. To know itself the Christian soul must escape from the confusing "now" of temporal sequence. Prophecy was the way out of time. An "interpreter & relater" of heroic events, Milton found in the very conditions of his own inspiration both the mercy of God and the difficult resolve of great men in labor.

The creative life of Milton himself can be understood as an attempt to disregard the illusions of immediacy, elude his swarms and fulfill a design of continuous purpose. He held the great ambition at an early age. Even then he was threatened with an uneasy conviction of belatedness, his present inaction ill-sorting with his projected future. On his twenty-third birthday he eased this sense of spiritual and literary sloth with the apprehension of "strictest measure" (Sonnet VII). His accomplishments must come in time, all his actions synchronized against a divine schedule: "All is, if I have grace to use it so, / As ever in my great task-Master's eye." The "grace to use it so" was relaxation in thieving time, the ability to unfold in an unhurried present that future, be it high or mean, resting already complete in the eye of God. The good servant was led by the "Time" that he shaped and the "will of heaven" that shaped time. Later, having abandoned the sacred song he loved, Milton tried once again to integrate his present with his destined future. The pamphleteer halted in the midst of hoarse dispute, banished rude ears, and laid his great works to come before him in *The Reason of Church Government* and *An Apology,* interrupting the swarm of topical controversy to descend within and promise his future to the knowing reader. But Milton was troubled by the extreme disjunction between now and then, what he was and what he hoped to be: "I trust hereby to make it manifest with what small willingness I endure to interrupt the pursuit of no lesse hopes than these" (CE III, 241). He prattled with lesser minds for twenty years, and his tactics were often as small-minded as those of his opponents. One can feel the tone escape from his command in many of the pamphlets. The voice turns strident, impatient, defensively proud. When, well on his way toward political isolation, Milton considered his blindness in Sonnet XIX, the early fear of belatedness had evolved into the threat of "useless" inaction; "patience" prevented that "murmur." The God of *Paradise Lost* offers the therapeutic gift of prophecy to Adam and Eve only if they accept His judgment "patiently." God calmed those who began to calm themselves. Patient men carried out the tasks of heaven, submitting to the designs of their own time before apprehending the mysteries of divine time. "They also serve who only stand and wait"—so Milton stood ready for his future. Seen with the eye of God or the eye of a prophet, waiting was indivisibly a part of acting. His restraint was a deed of faith: he must wait with the belief that his future, complete in the mind of God, would come round before he died. Impatient restlessness, the most dangerous kind of inaction, was the abiding temptation to violate divine schedule. Forcing time, relinquishing himself to the motions of a guilty dis-ease, would have constituted a faithless indictment of God—and therefore an indictment of the life God held in trust. Waiting for God was waiting for himself.

As he wrote *Paradise Lost,* Milton must have felt that "Time" and the "will of heaven" had come due at once. Psychological, political, and literary decisions moved in harmony with divine inspiration. The blind man discovered an inner light, more precious and more pure. The political man recognized that his decision to defend liberty had not been either a deviation from his chosen future or proof that God had shaped him for tasks painfully different from those for which he had shaped himself. The literary man, for reasons not altogether literary, chose to abandon rhyme. Jangling endings were the "Invention of a barbarous age" and associated therefore with the "barbarous dissonance" of the secular Revellers—but, in the note on blank verse prefixed to the second edition of the epic, his objections extended to the psychology of poetic creation. Poets wrote in rhyme "much to thir own vexation, hindrance, and constraint." The pressure to rhyme created nervous "vexation," undue restlessness in the mind of a laboring poet. Freed of this "modern bondage," Milton facilitated the artistic commerce between the mind of God and the mind of a poet open to inspiration. That was the crucial business. Once he had chosen his subject, the need for divine assistance stood prior to all other artistic choices. His "unattempted" argument, bold almost to the point of excess, would require a prophetic experience greater than the one which resulted in Genesis. Though he could adjust his motives, prepare his art and dispose his spirit, the requisite decision belonged to God. As Milton and God both resolved "now," their prophetic collaboration rewarded the incessant care of a lifetime tending: "easy" and "unpremeditated" the epic came forth. Granting a style answerable to the subject, Urania purged satanic disquiet from his language, his audience, and himself. He was "beginning late" in the eye of man, not "an age too late" in the eye of God. Milton composed himself in the tone of *Paradise Lost* because now, at last, his readiness and his future converged. His "intended wing" completed, line by line, the intentions of God.

When Milton began a second epic, he suggested that his poetic career might, like the day of *Samson Agonistes,* be measured in two directions. The Virgilian allusion to the movement from pastoral to epic defined the relationship between classical and Christian genres; his New Testament pastoral exceeded his Old Testament epic as classical epic had exceeded classical pastoral. But the Christian poet who "erewhile the happy Garden sung" also indicated that his career was as much a construction of knowing art as his poetry. One wrote in the lesser genre to prepare for the higher. Because he had written *Paradise Lost,* he could now write *Paradise Regained;* because he could now write *Paradise Regained,* he had written *Paradise Lost.* Milton often claimed to have consciously fulfilled a pattern in time, minimizing the coincidental in his life. The author of the *Second Defense* rehearsed his public career with the unlikely contention that he had, with systematic rigor, defined the three kinds of liberty during the past fifteen years, writing first of religious liberty, then domestic liberty, then finally of civil liberty. In his preface to *The Judgment of Martin Bucer* Milton noted that after finishing his first pamphlet on divorce, he was led to discover similar opinions in the work of this Reformation theologian. Here was no blind contrition of events: "Certainly if it be in mans discerning to sever providence from chance, I could allege many instances, wherein there would appear cause to esteem of me no other than a passive instrument under some power and counsel higher and better than can be human" (CE IV, 11). His steps in history, like those of Adam and Eve, were both wandering and guided. If one followed the designs of Providence, what one had accomplished from the vantage point of the future could not be separated from what one had intended from the vantage point of the past. There were no random events when the veils slipped from the present, unmasking time. At the beginning of *Paradise Regained* Milton characteristically suggested that his subject long in its choosing had really been the Temptation of Christ. This prophet appreciated the continuity of his purposes. Responsive to the motions of God, he came to ponder time without disguise.

The Chorus of *Samson Agonistes* distinguishes between the great champions of heaven and the nameless unremembered:

> Nor do I name of men the common rout,
> That wand'ring loose about
> Grow up and perish, as the summer fly,
> Heads without name no more remember'd,
> But such as thou hast solemnly elected. . . .
> [Ll. 674–78]

Though not the phrase of a democratic humanitarian, "wand'ring loose about" brilliantly summarizes the small, marginal lives that most of us lead—so far from history, so near to oblivion. Milton had real contempt for the ways we live. As we fear above all the threat of our own uniqueness, never happier and more assured than when we behold our image reflected in another, Milton prayed for a conspicuous life. The holy prophets of the Bible were not to him, as they were to so many of his predecessors, examples of spiritual favor too exalted to be sought again. He marked his time in preparation for the bold attempt. Entrusting his life and his art to the author of history, he distinguished himself from those common men and common poets who wander loose about, grow up and perish in the confusion of discontinuous motives. Milton refused to be dispersed in time. It cannot have been restful to greet the immediate instants—all that distraction, everything calling attention to itself—while keeping in mind the purposes of God. He lived with the unrelenting pressure of a destined labor, uncertain when to begin, how long to wait. Nothing could be his alone. His decisions could not be momentary; his tastes could not finally be whimsical. He wandered toward an end and when he acted, springing in the fullness of time, the restless preparation flowed into the deeds. Milton did not impose himself and his private concerns upon the great events of *Paradise Lost, Paradise Regained,* and *Samson Agonistes*. A prophetic poet, he unveiled what was already there. His unique experience had clicked into an eternal pattern. Obedient to God and to the Word of God, Milton could freely invent the truth.

Prophecy made him coherent. To understand his prophetic creations we must engage in kinds of speculation largely unrecognized in the scholarship of the modern Miltonist. What the prophet knows may not always be surprising, every line an oracle fresh from the mouth of God. No doubt the Heavenly Muse inspired Milton with the humanist culture of the Christian Renaissance and the reformed theology of Renaissance Protestantism. We can recreate his knowledge from diverse sources, reassembling the many lost ideas that inform his art. But the mode of his knowing cannot be duplicated in the common rout of the uninspired; his cultural heritage was not familiar to his contemporary readers as it was familiar to him. Unlike the known, the mode of knowing is dynamic, psychological, and therefore biographical. Art and life are one in his prophetic verse. We should no longer find this art, this life, too pompous for our tolerance or too outrageous for our comfort or too supernatural for our taste —that is surely to play the invisible hypocrite, cowardly toward men and brave toward God. So many of us live with the vague feeling that we have not yet begun to live, that someday we will undergo the triumphant exertion of our hitherto untried capacities. We all have our great futures, and we wait them out right into the grave. We crouch down in time, ready to spring, until the weight of distraction buries us there, nameless and unremembered.

Index

Index